CHILDREN OF BETHANY

CHILDREN OF BETHANY

The Story of a
Palestinian Family

SAID K. ABURISH

INDIANA UNIVERSITY PRESS
Bloomington and Indianapolis

Published by arrangement with I.B.Tauris & Co Ltd, London

Manufactured in the United States of America

Library of Congress Cataloging-in-Publication Data

Aburish, Said K.
    Children of Bethany.

    1. Aburish, Khalil, d. 1936.   2. Aburish family.
3. Palestinian Arabs—West Bank—Bethany—Genealogy.
4. Bethany—Genealogy.   I. Title.
DS110.B398A38   1989   956.95′3 [B]   89-15414
ISBN 0-253-30676-0 (alk. paper)

1 2 3 4 5   93 92 91 90 89

The idea of this book originated with Kate who shared much of the journey of discovery. It is affectionately dedicated to her and to my Aunt Fatmeh.

Contents

Acknowledgements

Huge thanks are due to the members of the Aburish family who were generous with their time and counsel. Uncle Mahmoud's contribution went beyond his own vital recollections and included advice on my approach to reluctant participants. My mother insisted that the book 'may be good for the Middle East but it's bad for the family'. Her decision to contribute to my efforts is a true reflection of a positive awareness of the larger picture.

Aunt Mirriam Mahmoud was my gracious hostess for three weeks while I was in Jerusalem. She not only put up with my erratic schedule but opened her house for dozens of people to be interviewed there. She deserves special thanks.

My friends Loris and Paul Parker, Al Webb, Adel Dajani, Rima Sabbagh, Riad Hassan and Maher Othman understood my purpose and were most encouraging. They provided excellent sounding boards and friendly advice. My good friend John Bulloch lent a kind, helping hand and provided valuable advice every step of the way.

Finally, the most charming interview I conducted was with my nephews Ziad and Walid (Munif's children). Their confusion over their identity (they are six and five years old respectively) was confirmed to me while I sat cross-legged in the middle of a floor full of chocolate and other cakes, toys, children's books and bottles of orange juice and coca cola. I am deeply indebted to them for allowing me to interrupt their more immediate and natural pursuits.

CHILDREN OF BETHANY

Introduction

For me, no complete understanding of the turbulent modern history of the Arabs is possible without the human factor. This is a book about one family, a family unfortunate enough to experience most of the dislocating events which began in Palestine and the Arab world in 1917. I am not particularly interested in the politics of those events in isolation, but I am interested in the people caught up in them, in the wounds of change rather than the winds of change.

On the surface, this book is a study of the Aburishs of Bethany, my family, from 1917 until the present day. The choice of 1917 as a starting point is far from accidental; it represents the end of Turkish rule in Palestine and the arrival of the British and consequent western influence. Until 1917, little change had taken place there for centuries; after 1917 the problem was how to contain the effects of the rapid pace of change.

The Aburishs, in terms of achievements, do not deserve a book. However, they do represent a startling microcosm of the vast social changes which have transformed Palestine and the Arab Middle East from a rigid feudal society based on family and tribal links, to one with a disturbing lack of direction and continuity, suffering from an imperfect, often superficial, understanding of western thinking.

My grandfather and his family living a village life in
Bethany, just east of Jerusalem, provide good examples of
domestic, conjugal and religious life as it existed in rural
Palestine in 1917. Between then and now these children of
Bethany have produced heroes and been accused of
treachery. We have known poverty and shame and enjoyed
wealth and fame. Individual Aburishs have exercised political
power, suffered torture and become entrepreneurs. We now
live in twenty-two different countries. The only thing some of
us have in common is our name.

*   *   *   *

I am not in the business of pleasing people: presenting
naked truths very seldom does. This is especially so when
facts undermine national legend and interfere with accepted
illusions. The Palestinians and Arabs will object to reflections on their national character, as they always do. Some
fundamental Israeli claims will also be challenged and shown
to be empty, while the more elusive aspects of inter-Arab
relations will be seen for what they were and are. My answer
to all expected cries of protest is to stand by what I know to be
the truth.

And finally, to my own family. Blood relations – even when
the link is tenuous – cannot be reduced to statistical abstrac-
tions, so the likelihood of giving offence in a family chronicle
is forever present. I have tried not to render judgement in an
absolute sense and relied on the truth to speak for itself. But
always I have been driven by the notion that today's Middle
East can be better understood by understanding its people.
Here, for better or for worse, I have relied on my family to
shed a little light on what it means to be a Palestinian in the
twentieth century.

My grandfather, the man who founded the Aburish clan,
would have understood my purpose and applauded it. As for
me, I am fifty-two years old, but the journey between where I
was born, the Bethany of 1935, and now is centuries long. As
one of the children of Bethany I hope that my chronicle will
help to explain a period of Palestine's history.

1
A dynasty is founded

Khalil Aburish came home riding a mule and wearing the ill-fitting uniform of a sergeant in the Turkish army. For his young wife Rashedah, who saw him far up the dusty path, this was proof at last that the war was over. Her cousin had assured her that the fighting had ended, but she would only believe it when she saw her husband back home, and all the other men of the village. Now at least the living proof that her cousin had been right could be seen. As Khalil Aburish and his mule made their laborious way down the narrow path, Rashedah began a chant: 'Our beloved is back on his horse with his sword by his side', though all Khalil Aburish had was a knotted handkerchief with some bread and olives to sustain him on his way. No matter, facts should never be allowed to get in the way of a celebration, and soon Rashedah's step-daughter Hamdah joined in the song of praise, with all its extravagance and hyperbole, and Khalil's sons Ahmad, Mahmoud, Mohammad and Ibrahim lined up to greet the returning warrior. When he finally dismounted from his 'horse' they showed their respect by kneeling and kissing his right hand. The sons were followed by his daughter Hamdah, and finally his wife bent and kissed his hand. For his wife and daughter Khalil Aburish had merely a pat on the shoulder, but for his sons there were embraces and tears of joy.

Next in the ritual of return a hot bath was prepared. Water was heated in a big brass pot in a small fireplace outside the house, carried inside and poured on him with a ladle by Ahmad, the eldest son, who claimed this honour. There was no bathtub or anything resembling it: Aburish sat on a bare wooden seat and took his bath in the middle of one of the small rooms used for that purpose and also for dining. This was a luxurious affair in itself, for water was dear, but Aburish owned one of the four wells which satisfied the needs of all Bethany and he was known to take a bath weekly. The rest of the people bathed once every few months but wiped themselves with a wet cloth regularly to satisfy the need for ritual cleanliness before prayer on Friday, the Muslim Sabbath.

Aburish discarded his unbecoming soldier's uniform, put on his tunic and mantle (*kimbas* and *abba*), slippers with no socks and his Arab headdress and head band (*hatta* and *egal*). Over a special meal of rice and mutton – one of the three sheep kept by the family had been slaughtered – he regaled his family with accounts of his three-year adventure with the gendarmerie. Although he had been stationed in Acre, only a short distance away, his previous communications with them had been limited by the unreliable postal service and his difficulty with writing. They had known he was in Acre but did not know what he had been doing and could not make the journey to find out.

Aburish's first public act upon returning to the timeless atmosphere of Bethany in 1917 was to re-establish his pre-eminence in this poor community. His reappearance after such a prolonged absence was the occasion for people to go through explicit and implicit motions of respect and reconfirmation. These expressions of support could be encouraged but never solicited. To have value, respect had to flow naturally and could therefore never be demanded. So his eldest son Ahmad, aged seventeen, wandered around Bethany informing one and all that now the war was over his father had come back from his posting to strange lands a hundred miles away and was ready to receive visitors.

Most of Bethany came to greet their chief, who sat cross-legged in the corner of the largest room in the house on two mattresses as became his elevated position, and on this occasion he did wear one of the four swords he owned. The status of the members of the village could be recognized by their behaviour in Aburish's presence and his reaction to them: the elders walked in first and he stood up to greet and embrace them, but the young bowed and kissed his hand, with the number of kisses exchanged or implanted on the hand telling of the closeness of the party involved. No one called him by his first name, for he was Abu Ahmad, meaning father of Ahmad, his eldest son, the begetter of male heirs who are a source of pride. In contrast to Hebraic tradition, where a person is Ben, or son of someone, the Arabs proudly take the name of their first son.

There were exchanges of mutual esteem and affection and the guests sat on mattresses or cushions. Their lamentations as to how much their chief had been missed were many: 'Only Allah knows how much we thought of you' and 'We are richer knowing that you are once again with us'. Then there flowed the proclamations of allegiance like: 'Only Allah knows how we kept the faith'; 'You are our head and our crown and without you we are prey to the wild dogs; 'The eyes of your enemies haven't known sleep since your safe return'.

Aburish's response to each proclamation of affection was in equal measure, thanking everyone for their kind thoughts and enquiring about their health and families, complimenting all who announced an increase in the number of their household and consoling others who had lost dear ones. Turkish coffee with cardamom seed, bitter unsweetened Arabic coffee and mint tea were served to the guests by the Aburish boys.

His wife Rashedah received the women of Bethany in an adjoining room. On this occasion Rashedah wore a black silk *thaub*, a gown which reached the floor and was given shape by a damascene silk band tied round the middle. The front and sides of the *thaub* were hand-embroidered and she wore a white head-cover which fell down the back and over the shoulders. The ladies visiting Rashedah echoed their husbands' words and so it was with her.

Aburish thus had good reason to be pleased; Bethany was

still his undisputed domain. True, his sons were too young to protect this indefinable position of power, but he had left an indelible imprint on this little community, and as long as prospects of his return existed, no one had dared to encroach on what he had come to regard as his natural right.

The Bethany of 1917 was a small settlement, hardly even a village, of some 400 inhabitants, a cluster of hovels nestling in the south-eastern fold of the Mount of Olives. Its occupants were Muslim Arabs who had lost all sense of time and who carried on a lifestyle that had existed, with little change, for more than 2,000 years.

On 6 December 1917, the British Army entered nearby Jerusalem and accepted the surrender of the Turks, the previous occupiers of Jerusalem and Palestine and Germany's ally during the First World War. To the people of Bethany, semi-bedouin who inhabited the caves and huts of the tiny place and lived off herding and farming, this meant only one thing: the return of the young men who had been conscripted into the Turkish Army to fight a war which was beyond their comprehension. There was little to suggest to them that the replacement of the Turks by the British would disturb their centuries-old state of subservience and isolation: nor were they interested. The whole thing, the end of what people in the west called the Great War, was of little concern to them. They simply welcomed the return of their young men, which meant easing the work burden of the old, the women and the children who had to farm and herd by themselves during the war years.

Khalil Aburish was not part of the Turkish Army, but he had done his bit. Too old to be conscripted into the regular army, he had become a member of the gendarmerie, an ill-equipped, ill-trained force entrusted with keeping order within Palestine itself. His paramilitary days had come to an end at the ripe age of fifty-six when the British, with a simple stroke of a pen, disbanded the gendarmerie, disarmed it and released its members to their homes. So Khalil Aburish came back to Bethany to face the future under a new colonial government.

The house to which he returned stood alone, some 600 yards west of the group of ancient caves and stone huts which made up Bethany proper, a stone-walled village occupying an area of six acres. He had built it in 1910 against the advice of friends and relatives who feared for his safety and that of his wife and children and had urged him to stay within the security of the established community. Hyenas and jackals infested the surrounding land, and dogs maimed by the inhospitable natives were equally dangerous; so were roving bedouin who were known to raid isolated houses. My eldest uncle Mahmoud remembers the mournful howls of hyenas, how they forced the people of the village to stay indoors at night, and how the villagers built eight to ten foot traps covered with shrubs to capture these predators so that they might be battered to death with long sticks. Mahmoud also remembers instances of unwelcome passing bedouin demanding food or a bed for the night – often with implied threats of camping menacingly under one of the few olive trees near to the house.

Hyenas, jackals and bandits were but a small part of village life. Agriculture, the primary source of income for Bethany's people, was the same as it had been in Biblical times – ancient dry farming dependent on rain. Primitive tools were used to till and harvest small plots of land which seldom exceeded three acres in size and which produced just enough grain for the landowners to eat or to barter for other products. Poorer villagers herded a few head of sheep and goats and used them the same way, to eat or exchange. When the grain crops failed due to lack of rain, some people would revert to eating locusts. Olives, figs and almonds were grown, but there were few trees and the recognized varieties of citrus fruits did not arrive until later, introduced by foreign monks who came to Jerusalem and Bethany to establish their presence in the Holy Land.

Insects, particularly black fly (*barghash*), were insufferably abundant and so were lice. Snakes were known to seek warmth close to the bodies of sleeping people and to react to natural human movement by biting them. The unlucky met instant death; the fortunate had an adept relative who would suck out the poison and then apply a poultice of aromatic herbs and ashes of other venomous snakes to heal the wound.

There was a high percentage of blind and one-eyed people in Bethany in 1917 because there were no doctors and eye infections were not treated properly: few people over thirty had any teeth for lack of dental care and most relied on gums hardened by regular use. There was leprosy and there was mange. People shared their living quarters with their animals. Apart from Khalil Aburish's five-room house the biggest hut or cave came to no more than 500 square feet, accommodating husband, wife, children and often a jackass, a mule, a few sheep and goats or occasionally a camel, not to speak of the husband's and/or wife's parents.

Infant mortality was very high: a rough estimate would suggest that at least one out of every three children succumbed to disease and died before the age of ten, and a high percentage of women died in childbirth for lack of a trained midwife. Today there are people called Mohammad the younger or Mohammed the second, or little Mirriam, because they were named after an elder brother or sister who did not survive, and there are many men married to sisters of their first wives who did not live through a difficult delivery.

This was the Bethany to which Khalil Aburish returned when, in his own words, 'they stopped beating the drum'. He returned to reclaim his position as the 'face of the village' (*wigh blad*), the headman who, though neither elected nor appointed, assumed a position of leadership among equals, the *primus inter pares* of this tiny, uninviting piece of the Holy Land which had been continuously inhabited for over 2000 years.

We know Bethany from the Bible. Its most famous feature is the tomb of Lazarus, a vault lined with masonry, which history books speak of as 'a castle of Lazarus during the Latin Kingdom'. There are also the house of Mary and Martha and the tomb of Simon the Leper, and it is the place where Martha met Jesus and where he stayed before the last supper.

A mountain track connected Bethany with the outside world, winding up the Mount of Olives and then descending to Gethsemane and Jerusalem, a mere two miles away.

The primitive conduct of farming and herding as a source of subsistence was all Bethany people knew and, in this respect, Bethany was less lucky that other villages of similar size because the limestone of the surrounding land was not fertile. It had nothing else going for it – nothing else, that is, except the inherent value of its religious places, especially the tomb of Lazarus.

How had Aburish, an only child who had lost his father at the age of seven and who could not count on family background and connections, managed to dominate this small, conservative, ancient community? How had he created for himself a level of genuine loyalty and affection which made him the undisputed leader of the community? The answer is simple. Alone among Bethany's people he had recognized the potential of the place and exploited it; through his shrewdness he had attained wealth and status which he translated into a position of supremacy. Moreover, his achievements benefited the rest of the community, many of whose members depended on him, directly or indirectly, for their livelihood.

Before 1917 there were few tourists to Jerusalem, only a few scholars, orientalists and the odd adventurer. Of those who reached Jerusalem few considered it safe to venture further, even to a place so close as Bethany. But the handful who braved the journey around 1890 sent a signal which only Khalil Aburish understood, and which inspired him to turn the religious interest in the ancient stones of the tombs of Lazarus and Simon the Leper into gold.

Until this discovery he had inhabited a small cave like the rest of the people of Bethany, and lived off the two small plots of land his father had left him. He and his widowed mother lived precariously, helping each other with everything, which meant sowing and harvesting and bartering their meagre surpluses. His instinct, which led him towards developing Bethany's tourist potential, was complemented by luck, for he discovered that the Hamdans (his ancestral name) had always claimed the tomb of Lazarus as theirs and, indeed, that there were official documents going back 300 years appointing the Hamdans 'the guardians of the holy resting place of Lazarus'. He himself owned one-fourth of the tomb and his relations' lack of interest in the shrine was confirmed when they sold him their seventy-five per cent share for an unknown but small number of sheep.

Aburish hurriedly improvised a door to the cave containing Lazarus's tomb and proceeded for the first time to charge an entrance fee to anyone wishing to visit it. The visitors were few and the money wasn't much, but it was considerably more than he had gained from tilling the forbidding land, and it was a growing business. His new income allowed him to save enough money to build himself that five-room house and distance himself from the rest of Bethany. The new house was a grand gesture. It had Bethany's first water closet, flushed by throwing buckets of water on the human waste, and placed him ahead of the rest of the people of the village. Ushering tourists with candles in their hands to view the moist underground slab of stone over Lazarus's tomb was good business.

A few years later, around 1895, he built a khan, an inn or caravansarai called al-Houd, the puddle. It was about a mile and a half east of Bethany and was the rest-house for the ever-increasing number of adventurous tourists who descended to Jericho from Jerusalem, using the main road which passed through Bethany. Most of these trips were undertaken on horse or mule-back, but already the odd vehicle was making its revolutionary appearance.

Al-Houd had two unfurnished chambers for guests and a courtyard for their animals. Mats and cushions were provided for each visitor in accordance with rank, and there was a single carpet for guests of distinction, but no one, however exalted his or her position, had a separate room. Outside al-Houd there were barrels full of water, some for drinking, some for washing, and some for the animals. For Arab and non-Arab alike, al-Houd served the standard Arab meal of rice topped by chunks of lamb. Like all khans, al-Houd offered dried fruit, coffee, milk and unleavened bread to the guests who stayed the night, to others who rested for a few hours and to passers-by. But ever the innovator, Khalil Aburish introduced insect powder into his khan, something which led to a more comfortable sleep and which, uncle Mahmoud remembers, gave the place a lot of publicity.

Khalil Aburish expanded his business and opened another rest-house, the al-Khan, four miles east of al-Houd and closer to Jericho. By now he had stopped attending to his guests himself and elevated himself to supervisor, using relatives, in-laws and fellow Bethanites to do the profitable day-to-day work. This allowed him time to exploit the Christian tourist potential growing around Jerusalem, particularly promoting visits to the tomb of Lazarus: trinkets, postcards and water from the Jordan river fifteen miles away were sold to the hundreds of unsuspecting tourists who now ventured beyond the Holy City and were charged unreasonable prices.

He made it his business to know the local priests who occupied the monasteries on the Mount of Olives, with an eye to meeting their superiors, the bishops. And to the bishops he made offers which appealed to every religious ambition they had ever entertained: to buy them land close to Bethany's religious sites. This was an act of unusual daring for, in spite of their obvious poverty, Bethany's Muslims had resisted previous Christian attempts to buy their land and introduce an alien religion into their community. The various religious orders were kept a whole mile or so away, right on top of the Mount of Olives; but defying this tradition, Khalil Aburish bought local land and sold it to the Greek Orthodox, Roman Catholic and Anglican churches. The churches wanted to be in Bethany, close to its known religious relics, and were willing to pay five to ten times the going price to achieve this. His overnight profits from these transactions were enormous.

When the profitable religious possibilities around Bethany and other touristic endeavours were exhausted, Khalil Aburish turned to trade. He used his khans to buy wheat, barley and lentils from the travelling bedouin and transported

it back to Jerusalem by mule for sale there, again at considerable profit. He later ventured further afield and began
importing sheep and goats from Turkey and Cyprus, first
journeying himself to what were considered far-away foreign
places and then sending representatives to do his work.
Records show he never imported more than 190 head of
sheep at a time, but that was a considerable number not only
by the standards of Bethany and neighbouring villages but of
Jerusalem itself. At one point he used ten full and part-time
shepherds, mostly poor landless Bethany people.

Aburish became a successful man, the most successful in
Bethany and a name known to the people of the neighbouring
villages and to the well-to-do in Jerusalem itself. His success
was based on money which he enjoyed to the full and which
allowed him to claim the leadership of the village.

He began wearing silk tunics and the colourful clothes
identified with the rich, and his *abbas* were made of camel
rather than goat hair; he was the first man in Bethany to wear
the much-whispered-about underpants, and he took to wearing a sword in the style of tribal chiefs, eventually collecting
four of them. Daringly, he kept whisky at home in case of
visits by his Christian clients; his sons and daughters were
distinguished by their fancy clothes and the fact that – as distinct from other Bethanites – each owned a pair of shoes and
wore them often enough to avoid the blisters associated with
occasional use. Aburish's concern for his children went
beyond that – he even took them to see Jerusalem doctors
whenever any of them showed the slightest sign of illness; the
local healer was no longer good enough for him.

The Aburish women, Khalil's wife and daughter, were
ostentatious in their celebrations of his success. They took to
wearing gold thread necklaces and gold bracelets, and
Rashedah went even further: she attached small gold coins to
the rim of the cap she wore to hold in place her very light
white head-cloth. Gold, silver, copper and iron talismans and
armlets appeared: everything about Aburish and his family
spoke of money and its enjoyment.

Not only did Aburish have a five-room modern house with

a water-closet and his own source of water, but he also prevailed upon his wife Rashedah to make bread in their own
taboun (oven). The oven was a round pan made of clay, don-
key dung and straw, about two and a half feet high and two
feet wide with an open narrow top and no bottom. There was
a fire inside and the dough was put on heated stones until it
was baked, when it was pulled out and the small stones prised
loose. Rashedah baked wheat bread while the rest of Bethany
nearly all settled for barley bread in their communal *tabouns*.
Whether Rashedah's hedonism extended, like her husband's,
to wearing underpants is a question to which I can find no
answer.

Beside the manner of dress, food was the second most
important expression of Arab extravagance. The ratio of
meat to rice in typical Arab dishes in the Aburish household
was high, a sure sign of affluence, and Aburish's sense of
culinary adventure extended to serving fish, a novelty to
Bethany and a solid sign of sophistication. (Though local
legend has it that some Bethany people wondered whether
fish was edible.) For the rest of the people of Bethany food
was not abundant and many lived off dipping their barley
bread in onion soup (*basalia*) and eating yoghurt and its
derivatives, which they stored in skin bottles made from the
stomachs of sheep. Many of them went to bed hungry,
especially after a drought year.

His acquisition of relative wealth and his display of it does
not, by itself, explain the leading position to which Khalil
Aburish returned from the war – particularly in view of the
fact that he had not inherited it. His pre-eminence came,
above all, from that unknown, inexplicable, quality inherent
in men of all races who possess the gift of leadership. By all
accounts, first and second-hand, he was blessed with a sense
of grace, and he was a natural leader: kind, cunning, remote
and unafraid, with a sense of fun that did not detract from his
assumed status and elegance.

His headband was always at a rakish angle, his handlebar
moustache properly waxed, his waistband made of fine
damascene silk folded to contain his seal, a silver box of snuff

and sometimes small coins. He never left home without his walking stick with which he used to take long, deliberate steps. He was bald, light of skin and his moustache was brown, giving credence to the legend that he had crusader blood in his veins. He loved to sing and would indulge in folk dances at every opportunity, but he was not familiar, and insisted on ceremony and respect.

A more worldly man than most, he accepted the British opening of higher education unquestioningly and when the time came decided to send his sons to Bethany's Department of Education schools. His own narrow Koranic learning, consisting of two years of sporadic attendance at the local mosque school, had hampered his progress and often embarrassed him. Unlike his wife, Khalil Aburish could read Arabic, though with difficulty: he would often feign indecision about a certain contract and delay giving an answer for no apparent reason. In fact this gave him time to take the document to a learned scribe in Jerusalem who would explain its contents with greater precision. Writing for him was for special occasions, and when circumstances compelled him to do so he cleared a wide area round him and pulled up the sleeves of his Arab robes before committing pen to paper. The act became a minor ceremony often watched with awe by people around. Even then the inconsistency of his signature forced him to dispense with this elaborate performance and use a brass seal. Through dealing with the churches he spoke several languages, albeit badly – English, Greek, French, German, Italian, Turkish and Spanish.

So he towered above his village contemporaries, who began to defer to him in all matters affecting their lives. He represented them in the sale of land to outsiders, mediated in internal village disputes, advised them on how to conduct their communications with the government, lent them money when they needed it and eventually deputized for them in their land claims with other villages. Poor and docile, most accepted his suzerainty while the few who opposed him were mercilessly pressurized into submission. When the Khalafs, a local family, showed signs of disobedience he bought all the land surrounding theirs and denied them access to their source of livelihood until they gave in. He conspired to deny other enemies access to the local wells, prohibited others from using land for grazing while favouring his followers through equally cunning means. When the First World War broke out in 1914 he had earned the position of local chief, pushing aside the previous ineffectual claimant to the title, a relative on his mother's side, one Said Abu Zayyad. Unhappily for him this position carried no weight with the central government which still viewed him as a semi-literate villager, unfit for officership in the army, these positions being reserved for the bourgeoisie.

His behaviour at home was an extension of the way he conducted himself outside: he demanded and received obedience. His wife never called him by his first name but by the respectful Abu Ahmad, though Ahmad and Hamdah were the children of his first deceased wife, and his sons and daughters called him *yaba*, my father; they always stood up in his presence unless commanded to sit down, and they would always walk a step or two behind him. At meal times they and their mother would wait for him to begin and would vie to pour the water on his hands after he had finished eating with his fingers in the style of the Arabs. But he was a loving father who cared for their health and education and spent considerable time with them, telling them the old Arab legends aimed at instilling a sense of honour and hospitality in their minds and directing them to play with each other to avoid the pitfalls of lying and laziness, and to keep away from outsiders beneath their station.

Food, one of the first signs of Aburish's affluence, was served on a tray of brass or wood placed in the middle of the ground, and everyone sat on cushions around the tray. People, particularly the elders, always sat cross-legged, though some young people were known to sit on their knees. The main meal, which opened with a recital of a brief Koranic sura to thank Allah for his generosity, consisted of one course only, meat and rice or *kubuz* and *lahem* (meat pie) – breakfast would have been merely cheese and olives. When the meal included rice and additions, one would squeeze a handful into a ball or cylinder and then put it in one's mouth – hence the need to wash the hands. Wooden spoons were available but very seldom used, saved mostly for non-Arabs or visitors from the cities. The meal was accompanied by plain or flavoured water, often rose water, and the elders helped the young by tearing big chunks of meat into small pieces which they gave them to eat, and by pouring them water or tea – coffee was and is for elders.

Rashedah Aburish was typical of her generation, a proud matron who had already produced three male heirs. Having done Aburish proud by giving birth to three boys – the first two girls died in infancy – her other functions in life appeared to be to cook, to suckle her infants, to be utterly subservient to her husband's every need and to discuss whatever scandal there was in hushed tones with her female friends. She was thrifty, untiring, brave and honest. By modern western standards her husband treated her badly – lack of sharing, unequal status – but she never complained. On the contrary, she was happy in her way, proud of him and very much his equal in enjoying the fruits of his achievements – and in talking about it.

Having made sure that his position of supremacy had not been eroded by his involuntary absence, Khalil Aburish used the first Friday after his return, the Muslim Sabbath, to visit the local mosque and occupy the special corner which had been his ever since he became Bethany's leading citizen. He joined his fellow villagers in prayer and received the apologies of the few who had not come to pay him homage in person. His act of reaccession was complete.

The people of Bethany and his immediate family were very pleased to have him back. But although still the unchallenged boss of Bethany, he alone knew that this exalted position in his tiny domain depended on another equally important element: how the British government, which now ruled Palestine and Bethany, would treat him and his like, the local chiefs who spoke for whole populations of backward semi-bedouin villages.

Under Turkish rule the fortunes of the village had risen
and fallen according to his successes in dealing with the central government, and with other communities, but the British
were an unknown quantity, though there was a disposition to
think well of these new conquerors as a result of the dimly
understood third and fourth-hand accounts of the exploits of
'Laurans', who had helped the Arabs throw off the yoke of the
Turk in far-off Arabia. Aburish worried about his own position:
would the British allow him to settle local disputes, including
blood feuds, to act as banker, realize exorbitant commissions
from land sales and divide the meagre water of the village
wells among its inhabitants, or would they choose to interfere
at the lowest level of local affairs and usurp his powers?

This problem, unknown to most of Bethany, was upper-
most in Khalil Aburish's mind, for if the British were to ignore
his position as a local leader, the resulting loss of face would
undermine the whole basis of his authority and prosperity in
Bethany. Because British officialdom had not yet established
itself at such a local level, he again demonstrated unusual
initiative and sought his answer from the local Anglican
bishop in Jerusalem. Rightly, he assumed that the bishop
would be able to explain the attitude of the new British
colonial administration and, as in so many instances in the
past, his instincts proved correct. The bishop was quite
forthcoming, and assured Aburish that the British experience
in India and other places augured well for his like. The bishop
was right.

2
The golden years

Baksheesh is nothing more than the tip, the gratuity of money the British gave to poor Arabs who served them in the Middle East
                                                    Mohammad Aburish

The Anglican bishop's assessment of the attitude of the new administration of Palestine underestimated the British desire to perpetuate the village chief system. As it turned out, this commitment was total, and it affected more than 800 villages in which sixty-five per cent of the Arab population of Palestine lived. There was an interregnum of two to three years before British influence took hold, during which the daily life of most of the people of Bethany remained virtually unchanged, though this wasn't so for the daring, the aware and the exploitative who moved ahead relentlessly to benefit from the new government's relative wealth.

Khalil Aburish met British military and civilian officials – military rule lasted until 1 July 1920 – through the Anglican bishop; he wanted to discover the needs of the new rulers, to discover what co-operation and allegiance on the part of local leaders was expected or possible. He found that not only was he permitted to continue all his previous activities, he was also encouraged to enter into new ones, particularly to supply personnel, labourers, minor civil servants and even policemen. The British favoured slow change, so they did not infringe on Aburish's prerogatives, which now included the use of local people in untried ways.

The new wage-labour jobs introduced by the British were a

welcome substitute to subsistence through traditional dry farming and herding. Not only did no one among the local population object to the British as occupiers, many of Bethany's young men were anxious to help them build roads or houses for their officials or to serve them in other capacities, simply because the pay was considerably better than the income from farming. Very few Bethanites qualified for civil service jobs because of their lack of education, but some found positions as male receptionists, servants and men-Friday and derived pride from the name and position of their employer. Bethanites who worked for British Army officers bragged about the range of their empoyer's rifle – one claimed his boss's Enfield 303 had a twenty-mile reach! Two Bethany men met the basic literary-test requirements to become policemen and enjoyed the pomp and prestige which went with wearing a British uniform. Aburish considered this a tribute to his status with the new government – to the extent of lecturing 'his' two policemen about polishing their boots and ironing their uniforms. Within the group of villages east of Jerusalem, the Wadiya, only one village chief bettered him in this regard: Abdul Rahman Irekat provided five policemen from the village of Abu Dis, but then Abu Dis was three times the size of Bethany.

Having policemen from one's village was particularly important because it meant a distinct advantage when the village got into trouble with neighbours: this symbol of association with higher authority was supposed to deter would-be poachers on the village's rights. Indirectly, the importance of a village boss could be judged by the number of his people employed by the British, as well as the positions they occupied. As a result, village chiefs tried to ingratiate themselves with British officialdom, vying for attention and regard in different ways, including the dispatch of frequent invitations to weddings and other feasts. The results of one such effort almost backfired when a British official nearly fainted in the process of watching a circumcision ceremony sponsored by Aburish.

The use of locals, particularly villagers, in new, well-paid

jobs led to an improvement in Bethany's standard of living,
particularly that of its local chief. The direct beneficiaries of
the new employment opportunities owed their jobs to
Aburish, who always selected people loyal to him who
secured his position by ensuring that he represented them in
all their affairs, including keeping their savings – which he
converted into gold coins. The second phase of British policy
was to train mechanics, drivers and even waiters, and here
again, Aburish nominated the trainees; this redirection of
men of working age meant a further decline in farming and
herding and increased economic reliance on the cities, where
the duties were performed. One of the Bethany people
trained as a driver used to dazzle the rest of the villagers with
his knowledge of the various makes of cars. To the locals, he
was a very knowledgeable person, indeed some considered
him a genius. The first time he brought his employer's car
with him to Bethany he parked it in front of the local coffee
shop and chatted to everyone through the window.

An early British move which affected Khalil Aburish directly
was the creation in 1922 of a Census Bureau. The new
department demanded a more complete and exact personal
identification system than had existed under the Turks. Up
to this time semi-bedouin and bedouin people had seldom
used family names: a person was called after his father and
identified by his profession or place of residence or work, or
in the case of the bedouin, by his tribe. So there was Mohammad, the son of Abdullah who herds goats and lives in the
third house on the left; and if that wasn't enough identification then he became Mohammad son of Abdullah son of
Ibrahim who lost one eye in the Turkish–Yemeni War and
who qualified for the rest of the description already given.
The collection of names and descriptive adjectives went on
until the person in question was recognized.

Khalil Aburish was born Khalil Ahmad Hamad, where
Ahmad was his father and Hamad his grandfather. Available
documents indicate that he used Hamad the way people use a
family name, though he also used the name Khalil Hamdan,
Hamdan being the name of the tribe from which the Hamads

came. There are other contemporary documents in the name of Khalil Aburish Hamad, Khalil Aburish Hamdan, and Khalil Hamad Aburish.

Clearly, when it came to a last name my grandfather was having an identity crisis, which was forced into the open by the new Department of Census requirement for a family name. He finally registered as Khalil Ahmad Aburish, adopting the nickname Aburish as a family name: literally translated, Aburish means 'feathery person', which colloquially means one with money, 'a downy bird'. That is what the admiring villagers called him and it became the name he chose.

The British liked Aburish and he liked them. He spoke broken English, drank whisky, was full of bonhomie, generous to a fault and appreciated their exactness and punctuality. He was a man of his word and, to him, so were they: he was fond of saying, 'The English don't lie.' His pretty wife Rashedah didn't speak English, but unlike most Muslims he didn't keep her under lock and key, and she was known for her sweet smile and over-use of 'hello' and 'welcome' – her total acquaintance with the English language. Besides, she was a superior cook, something which endeared her to Aburish's many English visitors. Even so, Aburish's break with tradition didn't go so far as to include his daughters, who remained in the background, avoiding all contact with outsiders; indeed, they were under strict orders to report attempts by men to speak to them.

In addition to his other activities Aburish became a small-time supplier of provisions for the British Army, as all his connections with the British appear to have been unhindered by anything resembling nationalistic or anti-British feeling – nor did anyone in Bethany have such an attitude. His concerns were limited to Bethany and its surroundings, which included Jerusalem in so far as it affected Bethany. His contacts outside Bethany were with other village chiefs, his regional counterparts, and no one can recall him expressing specific attitudes towards a country called Palestine, let alone who should govern it. He was Arab through and through, religiously, culturally and in attitude. Even the 1920–1 anti-Jewish riots in Jerusalem, Jaffa, Haifa and other towns appear to have left him unmoved; he viewed them as town, not village, problems, though if pressed he would undoubtedly have sided with his fellow-Muslims. Uncle Mahmoud remembers him discussing the riots with his friends Sheikh Hassan Othman of Beit Safafa and Sheikh Ghazlan of Silwan and insists that all three were agreed that they liked the British better than the city bourgeoisie (the *effendis*).

Rashedah, already the mother of three surviving boys, continued her winning ways and added to Aburish's pride in October 1918, but giving birth to another boy, Ali. Being neither a first nor second son, there was little fuss surrounding his arrival, except to celebrate the fact that it was a boy and not a girl.

Preference for boys over girls was deep rooted because boys carried the family or tribal name, helped their fathers with their work and in their old age, and, importantly, were useful in fights with other families, which often developed into blood feuds. A man's tribal status was often judged by the number of men behind him, his *azzwa*. A woman could be divorced if she didn't provide a son and heir for her husband, sometimes if she didn't provide more than one son. Being an only child, Aburish had more reason than most to want male children who would stand by him in case of trouble.

Like all Arab babies of his time, Ali was wrapped in swaddling clothes, with his feet tied together and his arms folded across his chest. His nappies were boiled in hot water, and olive oil was used on his bottom to avoid skin rash. Rashedah was up and about two days after his birth, breast-feeding Ali day and night with little regard to schedule or need.

Mousa, another son, was born in 1919, and so the five-room house had to accommodate six sons, one daughter, Rashedah, Khalil and Rashedah's mother and sister, Hasna and Mirriam-the-elder. In addition, Khalil's legendary hospitality meant guests were always present, and often stayed the night. Even by the standards of those days, the house became too small to cope with Aburish's family and hospitality.

Thus it was for practical reasons as well as those of ostentation that Aburish decided in 1921 to build a much larger house above Bethany, on the southern slopes of the Mount of Olives. It was positioned at the same altitude and in full view of the biggest house in the area, the one which belonged to Abdul Rahman Irekat, the chief of Abu Dis and the undisputed leader among the notables of the villages east of Jerusalem. Irekat was temporarily annoyed that Aburish considered himself his equal but he and Aburish eventually kissed and made up. Gossip had it that Aburish had considered building higher than Irekat but decided against it to avoid causing a feud.

There was no architect or designer involved in the new house, for Aburish knew exactly what he wanted: he hired a builder, told him he needed a large living-room and two small ones, a big kitchen, two storage rooms and six bedrooms. Naturally, the exterior was of hard stone in keeping with the grandeur of the house; the much cheaper soft stone was for others. There was no inside bathroom, just two sinks and china jugs for hand-washing purposes; the two lavatories and the *taboun* were built outside, just as in the old house. To give the new building a greater air of luxury Aburish built two small water wells, though one big one would have sufficed and been cheaper.

One of the bedrooms was used for bathing: it contained a round brass tub large enough for a normal-sized person, who needed the help of another person to wield the jug. Normally, one of Aburish's boys waited on him, Rashedah's stepdaughter Hamdah waited on her while the boys helped each other. Bathing took a long time as water had to be heated on a kerosene cooker, but cleanliness is commanded by the Koran.

This unimaginative piece of architecture was a square four storeys high – a basement and three floors. In line with custom there was a big to-do every time one of the floors was finished – an act denoting completion – and the people of the village came to help put the roof in place and celebrated the occasion with special songs of praise; the volunteers and regular workers usually stayed for lunch, when their talk consisted of praising Aburish and his achievements. After the house was completed, the people of Bethany briefly took to calling the biggest building in their town 'the palace'. Aburish didn't discourage the use of this misnomer; he thrived on it and ever after referred to the deep foundations of the place suggesting he might build one or two additional storeys.

Without doubt Aburish was a major beneficiary of the arrival of the British; his life was an expression of the golden age of *baksheesh*, a gratuity or present of money (nowadays often a bribe) which people give to others less fortunate and which lies at the heart of the relationship between giver and receiver. Not only did his connections with the British allow him to build the big house, his pioneering activities included sending Mahmoud, Mohammad and Ibrahim to schools in Jerusalem, thus sparing them from work at an early age. Another distinguishing feature was their western-style dress. He would haul them in to greet some of his British visitors, prodding them to try their few words of English on the guests, and the boys always asked the visitors to send them postcards from faraway places. On one occasion when their wish was granted, and a card arrived, it took two weeks to find someone who could read it, but receiving a card appears to have denoted the worldliness and sophistication represented by the visitors to the tomb of Lazarus.

This was the atmosphere which formed the character of the Aburish children. As the eldest child of Rashedah and Aburish, Mahmoud was encouraged to be a model for his brothers and sisters: he walked ahead of them and was introduced to outsiders first; he accompanied his sisters when they went to visit relatives or friends and refrained from 'childish' games. He both explained and transmitted his parents wishes to his brothers and sisters, and even at this early age it was he and not his mother who greeted visiting strangers when his father was absent and who joined his father in attending weddings and funerals. He was already in training as the future head of the family, the senior member of the clan.

Mohammad who, unlike his father and older brothers Ahmad and Mahmoud, was dark haired and brown eyed, was sandwiched between the dignity of Mahmoud's position and the glibness and naughtiness of Ibrahim, but he didn't compete with either. Instead he worked at being the obedient work-horse of the family, spending considerable time helping his mother and playing with his younger brothers and sisters. Today, Mousa speaks of this affectionately: 'Mohammad was always nice to us, while the others thought playing with us was beneath them.' Daoud takes his praise a little further by describing him as the family's 'Mr Reliable'. There is a good case to be made for explaining his future revolutionary activities in terms of a search for self-expression which he never had as a youngster, to compensate for his shyness and the inherent feeling that the elder Mahmoud and the younger Ibrahim appeared to outshine him.

'Bombastic' is the word everyone uses to describe Ibrahim, two years younger than Mohammad. He appears to have been born that way: among other thing he was always 'punishing' his younger brothers and sisters. He was so impatient to grow up he once stole one of his father's swords, tied it to his side and made a celebrated visit to the coffee house. This earned him a beating from his father, but suspicion lurks that Aburish wasn't altogether disapproving of Ibrahim's macho image and activities, which twenty years later found expression during the 1948 Arab–Israeli War.

Ali and Mousa never had their elder brothers' presence –as was common the older boys got more parental attention. According to uncle Mahmoud, Ali very seldom spent time with his brothers, for reasons difficult to judge, preferring his sisters' company. Amneh confirms this, saying: 'He wasn't very communicative but he was very helpful. He was good with his hands; he wanted to do carpentry work all the time but father discouraged him; he did not want him to become a worker.' Ali's idol was his brother Mohammad, the other introvert in the family.

Mousa was everyone's errand boy. He was an 'outsider'; he looked and behaved differently, never completely adopting the haughty Aburish attitude, but happier being one of the boys of the village. Even his parents appear to have shown little affection towards Mousa: all menial jobs went to him. Whether he resented his position or not is something he refuses to talk about to this day.

Daoud and Hassan were twelve and fourteen years younger and as such received little attention from Aburish. Daoud grew up inward-looking, like Ali and Mohammad, while Hassan's position as youngest child guaranteed him extra maternal attention; he was spoiled by Rashedah. The discipline exerted by Aburish to his older boys didn't reach him.

Hamdah, Amneh and Fatmeh were second-class citizens, like all girls of their age. Even younger brothers had the right to order the girls around; to ask them to fetch a glass of water or polish their shoes. So universally was this accepted at that time, they never complained. Amneh and Fatmeh were very close to each other and their rare quarrels resulted from competition over who did more for the males, served the tea or the coffee; while poor Hamdah, the much older half-sister, and therefore now a sad outsider, had to find her own way to please the young men in her household. The sisters were invariably obedient and never had a chance to show initiative, though they obviously appreciated kindness and remember those who treated them well. Still they were total persons and my mother who has known them since their early 'teens speaks of 'two of the most gracious creatures I've ever known'.

The girls' subordinate roles as resident maids and the boys' willingness to be helpful around the house allowed Rashedah to follow an active social life – attending weddings, funerals, births and circumcision ceremonies as well as visiting friends and relatives. While Aburish's world was public and regionally political, her life was more confined, essentially domestic and private. Rashedah bought the food for the household and either cooked or supervised the preparation of meals, exercised the authority of motherhood by telling her children how to behave and bought the girls' and her own clothes, which remained native. Aburish bought the clothes for the boys because Rashedah didn't know anything about western dress and, to Aburish, didn't buy good enough material for the *kimbases* the boys occasionally wore.

All the Aburish children remember his definite attitudes towards his surroundings, something which he tried to transmit to all of them, the girls included. Aburish thought the British were superior, the city Arabs were not to be trusted because they disliked villagers and were rude to them, and lastly that one should always be kind even to the most lowly person because 'better the dog that barks with you than against you' (*ahsan al-kalb illi be'wi ma'ak wala aleik*).

Rashedah's independence in her social activities was considerable. According to Mahmoud and my father, she danced at weddings, wept at funerals, gossiped with friends and went as far as checking on the welfare of the poor on the occasions of religious feasts. Her independence extended to visiting people Aburish disliked. Says Mahmoud: 'Let's face it; she was a busybody, and nothing pleased her more than when father was away. She wandered all over the place – even walked to other villages for a bit of gossip. Father hated her excursions but she didn't care.'

* * * *

Unpleasant as it may now appear, the Arabs of Palestine in the 1920s lived and died to one tune – *baksheesh*, that the British colonizer gave them. This was true of villagers and city folk, of Muslim and Christian alike – with the exception of the proud bedouin of the desert, a mere seven per cent of the population. This semitic tradition – first spoken of when one of the Pharaohs bribed Abraham – was reaching unprecedented heights. What seemed to the British colonialists to be small amounts represented a fortune to the native, whether bureaucrat, shopkeeper, labourer or servant. Everyone's income was complemented by outright tips and gifts of clothes and food. In addition, the well-meaning British lowered the rate of taxation which Turkey had imposed during the First World War, helped people educate their children and get proper medical care and paid special attention to the disabled. There was no shame attached to being on the receiving end of British generosity, and labourers and other menial workers became identified with the names and positions of their bosses – Mr Harvey's servant or the mayor's doorman. Most of them proudly exaggerated the generosity of their masters, the value of the gifts they received. One spoke of his second-hand coat having been made in Ondon, ignorance eliminating the 'L', while a second whispered to everyone that his employer corresponded with the King – he had seen a letter from His Majesty's Government.

Aburish did not descend to the level of accepting *baksheesh*, but much of his money depended on acting for Bethany people, and what he eventually received was a reflection of what they got. They paid him for representing them in disputes, interceding on their behalf with the government and having their documents certified. His income from the sale of land and trading also rose, because the general well-being meant an increase in prices and profits.

For Aburish this happy state produced further improvements in his home. Rugs replaced the mats the Aburishs had previously owned, and he started sending his son Mahmoud to Jerusalem to buy him tins of tuna, which he found to his taste. He even began adopting British mannerisms, insisting upon using genuine Ceylon tea in place of the traditional mint tea, at first to foreigners then to Arabs – with an explanation of why it was better. He served chocolate to foreign visitors, *baklava*, *knafeh* and other local sweets to Arabs. But this period was far from being trouble-free, for Aburish's role as head of the village was constantly tested by new and different problems created by the British and their ways, and some of the problems were close to home.

In 1923 a Bethany man died as a result of an accidental fall off a big rock in the middle of his own land. There was a chance that the poor man might have survived had he been discovered in time, but he wasn't found until the day after he went missing. The narrow-minded British official (a mere constable) in charge of Bethany affairs wanted the corpse taken to Jerusalem for an autopsy, but this conflicted with the Muslim custom requiring burial before sunset on the day of death, and the situation was made more pressing as the man had died the day before. Aburish, representing the deceased man's family, wanted to follow tradition but the official would not be moved. So Aburish appealed to the local British Army major, pointing out the possible consequences of violating religious custom, and the major reluctantly rescinded his subordinate's decision.

The army officer was one R. E. Wallace, who recorded his impressions of the villager's funeral in a diary which, for unknown reasons, is with my uncle Mahmoud. The diary records:

> Women tore their clothes and scratched their faces repeating unintelligible mournful dirges. Men cried and sobbed openly. Then the body of the dead man was laid on a table and washed in full view of all the men and the apertures were closed with cotton and cloth. Afterwards the body was wrapped in a winding sheet, placed in a bier and carried by four men, who were relieved frequently on their way to the graveyard, the men repeating what appeared to be Koranic sayings, and walking immediately behind while the women followed the men. The corpse was lowered into a grave which was covered by slabs of stone and then earth. The whole thing was over in five hours and I understand Sheikh Aburish invited all the mourners to lunch and provided food for the members of the dead man's family for three days. The latter were supposed to be too grief-stricken to cook for themselves. It is all very dramatic but we will never know the real cause of death.

Major Wallace's account failed to mention that the dead man was Abu Zayyad, one of Aburish's relations on his mother's side and that it was customary to invite a dead man's family and other mourners to lunch. Furthermore, because the man was from an important family, it meant that the chiefs of other villages attended the funeral at the head of small delegations to pay their respects to the family of the deceased and the village head, Khalil Aburish.

The conflict between autopsies and Muslim burial rites and habits continued throughout the country for a long time, until no less a person than the High Commissioner of Palestine decided in favour of custom, 'except under the most unusual circumstances'.

Problems of a religious kind were greater under the British than the Turks, as the Turks were Muslims who subscribed to Koranic teachings. Under strict Islamic law a son is legally bound to support his parents in old age, so when one renegade Bethanite refused to do so, he offended the sensibilities of all the villagers including their chief. Aburish was so incensed by this act of discourtesy and violation of custom, that he summoned the young man in question and flogged him publicly, in the coffee house, ordering him to live up to his duties. After all, the young man's action could be contagious.

It appears that Aburish's cane did more damage than was intended and the guilty young man somehow managed to reach the local British officer, show him the lacerations on his back and lodge an official complaint against Aburish. This was the test of tests, a direct confrontation between British and Islamic law, between a British official and a local village chief. Although the British had no intention of arresting Aburish or charging him with an offence, some action had to be taken: a citizen's rights had to be protected. The British officer had to find a solution to the dilemma, so he went direct to Aburish to demand an explanation.

Khalil Aburish was nothing if not resourceful. He invited the major to dine with him in two days time, along with Mohammad Abu al-Hawa, chief of al-Tour village, and Abdul Rahman Irekat, chief of Abu Dis village and a leading regional notable. During the dinner Aburish told the story to the other two chiefs and asked them to give the major the benefit of their opinion.

Not only were both men friends of Aburish, they felt as threatened by the incident as he did. Their verdict was a clear one: a village such as Bethany was a self-contained community with a rigid structure which demanded a firm adherence to custom and tradition. According to Irekat, Aburish and Abu al-Hawa, the moment outside hands began to tamper with the structure it would be destroyed and everyone would lose. The *status quo* could only be maintained by supporting Aburish. The result was that the British major told the young plaintiff to apologize to Aburish, and upbraided him for being a bad son.

The third dramatic problem Aburish faced was closer to home; it involved his eldest son Ahmad, the child of his first wife Abde'. The year was 1926, after Rashedah had given birth to four more children, Amneh, Fatmeh, Daoud and Hassan. The strain of attending to nine children and a stepchild must have shown, even on one brought up to cope with big families.

Ahmad, unhappy over the way Rashedah had managed to marry off his full sister Hamdah to a failed local farmer, had good reason to suspect Rashedah was conspiring to get rid of him the same way. But Ahmad, twenty-five and restless, did not feel bound by Rashedah's plans for him, something which produced a cool relationship and an atmosphere of tension between him and his stepmother. Though Ahmad was doing well managing one of his father's khans, he had heard about America from tourists and city folk from Jerusalem. It wasn't long before he began to talk about emigrating to that strange and wealthy land to make a life on his own. Some people from the nearby villages of Bethlehem, Ramallah and Beit Jala who had gone to America had written to tell their relatives of the fabulous and easy wealth waiting to be acquired there.

Aware of his son's unhappiness and quiet planning, Aburish approached the authorities with a request that no passport be issued to Ahmad to facilitate his escape, but this time he failed, for Ahmad was judged to be an adult capable of making his own decisions. The authorities did not see fit to bend the law in favour of traditional obedience to a father.

Using his meagre savings, Ahmad managed to obtain a passport and US visa and left Palestine secretly on a ship bound for New York. Aburish was stung by the triple blows of loss of control over his son, shame within the community because of his inability to manage his own household and an awareness of the limits of his influence with the authorities. He continued to speak of the incident with considerable sadness and pain to the end of his life; he died without knowing Ahmad's whereabouts, never forgiving himself or Rashedah for not having paid proper attention to his eldest son, or for that matter his eldest daughter, Hamdah.

British efforts in Palestine from 1925–30 yielded marked signs of improvement in many fields. Tinned goods, including Aburish's favourite tuna, appeared in the local store. More cars and buses resulted in a shrinkage of distances: some of Aburish's gendarmerie comrades came and visited him, to hold the equivalent of a veteran's reunion, from places as far away as Tiberius, 120 miles distant – a journey beyond contemplation under the Turks and still a dramatic trip in the 1920s. Aburish's various enterprises so benefited from the influx of tourists that he hired no less than eight of his in-laws, the Khatibs, to work for him, with all of his sons helping when not at school. Variations of western dress were being adopted by more and more people and were incorporated in traditional costume – a jacket worn under the *abba*, for example. Aburish bought a dining table and a set of china and steel knives and forks – he insisted on Sheffield – which he saved to serve food to British and other western people, while he and his family continued to eat in Arab style. He bought himself a large bed and slept on it while poor Rashedah continued to use a mattress in the same room because she insisted it was more comfortable. The children too had no beds of their own, just mattresses which they laid on the cement floor.

Most basic, traditional, relationships remained unaffected by the new economic well-being. Respect for elders, even when the age difference was only a year or two, remained near total. It was a situation beyond question, to the extent that uncle Mahmoud used to prevail upon my docile father,

Mohammad, to carry him piggy-back whenever he became tired, because Mahmoud was older, and my father couldn't say no. Even wild Ibrahim toed the line and would accept reprimands uncomplainingly from Mahmoud and my father; occasionally he apologized and kissed their hands. When not playing marbles or soccer (using a tennis ball instead of a football), the children helped around the house whenever commanded by their mother, and were beaten into obedience by their father, the sole administrator of punishment, if they questioned her orders, which was seldom. Aburish's own orders to them were never questioned, even the orders to cram before examinations and not to mix with village boys of whom he disapproved.

The Muslim feasts were occasions when money, 'eidiah, was given to the young and the women of the family, who always responded by kissing the hand of the donor. Those who could afford it sent 'eidiah to the poor of the village who responded with glowing praises of their benefactors to Allah. The imam at the local mosque preached goodness and adherence to the old ways, including honouring one's parents, assisting the poor and showing consideration to the maimed. Whatever changes the British brought fell short of a direct challenge to custom: they mostly went along with the old ways and made no attempt to turn people to new, western ways of self rule. Conversely, even when the benefits of wage labour became known and people celebrated their bosses, the British received little credit – people still attributed the results to Allah who alone governed these things, especially since they couldn't give the credit to 'infidels'. Even tips and grants came from 'Him who governs all things', and not from the pockets of the British.

The improvement of everyday life brought about by an enlightened British administration was accompanied by a new phenomenon, a new force which affected life in all Palestine. The small oriental Jewish communities which had lived separately in Palestine for centuries were being joined by a new, more aggressive type of European Jew, Zionists who believed that Palestine belonged to the Jews. The new arrivals – the Jewish population of Palestine increased by 250 per cent between 1917 and 1930 – were not content to occupy traditional ghettoes like the one in the old city of Jerusalem. Instead, with the tacit approval of the British government, they sought to buy land from villagers such as the people of Bethany to establish new, modern settlements in the countryside, and there were about eighty such settlements by 1930. The prices they offered for land were higher than the going rate, sometimes ten times more.

Bethany and Khalil Aburish provide an excellent glimpse of Jewish plans and Arab reactions. A representative of the Jewish Agency, the organization which represented the new Jewish immigrants, visited Aburish in 1928 and, without any preliminaries, the usual lengthy niceties that precede straight business talk, expressed an interest in buying any land east of Bethany, along the road to Jericho and the Dead Sea. Aburish was both local chief and land broker, and the villagers harboured no prejudice against Jews, nevertheless they were regarded as 'belonging' to the cities and the Jewish representative's offer to 'take care of Aburish handsomely' made the visit unusual. The Jewish gentleman claimed that the land was needed for agriculture with only a few houses to accommodate the farmers. There was a promise that new, better ways of farming would be introduced which would benefit everyone, including the Arab inhabitants of Bethany, and the gentleman was not short of examples of where such projects had worked well – the villages of Lifta and Abu Ghosh being known to Aburish.

Uncharacteristically, Aburish asked for time to consider the request. He had seen the benefits from the presence of the monasteries: the new varieties of citrus fruits, the success of crop rotation, the better use of water. But the situation confronting him was not so simple: the townsmen who organized anti-Jewish riots in 1921–2 and 1927, and later, more seriously in 1929, spoke of Jewish designs on Arab land and of how the Jews basically did not like Arabs. Taking this into account was particularly important because Aburish knew that the land in question was unfit for farming; he decided that the time had come to consult a more worldly, educated friend in Jerusalem, so he arranged a meeting with an Arab judge by the name of Aref al-Aref.

Al-Aref, unlike Aburish, belonged to an educated city bourgeoisie who saw Palestine as a country, a national entity which belonged to its Arab inhabitants. He even viewed Palestine as part of a larger Arab world, perhaps a single state in a huge federation incorporating all the Arab countries. Wisely, al-Aref did not try to turn Aburish into an Arab or Palestinian nationalist; instead he spoke to him in terms Aburish could understand.

To al-Aref, 'the foreign Christians wanted to be in Palestine to worship, but the Jews wanted to colonize' – the Arabic word *isti'mar* doubles for imperialism and colonialism. He cited the Bible, particularly the Old Testament, and in the end convinced Aburish that any sale of land to Jews was dishonourable – much, much worse than sacrificing the interests of Bethany to another village leader, because it would be an irredeemable act. He blunted the argument of the Jewish Agency man by recalling how the same promises had been made to others but never fulfilled: unlike missionaries the Jews didn't try to help anyone except themselves.

When a convinced Aburish refused to co-operate with the Jewish Agency's representative because he felt Bethany was threatened, the Agency turned to individual landowners in an attempt to buy their land. This was an unforgivable encroachment on Aburish's assumed authority, and when one of the Khatibs, Aburish's in-laws, showed signs of weakening and not listening to his advice to reject the Jewish Agency's generous offers, Aburish secretly organized the burning down of the man's orchard. (As recently as 1985 one of the Khatibs approached me and asked for compensation.) That sealed the issue, forcing the Jewish Agency to re-direct its energies to other places, and to easier village chiefs.

So, the golden age of baksheesh saw Aburish maintain and expand his hold on Bethany, deal with new 'imported' problems beyond his own expectations, and fully enjoy the fruits of his prosperity. His responses to the challenges of the times

were marked by an incredible ability to cope; except for the
sadness of Ahmad's emigration he translated potential dis-
asters into exploitable opportunities.

This journey through uncharted territory was done with
Rashedah at his side. Was she the docile, obedient Arab wife
of legend, or was there more to this woman than met the eye?
It is the unanimous opinion of all who remember them
together that Rashedah was an equal partner in formulating
Aburish's approach to life, though she shied away from day-
to-day interference and he despised her gossip.

True, she did chores which could be described as menial
and was dragged down by having to care for too many
children. Nor did she in any way keep pace with his march to
worldliness through exposure to foreign ways. For his part
Aburish never made any attempt openly to express appreciation for her efforts. Yet she was party to all the major decisions he took. Perhaps he kept his regard for her strictly
private to avoid any appearance of unmanliness.

Rashedah had a hand in nominating Aburish's candidates
for work with the British, naturally favouring members of her
own family; she determined who received 'eidiah and selected
other members of her family for Aburish to hire in his khan;
she warned him about his spendthrift ways and, according to
Mahmoud, prevailed upon him to see al-Aref because, 'you
don't know anything about this, Abu Ahmad – see that lawyer
in Jerusalem'. With no close relatives or sons old enough to
help him, Aburish appears to have depended far more on
Rashedah for advice than at first meets the eye.

If the security of Bethany and the well-being of its people
represented the limits of Aburish's concern then it is well to
remember how seriously he guarded them: they were his life,
which was definitely Arab, and not negotiable. The British
presence did not threaten him, he said. Naively or not his
view of the British was relative rather than absolute: they
were better than the Turks and city Arabs. In moments of
cynicism he spoke of how the British built schools while the
Turks built mosques to keep the people occupied with
religion. The idea of the Arabs running their own country was

still alien to him, as no one had ever tried to arouse any national sentiment in him. Unavoidably, this issue came to occupy a central place in his last days. The first Arab political daily papers came into being in 1929, about the time when the Jews were becoming more open about their eventual plans, and when the elder Aburish children were developing a sense of political awareness. The bourgeoisie's discovery of vehicles to reach the villages coincided with the emergence of a new generation of relatively educated Arabs, whose ambitions were moulded neither by Turkey's legacy nor Britain's largesse.

3

A country and a family come of age

The 1930s were years of recognition and discovery for us and for everybody in Palestine. My father discovered that his relationship with the British was hampered by the natural conflicts between master and slave; we discovered and adopted our Palestinian identity; and the British recognized the Palestinians as a people with stronger hopes and aspirations than they had expected.

Mohammad Aburish's words give an excellent portrait of Palestine in the 1930s, particularly of how the children of Khalil Aburish experienced the formative years of their independent, colourful lives.

They attained the level of education permitted by their father's means and the schools available to them. They began to earn a living, married and produced children and became irretrievably exposed to a world greater and more complex than the Bethany-centred one known to their parents.

With an average of two years of high school education behind each of them, Mahmoud, Mohammad and Ibrahim left their schools in Jerusalem during 1929–30, at the ages of seventeen, fifteen and fourteen respectively. By Bethany standards, they were highly educated, though they were only average when compared with their father's equals in Jerusalem and other cities, and well behind the sons of the bourgeoisie. Khalil Aburish was as proud as he could be of his children's educational achievements, and as expected at that time, he, as their father, proceeded to try to find them employment – even fourteen-year-olds were considered to be of working age.

The natural thing to do would have been to use them at al-Houd and al-Khan, where they had worked during their school holidays, but the inns had been almost put out of business by the car, which now allowed people to travel from Jerusalem to Jericho and other places without need of Aburish's hospitality. The only business he conducted from his caravansarais was buying and selling grain and that, too, was adversely affected by the recession of 1930 – not being an industrial country Palestine suffered a recession rather than a depression. So Aburish followed the alternative available to him: he found his children jobs working for various British people and organizations.

In 1931 Mahmoud was hired as an assistant to a certain Mr Edwards, a member of the British colonial administration secretariat; Mohammad became a bell-boy, a hotel trainee at the Scotch Hospice in Jerusalem; Ibrahim was taken on as an errand boy for a certain Mr Harris, another official of the colonial administration and a close friend of the elder Aburish. Except for Mahmoud who was eventually expected to succeed his father as head of the village, the boys had no career plans or particular ambitions and would have accepted any job their father secured for them. However lowly the position, jobs away from the village's traditional sources of income were hard to come by and many a Bethanite complained bitterly about Aburish having 'all three children in well-paying jobs'. What made these humble jobs doubly desirable was that they were with the British, who were unquestioningly looked upon as masters, even by the sons of a successful village chief; it was quite acceptable to Aburish to have Ibrahim working as an errand boy for an Englishman, though he would never have allowed him to do the same job for an Arab.

The boys branched out in different directions. Mahmoud accompanied Edwards for years in his travels throughout Palestine when he was appointed a roving official entrusted with gauging the political and economic pulse of the Palestine Arabs. Mahmoud's work with Edwards widened his outlook; among other things he helped his boss prepare reports about the basic industries of the country – olive oil, textiles, soap and citrus fruits. Mahmoud still remembers with awe

Edwards' handling of thorny problems, his coolness under
pressure, his impartiality and his lack of familiarity. Edwards'
advice to Mahmoud included down-to-earth homilies such
as, 'An Arab feels much better after he lets off steam – always
allow them their say in full – even when you know it's a load of
nonsense'. The knowledge he gained from Edwards helped
prepare Mahmoud for his position as head of the village as
much as his father's influence did, and he retains a certain
Englishness to this day: a bushy red moustache, suede shoes
and a certain way of being relaxed while standing ramrod
erect.

His travels with Edwards opened Mahmoud's eyes to
marked differences among the people of Palestine. According to him: 'In the thirties the closer you got to the sea shore
(Mediterranean) the looser the morals. Even neighbouring
villages had different accents and, believe me, the people of
one village would be handsome and those of another ugly.
Let's face it, they very seldom intermarried.' He is still full of
stories about how the people of Abu Dis mistreated their
women and pays tribute to native intelligence by stating that
villagers can tell Americans from British even though they
don't speak English.

Mohammad, as usual, substituted hard work and solid
qualities for flair: he worked long hours, became everyone's
friend and confidant, helped his fellow workers and began
polishing his English. It took him a mere six months to
become an assistant concierge, two years to become a full
concierge, three years to own the first private car in Bethany,
five years to build a house and marry, and six years to become
my father. He was helped every step of the way by hordes of
admirers who appreciated his honesty and straightforward-
ness. Nobody disliked him, but then, unlike Mahmoud and
Ibrahim, he never sought a primary position in life; he was
always unassuming and self-effacing – almost un-Arab in his
lack of temper, doing a secondary job exceptionally well. He
endeared himself to fellow Bethanites by hiring five of them
to work at the hospice, though his employment there slowly
distanced him from Bethany and its ways.

Ibrahim continued to be the naughty boy among the brothers. He worked for Harris for six months, drove the official's car without permission, smashing it into a lamp-post: he escaped injury but was fired. Again he was fired when he pinched his next employer's wife on the bottom, a third time when he broke the nose of his boss's cook. Still he was a proud, inventive man who always managed to make enough money to buy flashy suits and visit night clubs. Aburish, stern, scolding and critical of Ibrahim's behaviour in his presence, told Mahmoud and Mohammad: 'Why not? Every family needs a tough guy in case of trouble. Ibrahim has earned the job . . . everybody fears him.'

Whatever their behaviour in their jobs and *vis-à-vis* other people, the elder Aburish boys were obedient sons. Mahmoud always kissed his father's hand whenever he returned home, even after a two-day journey; Mohammad took his salary intact to his father, and when the latter refused to touch it, he asked his father's advice on what to do with it. Even Ibrahim showed his affection in his inimitable way by, in Mahmoud's words, offering 'to kill anyone who gave father any grief'.

The attitude of the elder Aburish boys toward Bethany differed as well. Mahmoud, like his father, thought it beneath his dignity to go to the coffee house, the one and only men's gathering place – people had to seek him out even then. Mohammad was taking the first steps towards becoming a workaholic; he didn't have time for anything except his job in Jerusalem and was already cultivating contacts with the rich and powerful in Palestine. Ibrahim, on the other hand, was a coffee house regular who took to demonstrating his learning by reading aloud from a Jerusalem newspaper to the other, mostly illiterate, regulars. They would gather around him while he conducted a recital, spicing whatever he read with snide comments as he went along and occasionally making up stories completely. An Ibrahim-invented story which everyone still remembers had the British giving Palestine back to the Turks because the Palestinians were 'ungovernable'.

Jerusalem newspapers were introducing two new worlds to Bethany. The Arab press was urging Palestinian Arabs to follow the lead of their neighbours in Syria, Egypt and Iraq in demanding independence from foreign powers. Then in 1933, following the instructions of the Palestinian leadership in the cities and in an act of ultimate disservice to the Arab cause, the press praised the rise of a man called Hitler, describing him as a friend who would put Germany's weight behind Arab demands for independence. Until then, the villagers' knowledge of Germany was based on the stories of veterans of the Turkish Army who told them that German arms and officers were better than those of the Turks.

Newspaper tirades alone were not enough to inspire the mostly uneducated inhabitants of backward places like Bethany. However, the ideas they were disseminating took hold, because nationalism was being preached in schools to the educated elite and in mosques to the ignorant faithful. Advocates of an independent Arab Palestine began to pay attention to villages the size of Bethany through special representatives who sought to generate a religious and nationalist fervour against the British and the Jews. The man responsible for introducing nationalism to Bethany and neighbouring villages was Sheikh Mousa Shahine, a judge of the High Islamic Court, and a member of the Arab Higher Committee, the city-based organization opposing the British occupation and Jewish plans. Bethany became part of his territory because he lived nearby, above Gethsemane, on the Mount of Olives.

Shahine's efforts were successful, aided by a marked rise in the number of children exposed to the idea of nationalism in schools. By the mid-1930s, no less that 30 per cent of Bethany's boys were attending schools, many following the pioneering efforts of the Aburishs by going to Jerusalem. Ali and Mousa attended schools in Jerusalem until 1935, while Daoud and Hassan were still in Bethany schools; the girls, Amneh and Fatmeh, were at home helping their mother in the daily chores of keeping house and attending to the needs of the male members of the family.

Khalil Aburish and his children had a bigger problem than most people in deciding whether to join the rising tide of nationalism: their connections with and their indebtedness to the British colonial administration were much more direct than most. So Khalil Aburish's Arab identity was pitted against clear financial considerations which he couldn't dismiss lightly; his concern was for his children, for al-Houd and al-Khan were closing down, his land brokerage business had come to a halt because of the prospect of political turmoil, and he himself was now unwell, suffering from old age and over-indulgence.

On the other hand, Mahmoud's salary had increased several times, allowing him to satisfy his weakness for fancy clothes: more suits, shoes, silk shirts, and colourful silk ties as well as expensive native clothes. In addition, Mahmoud was beginning to show promising signs of being a worthy successor to his father in his relationship with the British and handling of local people. The elder Aburish encouraged Mahmoud to develop his own personal contacts with the British and he relieved his father's work burden by presiding over minor *sulhas*.

Financially, Mohammad was doing better than his brothers, augmenting his income as concierge by buying two taxis for hire by the guests at the Scotch Hospice. Unlike Mahmoud he was frugal, dressed soberly and, at that time, had few interests outside his work. Even Ibrahim's income was high by the standards of the day, in spite of repeated problems with employers and minor brushes with the law. He always improvised a way to make money.

The general well-being experienced by Bethany under the British extended beyond the Aburishs. The policemen and other employees of the British built themselves houses, owned bicycles, no longer rolled their own cigarettes. Others reaped the benefits of better farming methods as well as the introduction of new varieties of crops. Khalil Aburish's existing worlds, his family and Bethany, were doing well when suddenly challenged by the new, untried world of nationalism, the demand for allegiance to Palestine calling for an active confirmation of his undoubted Arab patriotism. The issue of allegiance was decided at the end of 1935, when the Aburishs

put their loyalty to their culture above immediate considerations; the reasons for the decision differed but it was
unanimous.

Khalil Aburish began to lose his affection for the British
during 1933–4, formative years for the nationalist movement
as represented by the Arab Higher Committee and its head,
the Mufti of Jerusalem, Haj Amin al-Husseini, the pre-
eminent religious leader of the region. The British, responding to Arab agitation and sporadic acts of violence, took to
employing methods which offended Aburish's sense of tribal
honour and fair play. The British had committed themselves
to a policy of 'collective punishment', which on occasion
meant arresting the entire family of anyone suspected of
being a rebel, or blowing up the houses of absentee
revolutionaries. They made other serious mistakes by
appointing 'local spies' to keep them apprised of the spread
of anti-British feeling. The 'spies' spoke in their master's
name, circumventing Aburish's role as the link between
Bethany and the British.

It was the appointment of one of these people in Bethany
that finally alienated Aburish, who had refused to inform on
revolutionaries or sanction collective punishment. The
British put in one Hussein Kadah in 1933; not only did Kadah
behave badly to Bethany's 1,000 inhabitants but he was also
a showy person who took pleasure in undermining Aburish's
tribal authority. To Aburish, the British betrayal was total;
they had shown themselves to be insensitive outsiders badly
at fault in their judgement of Arab character and temperament. Ancient loyalties took over, and he became a Palestinian nationalist.

Because of age and illness Aburish's nationalism never
went beyond preaching opposition to the British, the Jews,
and 'their stooge, the mangy son of a dog Hussein Kadah'. A
much more important development was the adoption of their
father's attitude by the Aburish boys for they were young
enough to give concrete shape to their feelings.

Initially the nationalism of Mahmoud and Ibrahim was confined both in depth and geography; they never ventured

beyond Bethany, nor did they resort to active resistance. Mahmoud, as heir to Khalil Aburish, was concerned with undermining Kadah's growing British-sponsored authority while Ibrahim threatened daily to shoot him. Their nationalism was local, a reflection of the conflict between their father and Kadah; certainly it had no ideology. It was the quiet members of the family, Mohammad and Ali, who became fully-fledged, active members of the Arab resistance movement, followers of the Arab Higher Committee, believers in Arab dreams and aspirations, the call for the creation of an independent Arab Palestine.

The catalyst in moving the Aburishs from passive dis-approval of British perfidy to active and, eventually, armed resistance, was Sheikh Mousa Shahine, local representative of the Arab Higher Committee who in 1937 struck a rich vein of hitherto undetected and untapped nationalist fervour in Mohammad Aburish, who had become his son-in-law in 1934 (see next chapter). So the chief beneficiary of British largesse among the Aburish children became their leading revolution-ary; he implicitly subscribed to Sheikh Mousa Shahine's teachings that the British wanted to give Palestine to the Jews, a feeling given impetus in Mohammad's case by the humiliation they administered to his revered father. He says: 'Sheikh Mousa was an outstanding spokesman for the revol-ution. Not only did he try to resurrect the Arab sense of honour, he said an independent Palestine would mean own-ing a hospice instead of being a concierge in one.'

Mohammad's first act of rebellion was not the stuff of high drama. At the suggestion of his father-in-law, Mohammad would roll into Bethany in one of his taxis in time for the all-important 6.00 p.m. radio news. As the taxi was equipped with a radio, one of three in the whole of Bethany, he would turn it on with the doors of the car open so that the villagers could gather around to hear news about Palestine, Hitler and Mussolini. This surpassed Ibrahim's readings of the news-paper in the local coffee house which were irregular, less dramatic, unreliable and in any case reached a smaller audience. Ten, fifteeen, occasionally twenty people would gather around the black Plymouth as night descended, then disperse into smaller groups to discuss what they had heard. This was the first stage of rebellion, the indoctrination phase: a raising of awareness through exposure to news, usually followed by an interpretation of it provided by Mohammad and Ali Aburish after consultation with Mousa Shahine. Surprisingly, the Aburish revolutionaries found Bethany fertile ground; there were converts. What was originally an abstract threat had become real and obvious; among other things Nazi policies led to a massive increase of European Jewish immigrants to Palestine. My father sums up his initial revolutionary activity by stating that: 'The lack of national awareness did not preclude identity; the people of Bethany didn't understand nationalism but they were Arabs and they were beginning to see the threat to their Arabism.'

If the indoctrination process into nationalism was basic, then the armed rebellion which erupted in 1936 and continued through 1939 was simply naive and resulted in the death of 3,000 Palestinians. Rebellion in the cities took the form of acts of civil disobedience, while the rural hill districts like Bethany were the areas of the armed uprising, which continued well after the townspeople gave in. Mohammad Aburish was Sheikh Mousa Shahine's chief lieutenant not only for Bethany but for the neighbouring villages of Silwan, al-Tour and Abu Dis. It was necessary to communicate with other rebels, a task which was rendered difficult by the night curfew introduced by the British.

Ali Aburish was his brother's willing messenger to other villages, and was joined in this activity by a close friend, Ali Abu Zayyad. Mohammad followed no coding system to get messages to other villages nor did he believe in oral messages. Instead he used onion juice to write to other revolutionaries. The onion juice didn't show until the paper on which it was written was heated over a flame – a cumbersome way of communicating for there was a danger of losing your place when writing the message and a chance of burning the paper when it was read.

Late in 1936, Ali Aburish and Ali Abu Zayyad were intercepted by a British Army patrol while cycling to Abu Dis with
found onion juice messages. Uncle Mahmoud recalls that
when asked why he smelled of onions, Ali replied that he
liked onions because 'they are healthy'. The British who were
up to all these tricks, arrested the two Alis, easily read the
incriminating mesages, then arrested Mohammad and the
addressees the following day.

This was the first of many arrests, the beginning of count-
less revolutionary adventures. In this case, Mohammad and
his messengers were exchanged for a minor British Army
officer who was kidnapped by the revolutionaries, and the
lenient British looked the other way when he resumed his
work after his four-week prison stint. However, things would
never be the same again; he had become a marked man,
under constant surveillance by the police, who were confronting broader opposition from the Arabs than they had expected.
Besides, he had by then become personally known to the
Mufti who admired the young man's 'honesty and reliability'.

Whether Mohammad's activities elevated him to the 'most
wanted list' of the British is confused by family legend, but
that he had to go underground during the 1937–9 period is
beyond doubt. Also beyond doubt is the high esteem in which
he was held by active revolutionaries who accepted his
leadership over other local notables such as the Irekats. It
was at this time that he resorted to using several aliases
including Mohammad Hamad, a simple reversion to his
ancestral name. Now he speaks nostalgically about the
rebels: 'Most were illiterate and more than half were
barefoot, and would only attack when the moon was out, but
by God they were committed men of honour.'

The most curious aspect of the Aburishs' adoption of a
nationalist identity is their continued social and business
intercourse with the British, which appears to have been typical
of others as well. How they reconciled the two is important for
a number of reasons; it identifies the nature of the rebellion
as well as the overall Arab–British relationship.

To Mohammad, who became universally known as Abu

Said after my birth in 1936, the issue between the Palestine
Arabs and the British 'had nothing to do with individual
Englishmen: we just wanted to be free. The British weren't
abusive to people but they were favouring the Jews at our
expense, helping them buy more of our land.' The question as
to why he had continued to work in their establishments gets
a ready answer: 'Revolutionaries had to earn a living.'

Mahmoud's assessment differs substantially – perhaps
because he lacked Abu Said's exposure to the Mufti's
idealogue revolutionaries. To him,

> the rebellion wasn't anything serious, and nobody, but nobody
> opposed the British, except a handful of members of the Arab
> Higher Committee. The rest of the people secretly admired the
> British though they genuinely worried about Jewish land
> purchases. My sympathies were and are totally Arab but there
> was no way to run Bethany or anything else without dealing with
> the British.

Ibrahim continued to work with the British while condemning
them, whereas Ali blindly followed his favourite brother,
Mohammad. Mousa, Daoud and Hassan were never involved.

The thorny issue of working for the British was avoided by
the Arab Higher Committee which decided against calling
upon people to quit. After all why alienate supporters by
inflicting economic hardship on them? Even highly placed
nationalists such as Mousa al-Alami and Ishaq Mousa al-
Husseini continued in the employment of the British Mandate Government.

The attitude of the women was equally revealing. Rashedah
was full of worry, totally opposed to her children's involvement in any anti-British activity. She remembered the bad
times under Turkish rule, along with the improvements in the
standard of living and general well-being the British had
brought. Besides, she wanted her children to make money.
Neither Amneh nor Fatmeh were old enough or educated
enough to have their own opinions, though both say they
hated Hussein Kadah because he encroached on the preroga-

tives of Mahmoud and Khalil Aburish. To them, the only reason the British were bad was because they supported Hussein Kadah.

The one female member of the family who had original thoughts on the rebellion was my mother, Umm Said. The desire to rid Palestine of the British was something she had learnt from her father, so her husband's conversion to the rebellion made her doubly proud: she felt like her father's true daughter, her husband's true wife. Now she speaks of the local rebels as,

> ... naive, almost stupid in the way they did things. They did everything except carry badges saying 'we are rebels'. On the other hand, the British had to be stopped from giving the country to the Jews. We tried to stop them and we failed ... at the end of the day, you can't condemn people for being stupid. After all, they did put their lives on the line – just think of how many of them went hungry until a local villager shared his food with them. God bless them.

It is obvious that several factors, often conflicting, were at work at the same time. First, people were as occupied with personal well-being as with nationalism and rebellion – even the Arab Higher Committee realized that. Abu Said had managed to build the first house with an indoor lavatory in Bethany, a much talked about achievement and a source of pride, so this and other manifestations of British influence conflicted with his revolutionary commitment. Mahmoud was still better off under the British than his father had been under the Turks but he resented Hussein Kadah. In its pure form the overall rebellion preached by Mousa Shahine didn't appeal to most people: they didn't understand nationalism and independence at all. There is solid support for the thesis that the 'revolution was exported to the villages' by the educated bourgeoisie in the cities, that the villagers were concerned with lesser issues, and that Hussein Kadah's 'corrupting' of their local government mattered more than Haj Amin al-Husseini becoming head of an independent Arab

Palestine. With this background, it is impossible to explain why people worked for Mousa Shahine and with Abu Said in the early 1930s, except in terms of their blind acceptance of what the educated bourgeoisie advocated. In other words, they thought the Mufti and members of the Higher Committee were right because they were educated and knowledgeable. They surrendered themselves to the rebellion rather than joined it, a feeling underpinned by their kinship to their compatriots in the cities. The surest way to overcome occasional objections to orders was to whisper that they were 'the wish of the effendi (Haj Amin)'.

The year 1937 saw the total transfer of allegiance from local to national leaders, to the Mufti of Jerusalem. This was caused by the publication of the recommendations of the Peel Commission, a British Government study group, which advocated the partition of Palestine into two states, one Arab and one Jewish. To the average person, even the humblest villager, this confirmed the promise in the Balfour Declaration of 1917 to give the Jews a national home in Palestine. As Mahmoud says: 'The Peel Commission's report reduced the problem to simple essentials. If there was anything the Arabs felt close to, it was the land, and that was what was threatened in actual everyday terms – not vaguely as in the Balfour Declaration.'

The year 1936 was as dramatic for the Aburishs as it was for Palestine as a country. It was the year of Khalil Aburish's death and this forced a number of new arrangements. Mahmoud took over as provider for his mother, sister Amneh and brother Daoud, while Abu Said assumed responsibility for Fatmeh and Hassan. Daoud and Hassan were at school in Jerusalem, Ibrahim had finally settled in a job at the ministry of agriculture while the brothers Ali and Mousa were found minor clerical jobs in the ministry of public works.

The Aburish family's attention centred around three things: maintaining Rashedah in style, finding brides and bridegrooms for the eligible members of the family and celebrating the family's continuity by focusing on the new generation which, for a while, consisted of only one grandchild, myself. Rashedah was the object of genuine love and respect, with the elder Aburish boys vying to see who could do more for her. In turn Rashedah's preoccupation was to get Mahmoud, Ibrahim and the girls married: to her, Mahmoud was getting old at twenty-six and Ibrahim was eligible at twenty-two. All of them took pride in my existence. According to my mother: 'Left to their own devices I'd never have seen you. Everyone wanted to have you with them. Until Khalil Ibrahim was born in 1940, you had a monopoly on their affection: you were the first grandchild, and a healthy male.'

Mahmoud's dual role as head of the family and village and an employee of the British continued, something which was not unusual: many like him had regular jobs as well as being family and village chiefs. His primary concern in Bethany was to continue as undisputed head of the village in the face of a general increase in the villagers' level of education and consequent awareness and expectations. He managed well, aided by Rashedah who, though still in the background in the way of all women, had a great deal to say about everything, particularly in the crucial area of distinguishing friend from foe.

Abu Said's revolutionary commitment took root. His exploits included organizing and participating in a raid on trucks (owned by the British Palestine Potash Co.), carrying potash from the Dead Sea to the port of Haifa. His group burned four trucks. Some of the revolutionaries were caught and imprisoned – one was killed by the guard of the convoy.

On another occasion Abu Said was given the job of assassinating Hugh Foot (now Lord Caradon), then an up-and-coming colonial administration official. Abu Said learned how to use a gun and for over a month he went to the hills around Bethany for target practice. He had problems deciding how to carry the 7mm. gun – on his right or left side, under his left arm or up the leg of his trousers – and whether to do the job in broad daylight and then surrender or to make a run for it. In the end Abu Said and his fellow revolutionaries decided in favour of a hit-and-run scheme which did not work. Many years later Lord Caradon described the young man who had circled his house on a bicycle as 'rather amusing', for the British had known of the assassination scheme and advised Foot to enter and leave his house only when Abu Said was not circling it. The British decision not to arrest him was typical: they preferred compromise to confrontation whenever possible, to avoid inflaming local feelings.

When 1938 came, Abu Said willingly gave up his regular work to join his father-in-law and the Mufti in exile in the small Lebanese village of al-Zoug. He became a full-time revolutionary, carrying messages from the Mufti to co-operatives throughout Palestine. Abu Said remembers the Mufti's directives as being general to the point of incoherence: 'He merely told everybody to keep the faith and make as much trouble for the British as possible.'

It was at al-Zoug, at the early age of four, that I was first exposed to political violence, when a wounded Palestinian revolutionary staggered into our small house and asked for an immediate meeting with the Mufti. My father left my mother to attend to the man and disappeared into the night to consult the leader; when my father was late in returning, Faris al-Azouni, the wounded rebel, became agitated, in spite of my mother's assurances that all was well. Soon he opened the door and ran into the street, and a minute later we heard machine gun fire – Faris al-Azouni was no more. A French Army patrol – Lebanon was a French mandate – tried to apprehend him and shot and killed him when he didn't heed their warning. I remember my mother looking at me in horror and saying, 'I don't think it's your father. He wasn't armed when he left'.

Our time at al-Zoug produced another indelible impression, an example of how Palestinian leadership viewed its lowly followers, the intrinsic disdain with which they viewed human life. The Mufti summoned the young Abu Said, then twenty-nine years old, and entrusted him with a most important mission: to go to Jerusalem and bring back a small package from a trusted fellow revolutionary. Though the delicacy of the mission was emphasized the Mufti never mentioned the contents of the package nor did Abu Said see fit to ask.

During the two-week trip to Jerusalem and back Abu Said used car, train and bicycle, and exposed himself to the constant danger of arrest and imprisonment; but it was only when he delivered the package to the Mufti that he knew its contents. Beaming with satisfaction the Mufti opened the package and showed Abu Said the fez wrapped in a white sash – his ceremonial headdress. According to His Eminence nobody could compare with his tailor in Jerusalem who had a way of wrapping the sash so beautifully. After that he mildly thanked the bewildered Abu Said.

Ibrahim's progress was different; it centered around his life style. He abandoned the Bethany coffee house for Jerusalem bars, dropped his village pronunciation, chased girls, wore flashy Miami Beach neckties, ate pork (forbidden by Islam) and smoked cork-tipped Craven A's. Overall, he wanted to sound like, look like and live like a city Arab who appreciated things western. Unlike Lebanon, where social divisions followed religious lines, in Palestine there was a distinct separateness between the cities and the villages; the townsmen considered the villagers backward and uneducated and while the villagers made fun of the townsmen's effete ways, nevertheless being accepted by the townsmen was considered an achievement for a villager.

Ali and Mousa, as was their wont throughout their lives, unsuccessfully tried to emulate their elder brothers. Ali, also working with the British while being a revolutionary, never attained Abu Said's level in either business or revolutionary achievement, for he was a difficult taciturn man, a brooding introvert, though a loving uncle who spent much time playing with me. Mousa tried Ibrahim's ways without success, for he did not possess Ibrahim's aggressiveness and charm.

Apart from the revolutionary atmosphere enveloping Bethany as a tiny component of Palestine, the second formative influence on the Aburishs was marriage. Not only did my father's revolutionary commitment obviously come through

his father-in-law, his immediate surroundings were markedly
influenced by my mother. She says: 'In many ways, he was a
bedouin, with all the charm which goes with that. I influenced
everything in his life, all the way from introducing him to new
food to stopping him from bragging too much about his
achievements. He was a fast, instinctive learner; he grew all
the time.'

Ibrahim's days as a tough man-about-town in Jerusalem
came to an end in 1938, when he married Salha Hamad. She
bore him a son in 1939 who was named Khalil after his late
grandfather, and Ibrahim, like the proverbial film hoodlum,
became a devoted father incessantly regaling people with
stories about the brilliance of his first son. This attractive
trait did not interfere with him becoming a disciplinarian; it
resulted in a carrot and stick attitude which he used with his
children all his life and which led to many a heated argument
with his wife when she objected to his harshness.

Amneh and Fatmeh married second cousins at a very
young age. In line with accepted custom, they continued to be
referred to as Amneh and Fatmeh Aburish, a label which
meant greater identification with their family than with their
spouses. They took singular pride in their brothers' achievements and deferred to their mother in everything. In a way
they were their husbands' superiors, and acted the part.

Rashedah's role during the late 1930s was an intriguing
one which belied the accepted outside view of the place of the
woman. She was in her sixties during this period but had
refused to move into the background with the loss of 'her
man'. She had been her husband's trusted partner, her
children's adored mother and, like many others, she did
interfere and exert influence. Her children were 'the face' of
the family, but they listened to her, particularly Mahmoud in
his position as head both of family and village. To my father,
she said: 'The British let your father down, but you can't beat
them; they are too smart.' According to Salha she told
Ibrahim: 'I am very pleased with your attitude towards your
wife and child – it's time you settled down.' She constantly
advised her daughters 'to obey their husbands . . . a man is

easy to please, just praise him'. She spent untold hours with me telling me endless stories full of parables of fidelity and perfidy, courage and cowardice. My favourite was called: 'Is it an Ox Tail or a Goat's Tail?' It took her a whole month to finish telling me this allegorical fable on the value of honesty.

The 1930s ended without excitement, but they were the critical years whose influence determined the future of the Aburish family. In the shadow of the turmoil enveloping Palestine, Mahmoud was confirmed as head of Bethany: for though undermined by Kadah, the rest of the village took him to their hearts. Abu Said's revolutionary commitment infected other members of the family and has had a marked influence on all of them to this day. Ibrahim's ways were only exaggerations of a widespread craving to shed the limitations of Bethany's attitudes and adopt broader, more western ones. Rashedah's matriarchal bent took hold; to this day the women of the family, even the Bethany-bound ones, interfere in their children's affairs more than the men. The name Aburish, the family name in which my generation was born after Khalil's children got married, now truly became a family name which people bore with pride. It superseded its Hamad and Hamdan origins and perpetuated the small time legend of a 'downy bird' who had cast a shadow slightly bigger than life.

4
Courtship, marriage and village life

All I knew about my future husband was second-hand: he was a distant
relation and he was sixteen years my senior. He gave me forty unhappy
years but we weren't brought up in a way which tolerated divorce. Allah
bless his soul; he was a miserable man.

Fatmeh Aburish Azzem

The first of Khalil Aburish's children to get married was my
father, Mohammad, the second of the sons who lived in
Bethany. There is little doubt that Mohammad got married
to please his father, who in 1934 was in his seventies and ail-
ing. Khalil Aburish and his wife wanted male grandchildren
to perpetuate his name, and he wanted to see that before
dying. After all, he came from a society which endowed male
descendants with all honour and power, where the absence of
sons was tantamount to an enduring stigma.

The privilege of the first to wed should have gone to
Mahmoud, who was the oldest son, but Mahmoud, whose
eyes retain an irresistible twinkle to this day, was suffering
from two handicaps. The Muslim girl he wanted to marry was
already engaged to her first cousin who had a prior claim
which he would not renounce; and he was secretly in love with
a Christian girl who lived in Jerusalem proper – and inter-
faith marriages were out of the question. Mahmoud was
therefore happy to concede his primary position to his
younger brother.

Khalil Aburish was not a man to be fooled easily. He knew
the situation, so he turned to Mohammad and asked him to
honour him by choosing a bride 'from a good family'. At
twenty-three Mohammad was a most eligible bachelor, gain-

fully employed at the Scotch Hospice in Jerusalem, with a seven-room house he had built himself, and his own car. Besides, he was by temperament the most quiet and obedient of Khalil Aburish's boys, and so accepted without question his parents' decision that he should marry. His virile good looks never overcame the painful shyness which still haunts him.

Surprisingly, rather than follow traditional lines and allow his parents to choose his bride, he expressed a singular interest in marrying Soraya Shahine, the second child of Sheikh Mousa Shahine, a graduate of Cairo's al-Azhar and Istanbul universities, an Islamic Judge and a member of the Arab Higher Committee (the body created by the former Mufti of Jerusalem, which was in effect the PLO of the 1930s and 1940s – the political body entrusted to negotiate with the British for an independent Arab Palestine). Shahine was a tall, darkish man with a white beard and penetrating black eyes, an imposing, handsome man by any standards. Like the Mufti he always donned the black robes and the head-dress of a tarboosh wrapped with a white sash denoting his position as a qadi, a judge, and a graduate of al-Azhar. Unlike Aburish, the local notable with a penchant for flowing silk robes and an Arab head-dress worn at a rakish angle, he was a man of national stature. He had moved near to Bethany a few years before and was the first to commute to Jerusalem daily.

Mohammad's unexpected and unexplained selection of Soraya Shahine, presented two major problems: Mousa Shahine and Khalil Aburish disliked each other and had done so for years. Shahine accused Aburish of supporting the missionaries and introducing Christian ways to Bethany, including the consumption of alcohol. On the other hand, Aburish scoffed at Shahine's haughty ways and austere outlook on life, and resented his formality. But the lack of sympathy was not the only barrier, as Soraya had a number of eligible first cousins on her mother's side who were entitled to 'first refusal' rights by tradition and were thus able to stop outsiders from poaching on their relations. An unsatisfied first cousin could force a bride to dismount from the horse carry-

ing her to her husband-to-be (*ibn al'am be nazela al-Hsan*) on
the day of her wedding.

Khalil Aburish's desire to have one of his sons marry and
provide him with a grandchild overcame his hesitation about
dealing with Shahine; he was not a man to be deterred from
what he wanted. First an old lady friend of the Aburishs was
asked to determine whether Soraya had been 'promised' to
anyone, then a messenger was sent to Mousa Shahine to
inform him of Aburish's desire to visit him accompanied by
his wife Rashedah and his eldest son Mahmoud. Shahine responded by inviting Aburish to his home, and his ready
acceptance of the Aburish initiative suggests that from the
composition of the delegation he realised the nature of its
business. However, not knowing of Mohammad's selection
and Mahmoud's unusual relegation to second place, Shahine
thought that Mahmoud was the proposed bridegroom.

Khalil, Rashedah and Mahmoud went to visit Shahine late
on a Wednesday in March 1934. Shahine greeted them at the
bottom of the stairs of his comparatively palatial fourteen-
room house and led them to a living-room decorated in subdued cream and grey and containing only a brass tray, some
crystal flower vases and voluminous reference books. In line
with Islamic teachings forbidding the representation of life,
there were no paintings or art objects. Shahine's wife
Mirriam was already seated in the living-room waiting for the
guests, and, as was customary, she stood up and shook hands
with everyone. By all accounts this was the first visit the two
men had ever paid each other – certainly their first encounter
for years.

The meeting began with the usual flow of expressions of
welcome and enquiries about each other's health, welfare and
children. Aburish talked to Shahine, Rashedah talked to
Mirriam and Mahmoud sat stiffly speaking only when spoken
to. Coffee with cardamom seed was served first to the men
and then to the women, then sweet mint tea was served in the
same order, then sugar-encrusted almonds (*malabas*) and
sesame brittle – sesame seed and honey. This traditional
beginning probably took the usual ten to twenty minutes,

during which the principal subject matter was not broached and the conversation was full of assurances of mutual esteem punctuated by deference and thanks to Allah (God willing and thanks be to him – *inshallah* and *al-Hamdou lilah*) which were offered to a background of clicking prayer beads.

For the actual proposal of marriage, I am fortunate to have uncle Mahmoud's first-hand account as well as my mother's and father's and maternal uncle Rashid's verification of it based on recollections of what they were told. It went something like this.

Aburish: Sheikh Mousa, you are one of our leaders and a pillar of our community.

Shahine: It is very kind of you to say so. Only Allah knows how mutual this feeling is.

Aburish: Our son Mohammad is a good boy, he is gainfully employed, he does not drink nor gamble and his reputation is as perfumed as gum arabic. He has built himself a house and has a car, and all he needs to make his life easier is a bride. We have questioned him on this matter and he professes the utmost respect for your person and asks for the hand of your daughter Soraya in marriage. Naturally, we thank Allah that he is a thinking boy and that he wishes, with Allah's permission and yours, to be honoured by being related to you.

Shahine: The honour is totally ours. We thought it was Mahmoud who wanted to settle down but, of course, we have heard about Mohammad and his good ways. I have no objection myself nor does Mirriam. But there is a matter of the girl's maternal cousins, one of whom, Ahmad Abu Zayyad, has asked for her hand in marriage, being one of many suitors she has turned down. There are also her wishes, because so far she is disinclined to leave home. We shall think about the first and enquire about her wishes and, Allah permitting, send you a message with our answer tomorrow.

The exchange took a long time and ended with Aburish expressing his total faith in Shahine's ability to persuade Soraya of the 'right path'. A perfunctory invitation to dinner was offered by Shahine and politely refused by Aburish – the delegation then trekked back home to a waiting and anxious Mohammad.

Mousa Shahine's assignment of importance to Soraya's opinion was unusual. The girls of Bethany and the villages of Palestine usually had no option but to follow their parents' wishes, so Aburish told a confused Mohammad that it was no more than a ploy, an attempt to get more dowry (*mahr*) – in the Arab Middle East it is the man who pays the dowry, whereas in other places it is the bride's family. My mother insists no ploy was intended and that she and her sisters were all consulted regarding their marriage, pointing out that her father was 'an advanced man of learning' who believed that women had a voice in their own future and that was why she was consulted.

Shahine was true to his word: his message to Aburish was delivered in the afternoon of the following day, putting an end to Mohammad's restlessness. Soraya took her decision on her parents' advice and her sisters' secret reports and accepted Mohammad's proposal of marriage, while her father decided to use finesse over the problem of her cousin. Another meeting, one dealing with the difficult specifics of the dowry and other aspects of the marriage contract, had to be arranged hastily. This time the delegation included Mohammad who, in accordance with custom, brought an engagement ring, a simple gold band on the inside of which was inscribed 'Mohammad Aburish'.

This second meeting was tightly structured. The first item was to cover the financial arrangement: the dowry, and divorce penalty – *al-muta'kher*, the amount of money a man pays a woman in case of divorce, which is specified in the marriage contract. Shahine proved demanding on all accounts, asking for a Bethany record of £150 in dowry and for the marriage contract to stipulate £150 in *al-muta'kher*. Aburish, a tough and tried negotiator, brought him down. He kept repeating that Soraya's worth could not be measured by money but by the immeasurable strength of her character and that, in view of the absence of divorce in his family, both were token figures. In the end, he still agreed on a record £100 for each category – Rashedah later chided him: 'I knew she'd be expensive.'

Second on the agenda was to satisfy the oldest maternal uncle and the young men of Soraya's family – *radwat al-khal* and *radwat al-shabab*. A fee is paid by the bridegroom to both. The reason for paying the maternal uncle separately was to avoid giving him part of the dowry which belonged to the bride's father – occasionally the paternal uncle has to be paid as well. Paying the young men was aimed at acknowledging their esteem for the bride: they would not 'let her go cheap', as the higher the demand the greater their regard for her.

Soraya's uncle Hashem put forward a difficult request which amounted to £15, while the young men of her family asked for another £15. Records were falling all over the place, for Bethany's highest known demand by a maternal uncle or the young men of a bride's family up to that time was £10. Aburish had to agree to the figures, both out of a desire to satisfy all parties concerned and because paying a high *radwat* reflected his position of importance and wealth. Given his character, he probably enjoyed being party to the record-breaking costs of a wedding.

Next came the matter of the disgruntled cousin, Ahmad Abu Zayyad, and here Shahine was very direct. He told how he had had to summon Ahmad and inform him of Soraya's acceptance of Mohammad Aburish as a bridegroom and how Ahmad's tears rolled down his cheeks uncontrollably. Though he had stressed to Ahmad the need for good behaviour, he was still worried lest the boy did something to himself – suicide – or something nasty like throwing stones at the wedding procession or challenging my father to a fight; after all, many a blood feud was started this way. Aburish did not react but both sides invoked Allah to instil wisdom into Ahmad's broken heart and wished for peace to continue among all concerned.

After the monetary aspects and familial hurdles of the

wedding had been dealt with there came the arrangements for the three stages of a traditional Muslim ceremony. The engagement, everyone agreed, should be announced immediately in the traditional way by word of mouth. After that would come the second stage of the Islamic procedure, the religious ceremony, *katb al-kitab*, in which an Islamic judge declared the couple man and wife. This was followed by the actual wedding ceremony (*urs*), a raucous affair lasting two or three days, depending on the financial capacity of the bridegroom's family, and consisting of the respective families, the people of the village and friends from near and far participating in a near-endless song and dance festival celebrating the betrothal. Normally, a marriage is consummated after the *urs*, though legal obligations become binding after the religious ceremony.

Aburish was in a hurry, sick with worry about 'not living long enough to see a grandchild', while Shahine wanted a more moderate pace, 'to give the young couple a chance to reconsider if they so wish', and this was the one instance where Shahine prevailed. It was agreed that the religious ceremony would take place two months after the engagement and the wedding four months after that.

When all the points were agreed, my father did the expected thing: he walked across the room to where my grandfather Shahine was sitting, seized his right hand and, bending from the waist, kissed it three times, raising it each time from his mouth to his forehead in the traditional Arab gesture of respect. Rashedah and Mirriam intoned Allah's blessings on my father as he sat back in his chair. This came to an end when grandfather Shahine raised his hands to heaven and recited a short sura from the Koran with everyone repeating the words after him.

A few minutes later my maternal uncle Rashid joined the gathering and kissed the hands of all the elders in a manner similar to the one used by my father, and then hugged and kissed both uncle Mahmoud and my father. He was then ordered by grandfather Shahine to take my father with him to place the ring on my mother's hand. As she was sitting in an adjacent room, the ring ceremony took less than a minute with no words exchanged between bridegroom and bride: she extended her right hand for the ring to be placed on her finger and according to her, 'I looked at the floor and didn't see what he looked like'. According to him, 'she looked at me and giggled and hid her face with both her hands'. When my father came back Rashedah and Mirriam performed their role and shed tears of joy, mumbling unintelligible things about what a happy day it was. The Aburishs left with ceremonial embraces and kissing of the hands. Mahmoud ran out of the Shahine household like a demon and energetically climbed the side of the Mount of Olives to the Aburish's home, carrying the glad tidings to a waiting throng of Aburishs and their relatives, the Hamdans, Azzems and Hamads. By the time the rest of the delegation reached *Hamweh*, the Aburish family estate, the men were shooting guns into the sky in wild celebration of the event, and the women were doing their ululations (*zagrouta*). Not only had their boy Mohammad succeeded in winning the hand of the daughter of an important man, the occasion was made more special because he was the first of his generation to get engaged.

Much to the annoyance of the ascetic Shahine the young Aburishs, known for their enjoyment of life, sang and danced all night long while the rest of Bethany listened. Even shy Ali, to the amazement of his parents and relatives, is supposed to have danced non-stop for three hours. But Khalil Aburish, fatigued by the lengthy negotiations and away from the religious shadow of Mousa Shahine, ordered his son Mahmoud to make him a cocktail: he drank three of the only cocktail he ever knew, Black Label Scotch Whisky with water, and went to bed. Rashedah, a faithful Muslim, never handled the bottles of whisky.

The news of Mohammad and Soraya's engagement spread like wildfire. The local central news bureau was the coffee house in the eastern part of Bethany, where the men met to drink tea and coffee and play backgammon and dominoes. Because he was a coffee house regular, my uncle Ibrahim Aburish was sent there to tell fellow habitué's, who in turn told others until it was know all over Bethany. Special messengers, my uncles on both sides, were sent to inform the notables of the neighbouring villages of Abu Dis, Silwan, al-Tour and al-Sawahra and a number of friends in Jerusalem proper. This was the accepted method of communicating such a happening, for whatever postal service existed was unreliable and there were no telephones. Aburish relayed the news to British friends and the local priests and bishops in person.

Soraya got busy worrying about her trousseau (*al-jihaz*). Her father, a generous and well-to-do man, promised to match her dowry by another £100 sterling, and her sorties to Jerusalem to buy clothes became the talk of Bethany and neighbouring towns. The two leading seamstresses in Bethany were engaged to make two ⹂silk *thaubs* (native dresses), while Mohammad decided to change the furniture of his house. His new furniture was more expensive and more fitting for a married couple. Except for the occasion with the engagement ring, the bride and bridegroom-to-be did not see each other until the religious part of the ceremony (*katb al-kitab*) had been performed by a local qadi. After that, Mohammad used to visit Soraya at her father's house, though, in accordance with recognized custom, they were never left by themselves, and the only time she met him accidentally she ran away and hid in a neighbour's house lest she be accused of flirting with him. During Mohammad's 'official visits' grandmother Mirriam acted as chaperone and by all accounts whatever conversation took place was between her and my father, while my mother sat silently in a corner, throwing shy glances at her future husband without adding anything to the conversation, though she did serve the coffee, tea and sweets. When addressing my mother, grandmother Mirriam referred to my father as her cousin, another confirmation of the fact that most girls married cousins, and Khalil and Rashedah Aburish automatically became 'uncle' and 'aunt'.

Khalil Aburish's deteriorating health, and a premonition that this was the only marriage of any of his children he was likely to attend, made him determined to make this a memorable wedding. It was his responsibility as the bridegroom's father to give the wedding (again unlike other societies where it is the bride's family), so he made a major decision: the festivities would last an unprecedented five days. This, too, was a new record because until then the longest recorded Bethany wedding ritual had lasted three days. Mousa Shahine objected that such an affair would be too long, ostentatious and wasteful, but since this was Aburish's decision his objections fell on deaf ears. It was to be Khalil Aburish's show all the way, and it is something that the elders in Bethany talk about to this day.

The arrangements were elaborate. Relatives and close friends were expected to be there every night and absence required a valid excuse, while other people from Bethany attended on the first and last evening; they knew their place without any formal invitation. People from other villages were assigned specific times, and then spent the whole night with their friends, the Shahines and the Aburishs, and were given places to sleep in their houses or with relatives and friends – some slept on mattresses in the orchard near *Hamweh*. Important people had priority, and religious leaders, both Muslim and Christian, were invited on a specific evening, and displayed the amity which always characterized sectarian relations in old Palestine; they sat next to each other after greeting each other with subdued embraces and kisses on both cheeks. (Rightly the Palestinians pride themselves on the lack of sectarian conflicts such as afflicted the Lebanon. There were no issues of supremacy between Muslims and Christians.) Soraya was to move to my father's house early on the evening of the fifth and last day of the festivities.

Thus the Aburishs, the Shahines, their relations, friends and the people of Bethany began the five-day wedding feast. It was a time of rejoicing in which people who had feuded with the Aburishs and Shahines participated, for they had conducted a peace (*sulha*) for the occasion. Weddings and circumcision ceremonies were used as excuses to make up, and invitations were extended to people with whom one had had a quarrel; the happiness of the events was supposed to overcome differences between enemies and the mere act of extending the invitations and their acceptance meant a tacit end to any feud.

The men and women celebrated separately, each group having its party in a separate building or wing. Within the women's compound the dancing was individual: a woman would impulsively stand up and do her dance number while the rest of the women clapped their hands and sang an accompaniment. Whatever she did was a 'folk' interpretation of the belly dance but she was always fully clad. Occasionally, in addition to the rhythmic clapping of the other women, she was accompanied by the beating of a small drum, the *derbakah*. Naturally, there were some who were more adept at shaking the hips and you could hear the wild cries of appreciation miles away when one known for her exquisite interpretations was induced to give it a try. The *derbakah* would beat louder and the spectators' shouts of recognition would rise accordingly. Often a song in praise of the dancer was improvised or adapted.

The men's parties were noisier and had more variety. They not only had a drum but also a lute player who sang as well, and occasionally someone who played a reed pipe or a similar wind instrument made of steel, a *shebabah*. Individual men danced alone, sometimes with sticks or swords in their hands, then men would do dances together, like the *debkah* (which is still popular and is akin to the Israeli *houra* of today). The *debkah* would consist of a group of men, arms wrapped around each others' shoulders, forming a semi-circle that could take up to twenty. A number of different steps were used and the rhythm was created by the particular beat they made on the ground with their own feet. The third common dance men performed was the *sahja*: that could be done with up to fifty or sixty men standing shoulder to shoulder, hands in front clapping, in a human snake around a man who stood in the middle and sang while the rest of the group acted as a chorus.

The songs of both men and women followed two distinct

lines: they praised family and friends and condemned enemies. The beauty of Soraya and the good looks of Mohammad occupied a central place with extravagant phrases like 'her eyes are like pearls' or 'he is so handsome his mother desires him'. The verbal attack on enemies was even more exaggerated: 'They are mice not men and if they do not behave the Aburish and Shahine swords will chop off their heads.'

All this took place at or around the Aburish family estate. The elders, both men and women, were inside the house while the young were in two goat-hair tents temporarily erected for the wedding. Then, on the fifth and final evening the celebration split into two groups, one at the Aburish household and one at the Shahine's, the guests of each family going where they belonged. Early in the evening a singing, chanting delegation, led by the elders and notables, followed by the young men and lastly by the women, went from the Aburish household to the bride's home to fetch her. As usual they sang the praise and condemnation songs and fired in the air. When they neared the Shahine household duets developed as the lines they sang received a reply from the waiting party. Much of this was improvised: 'We have come a long way to see our beloved ones'; 'The tears of your beloved ones have run dry waiting for you'.

Soraya was ready. Her hands had been decorated with henna two nights earlier, her eyebrows were plucked the night before by a committee of female relatives and friends (hofouf) – very often a girl had never had her eyebrows plucked until the night before her wedding. The morning when she was supposed to leave her father's house for the last time, her make-up was applied by the 'decoration committee' and there was a special effort to make her cheeks look much rosier than normal, while the rest of her face was whitened with powder. Deep colour was applied to her lips as well. Members of the decorating committee would often sneak out to tell others not so privileged of the progress being made in the hofouf, normally embellishing on how good the bride looked.

Aburish's party milled around in the courtyard of Shahine's

house until, veiled and wearing a white satin dress which reached her ankles, with white stockings and white shoes, Soraya appeared, looking like a Japanese doll, and, with the help of her brother Rashid, mounted a white horse side-saddle. The level of both shooting and singing rose to the heavens, particularly when Rashid placed an unsheathed sword in her right hand. She held the reins of the horse in her left hand and the sword straight in front of her. The two groups of guests now came together, elder joining elder, religious men standing in line together, men joining men, with the young men and the women behind. The horse moved slowly, led by Rashid, followed closely by Mousa Shahine and Khalil Aburish leading the whole procession, nervously clicking prayer beads in their hands and praising Allah for this happy event.

Ahmad Abu Zayyad, the rejected and dejected suitor, did not commit suicide nor interfere; instead he climbed the wall of the local Greek Orthodox monastery and tried to throw himself down eight feet – a feeble expression of histrionics. Then he had a last minute change of mind, tried to cling to the top of the wall which was spiked with broken glass, and grabbing one of the sharp pieces managed to sever one of his fingers. The whole incident did him no honour but made him the laughing stock of the village and Mohammad Aburish very proud. Mousa Shahine refused to see 'the fool' for many years; fool or not, he never spoke to my father for the rest of his life.

When the party arrived at the Aburish house they were ushered into two huge tents, with the customary divisions between old and young. The dancing continued, men and women still separate, with Soraya staying in the men's larger tent, still veiled, seated next to my father who had stayed at home and waited for her arrival to help her dismount. After she had touched the ground of the Aburish territory his first act was to twist the angle of the sword she was carrying with dramatic deliberateness. The angle she gripped when leaving her father's house denoted her tribe; now she was on Mohammad's home ground and smilingly let him twist the sword to the angle of his tribe – another occasion to raise the level of song and offer thanks to Allah. After that the sword was taken away from her by her ever helpful brother Rashid.

Suddenly the singing stopped and a voice asked everyone to remain silent. The guests sat down on backless wicker chairs borrowed from the local coffee house, on rugs, mats and even on the ground, and my grandparents and special guests joined the festivities in the big tent sitting on mattresses. It was time to give the newly-weds their presents. This was done in public and was announced to everyone by the crier or *mukalef* who asked for silence, stood in the middle of the circle of guests, received the present, declared its value and passed it on to a trusted relative of the bride and groom.

The presents were mostly money (*nkout*) and there is no question that people vied as to who would give more. The bedouin of al-Sawahra brought fine head of sheep in accordance with old customs, while the Irekats gave four gold coins reflecting their regional position of leadership and importance; there were even a few sacks of rice and lentils. The *mukalef* would start his declaration with the sentence: 'May Allah recompense you . . . and these are so many pounds to help the newly-weds on their way.' This was followed by cheers and applause. The first present was from the young men of the bride's family, the people who had taken £15 from my father: impelled by Arab pride they matched their part of the dowry and so gave £30 to the newly-weds, which was yet another Bethany record. This event deserved more than cheers of appreciation so it was followed by a song praising the characters of the young men of the bride's family. Appreciation of the present-giving varied, with songs, lute solos, even a *debkah* or a *sahja*, and the whole affair lasted from five in the afternoon until one in the morning. A meticulous record of the gifts received was kept by my uncle Ibrahim so the Aburishs might reciprocate when the occasion arose.

Food was served throughout in a separate small tent; it consisted of *mansaf*, spiced rice topped by yoghurt sauce with chunks of meat, served on huge trays around which people stood. Guests would leave the present-giving ceremony and go to the tent to eat in groups. They ate with their right hand with no utensils while the left was put behind their backs in accordance with polite Arab custom. Some would tear chunks of meat and offer it to friends, another gesture of politeness. When they had finished eating, boys outside the tent offered them a bar of soap and poured water on their hands from a brass jug, while others handed them a towel to dry themselves. They would then rejoin the party to be replaced by another group of diners, with a new tray of *mansaf* brought the moment one was nearly empty.

One part of the arrangements displeased Mousa Shahine: Aburish, who had business connections with every Christian sect in Jerusalem, set up a special corner in the house to serve whisky to his Christian friends. By all accounts the locals participated secretly and, in all, four to six cases of Black Label Whisky were consumed. There were no incidents of bad behaviour but the alcohol certainly contributed to the jovial atmosphere.

At one in the morning Mohammad Aburish and Soraya Shahine disappeared to their new home, half a kilometre away, in a hail of song and bullets. Other guests went their own way, while a few young men continued the festivities until five or six in the morning.

At about ten o'clock the following morning Rashedah Aburish, accompanied by her third son Ibrahim, knocked on the door of the newly-weds. Her son Mohammad opened the door and they exchanged whispers which Ibrahim, a few paces behind Rashedah, did not hear. Eventually, she turned around to Ibrahim, and transmitted the message to him. Ibrahim, ever the colourful member of the family, reached to his side, pulled out a Luger pistol, cocked it and fired three shots in the air. In this way the message was relayed to the rest of waiting Bethany: Soraya Shahine was no longer a virgin and Mohammad Aburish had done the deed. He may have been shy and retiring but he had had an experience or two with women tourists and knew what to do. This was a source of pride to his family, for it was not unusual for villagers to take two or three days to deflower their brides, while sometimes it took even longer and became a source of embarrassment to all concerned. Rashedah went back home, without entering my parents' house, to be hugged by a proud Khalil Aburish.

By local standards Mohammad Aburish and Soraya Shahine were relatively old when they got married, for he was twenty-three and she was twenty-one. Most boys in Bethany married around the age of eighteen, while girls were even younger, sometimes as young as fourteen. Age notwithstanding, the idea of taking precautionary measures to delay the arrival of children was totally alien to Bethany society. Having children, particularly sons, was a singular source of pride, an extension of a deep-rooted cultural attitude, and in this instance much more so because Khalil Aburish had organized the marriage specifically to have a grandchild. In addition, Islam, like Catholicism, frowns upon birth control. Soraya and Mohammad obliged and I was born eleven months after their marriage. I was named Said after my mother's favourite uncle, and in line with Arab custom my father adopted the name Abu Said (father of Said) and my mother became Umm Said (mother of Said). They were the proud begetters of a male heir.

According to both my parents and uncle Mahmoud that was the happiest day of my grandfather's life. The birth was a difficult one and when the local midwife proved unequal to the job my mother was moved to the French hospital in Jerusalem. After the birth Khalil Aburish, who was bedridden, defied his doctor's orders, donned his best silk *kimbas* and camel hair *abba* and went to the hospital to visit my mother and 'inspect' me. Mother says that tears welled in his eyes and after seconds when he was unable to speak he proclaimed in a hoarse voice, 'I am ready to go now', and left hurriedly after kissing me several times.

Khalil Aburish died of an internal haemorrhage fourteen months after my birth, and his last wish was for me to be taken to his bedside. He patted me on the head, kissed me on both cheeks and asked that I be taken away. An hour later he passed peacefully away.

Ceremonially the funeral of Khalil Aburish did not differ from that of the simple Bethany farmer whose death had caused a confrontation with the British authorities, because Islam commands that 'all people are equal in the eyes of Allah'. But it differed markedly in the size and composition of mourners.

The word of mouth communication system was used, amazingly reaching the villages of Beit Safafa and Abu Gosh in time for Sheikh Hassan Othman and Abu Said Erbash to make it to Bethany in time for the funeral, before sunset the same day. The procession of about 1,000 people was led by Haj Yusuf al-Khatib surrounded by the Aburish boys and the heads of the neighbouring villages, with religious leaders of the churches with whom Aburish had done business, local representatives of the government, and other notables and guests from Jerusalem following the men of the village. Women and children as usual came last.

The Aburish men, though totally distraught by the death of their father, held back their tears and behaved in a manly way; according to custom the women wailed and spoke of the emptiness of their lives after the death of their 'protector'. An Aburish man, in accordance with tradition, turned to the women and commanded them to silence while a guest could be heard saying that a man 'who produced so many lions [referring to the Aburish boys] should not be mourned.'

After the burial the Muslims in the funeral read the *fatha*, the appropriate sura from the Koran and Abdul Rahman Irekat, the chief regional notable gave a brief speech in which, among other things, he said that Aburish's last words had been a plea to 'get the foreigners out of our land'. The Aburish boys headed by Mahmoud lined up to receive condolences, the most commonly used expression being, 'May you live and achieve as much as he did'.

A member of the Khatib family, Aburish's in-laws, stood up and announced that all those present were invited to their

home for a meal, but most people went home without eating –
only about 100 people did so.

Then for a period of three days Mahmoud, in full Arab
regalia with his brothers at his side, sat at home to receive
condolences, over hundreds of cups of coffee and tea. The
condolences of Bethanites were mixed with declarations of
allegiance. Rasheda, with her stepdaughter Hamdah, her
daughters Amneh and Fatmeh and her daughter-in-law
Soraya sat in another part of the house where she received
the women. Occasionally a man would stand outside the
women's quarter and shout his condolences to her and wish
her and her children 'a long and happy life'.

The Aburish tribe had lost its founder. Mahmoud was now
the natural and undisputed head of the family but at twenty-
seven he was still something of a young playboy; experience
and the authority which goes with leadership were lacking.
He was, by his own admission, determined 'to have a little
fun' before marrying.

On the other hand, the third boy, Ibrahim, aged twenty-
one, wanted to get married. The object of his affection was
Salha Hamad, an orphaned second cousin and the only child
of the late Ibrahim Hamad. She was fifteen years old and a
ward of Khalil Aburish, so unlike the then exceptional case of
Soraya, her wishes did not matter. Upon hearing of Ibrahim's
inclinations my grandmother Rasheda told Salha of the plans
made for her without the slightest consideration for her feelings. Luckily, the diminutive, pretty Salha liked Ibrahim.

The announcement of the engagement, the religious
ceremony and the actual wedding all took place within seven
weeks. In spite of her secret affection for Ibrahim, Salha was
so confused as to what awaited her that she kept weeping, so
my mother assumed the role of the experienced eldest
daughter-in-law and briefed Salha on the 'secrets of marriage'.
Mother didn't stop there: she chose Salha's wedding dress
for her and chaired the *hofouf* committee to pretty her up for
Ibrahim on the night of the wedding. According to mother:
'She really didn't know what it was about but she wanted to

be with Ibrahim.' According to Salha: 'I was scared but I liked Ibrahim. Many girls in the village wanted him.'

By all accounts Ibrahim's marriage was a more sedate affair than my father's. It lasted only two nights, the number of guests were fewer, and since Salha was already with the Aburishs they dispensed with the wedding procession, and Mahmoud acted for both bride and bridegroom. The only distinctive thing about this wedding was the amount of alcohol consumed, for Ibrahim, an outgoing bon viveur, had invited dozens of Jerusalem friends who enjoyed Black Label Whisky as much as he did.

My aunts Amneh and Fatmeh were the next to marry. Blondish and blue-eyed, they were the envy of the women of their generation and the object of desire of the young men of Bethany. However, since they had cousins who had announced their interest in them outsiders never approached the family to ask for their hand. Besides, both were (and are) quiet creatures brought up to obey orders without question.

Rashedah organized the marriage of her daughters despite the reluctance of Mahmoud, who thought them too young, at sixteen and fourteen respectively. To Rashedah an early marriage reflected the desirability of the girl and she knew she had two winners, so Mahmoud's objections were dismissed with a wave of the hand. Rashedah was the wily power quietly manipulating the family.

Mousa Hamad, a second cousin, married Amneh, and Ahmad Azzem, another second cousin, married Fatmeh. Mousa Hamad was twenty-five years older than his bride to be; he had been to America and had married and divorced there. Ahmad Azzem was sixteen years older than Fatmeh. Both were ne'er-do-wells but the custom of giving priority to the family, particularly cousins, prevailed. In Rashedah's words: 'My daughters are too good to give to strangers.'

Once again, my mother acted as instructor, but Fatmeh, the youngest and shyest, proved more difficult than the others. For a week she refused to have sex with Ahmad; each time he approached her she crawled into a corner and wept. Bethany-born and bred, his attempts to seduce Fatmeh became the talk of the local layabouts and his embarrassment was so overwhelming that he tried to conspire with Mahmoud to organize a false shoot-out declaring his success with Fatmeh. Mahmoud refused to co-operate, blaming Fatmeh's virginity on Azzem's incompetence – if not impotence – and went as far as wondering out loud whether Azzem was a man. Rashedah saw Fatmeh the day after the wedding and scolded her for not accommodating Azzem, but that didn't work; my mother continued her sermonizing but that got nowhere either. Finally, it was Fatmeh's sister Amneh who, on the basis of her one week's experience, persuaded her that sex wasn't all that bad. Fatmeh gave in and the marriage was consummated after seven days of pressure on an innocent, uneducated fourteen-year-old. To this day Fatmeh is reluctant to speak about the subject.

The three marriages which followed were in the traditional mould. Mahmoud finally took as his bride Mirriam al-Khatib, a first cousin on his mother's side, a girl sixteen years younger and a recognized Bethany beauty. Because he was a local notable they had a wedding resembling that of my parents. Mousa married Mirriam's sister Khadija in an uneventful ceremony. Ali, though older than Mousa, later married my mother's sister Nafisa, and except for a cousin who raised a mild objection all went according to plan. No real change came until Daoud and Hassan, the youngest boys, married. By then Rashedah was getting old and Mahmoud fully occupied his rightful position as head of the family and village.

Daoud wanted to marry a distant cousin, Mirriam Hamdan. The problem was she was promised by her father to a closer cousin, so Mahmoud, responding to Daoud's wishes, approached the immediate family of the bridegroom-to-be, told them to 'lay off', and threatened 'action' unless his demands were met. Being a diplomat he never explained what action he had in mind, merely emphasized that Daoud was a cousin too, and that his side of the family was weightier. The would-be suitor was intimidated by the Aburishs and their influence and gave up Mirriam Hamdan, whom he had never seen, and married someone else within a month. Mirriam Hamdan was not consulted as to whom she preferred. Daoud proceeded to have a normal two-day wedding with subdued ceremonies.

Hassan was a different case, as he was to prove all his life. He chose as his future wife the daughter of a total outsider, the head of the local school and a man who came from another village, making it plain that whatever Mahmoud thought, he had to negotiate for him. The situation posed a number of problems: his intended bride was more educated than Hassan, as she had completed high school; but, apart from the implied insult to eligible female relatives, something else worried the more traditional female members of the Aburish family. This newcomer wore western clothes, with all that implied. To make matters worse, Hassan appeared to be deliberately flouting local custom, for he made a point of frequenting places like Amneh's house where he might see the girl, if only to wink at her. Amneh was terribly concerned that Hassan's forwardness would cause an 'incident' – he composed his own love songs for her, though if, as rumour has it, they went so far as to correspond with each other, Allah alone knows. There was a lot of talk behind closed doors, a lot of tongue clicking, but Hassan was stubborn: it was Munira al-Hass'an or nobody. One thing was sure – this was love, a totally new phenomenon in the Bethany of 1951, the year of Hassan's betrothal.

Hassan's wedding reflected a change which had been gathering momentum since my father was forced into marriage sixteen years earlier. Munira, it appeared, needed no instruction on the facts of life: she seemed to know all that was needed, though there is little doubt she was a virtuous girl and a virgin. She refused to cover her face, and may well have been responsible for what Mahmoud described as 'the vanishing veil'. Shamelessly, by Bethany standards, she led the dancers at her wedding, and openly held hands with Hassan while others sang their praises. Not only that, she refused to have henna put on, and she walked from her house to his, head up, eyes twinkling, chatting to those accompanying her. She bought her own trousseau, applied her own make-up and even chose the flowers she carried in her right hand.

Hassan, the last of Khalil Aburish's children to wed, gave an indication of the shape of things to come in Middle Eastern family life. The rest of the family had weddings typical of the Palestine villages of their time, when the amount of money available governed how long celebrations lasted, and the structure of the ceremonies was always the same. Only in the case of the poorest people, who married each other's sisters to avoid having to pay dowries, was there a marked difference.

Courtship and marriage have changed since then and are now a mixture of traditional Arab values and adopted western ones, though the extent to which western mores have been incorporated in functions which are basically religious varies, and there is no longer a rigid set of rules governing courtship and marriage. Looked at through western and Middle Eastern eyes, immense differences can exist in the attitudes of two brothers who are close in age, with one leaning towards Middle Eastern and Muslim ways and the other to more 'western' ideas. My brother Afif had a Bethany wedding in 1964 while Wagih married at the local registry office in New York City.

It is important to examine the constituent elements which have direct bearing on the two related institutions of courtship and marriage, and which make contributions peculiar to this male-orientated society. These two elements are part of the male attitudes and indirectly influence female attitudes: I am referring to circumcision and homosexuality.

* * * *

Circumcision is part of religion, an extension of Old Testament Judaic teachings, but in Islam, unlike Judaism, there is no prescribed time as to when circumcision should be performed. As a result it was until recently done when a boy was between five and twelve years old and became part of his sexual awareness, although it is now usually done shortly after birth.

As in marriage, the ceremony surrounding circumcision is a direct reflection of the financial means of the parents. The feasting can last from one to four days before the actual performance of the operation, but the guests are relatives and close friends and very seldom include outsiders or people from other villages. While important, circumcision is not the ceremony that marriage was and is, and another difference is the fact that the feasting and dancing is often only for women – the men's celebration, if it takes place at all, is for one night only.

For days before the operation the boy would be briefed by an uncle or a father about how to behave 'like a man'. A brave boy wasn't supposed to cry, even though the operation was performed with a simple razor and without anaesthetic: he was supposed to make a statement of courage as the razor was applied. Cousin Khalil Ibrahim managed to squeak, 'we are Hamads and we are accustomed to pain'. Cousin Khalil Mahmoud bettered him by declaring, 'this is for the eyes of my father'. Boys are praised or ridiculed in accordance with their behaviour in the shadow of the razor and one is either a goat or a lion forever as a result.

The mother's role up until the 1950s was an intriguing one, for she was the true organizer of this affair. Yet, she spent most of her time weeping, loudly and rightly bemoaning the pain which would be inflicted on her boy. Mothers, my grandmother Rashedah included, are known to have gone to visit the neighbours at that moment of utmost delicacy, 'because she didn't want to see her children in pain'. Aunt Nafisa Ali went into her usual hysterics when her only son was the centre of the affair; uncle Ibrahim, a man who never suffered women's sobbing gladly, told her very seriously to stop it because, 'her son's wasn't the only cock in the family. How else is he going to become a man?'

When my father and uncles and my own generation were growing up, circumcisions were done by the local barber – who for some totally inexplicable reason was also the lute player at weddings. The razor he used was the same one he used for shaving the grown ups. It was a thankless job, for any ensuing complications were blamed on the poor barber. Nowadays, the job is done by a doctor, anaesthetic is used, and risks of infection are lessened. All this has affected the mother's role in a positive way: she doesn't weep or worry but she can have a celebration if she wants one.

The convalescence period was and is overseen by the mother, and before modern methods were adopted the wound often turned septic and inflamed. Grandmother Rashedah bandaged the penises of her children in ordinary cloth dressed with drops of sesame seed oil to prevent it from sticking to the wound. She put on a brave face and told her children that, 'their birdies were the envy of all the girls'. We were circumcised by the same barber who had accommodated my father, but my mother bought regular bandages from a pharmacy in Jerusalem. Interestingly, my mother's refrains were the same as grandmother Rashedah's and she spoke of our penises 'being the talk of the town'. Today there may be considerable improvements in standards of hygiene but little change in the sexual importance attached to the act of circumcision. The briefing of the father or uncle and the mother's subsequent refrains tell a boy that he is entering manhood; this is in fact the closest anyone comes to discussing sex with him.

Group circumcision is still very common in Bethany. When age differences are small, brothers, even cousins, are circumcised together in a single ceremony. Costs are reduced in this way, the mother is spared repeated suffering, and is often forced into character assessments of her children. I was circumcised with my brothers Afif and Wagih and my mother's concern was Afif because 'he is so delicate'. Aunt Salha Ibrahim noted that, 'poor Hilmi has not got much of a birdie ... what are they going to take away?' Aunt Mirriam Mahmoud, who denies it now, is supposed to have bragged about how well endowed her son Khalil was.

If circumcision is a boy's coming of age, his move from childhood to manhood, then the whole occasion revolves around what happens to his penis. Not only is the importance of the penis implanted in his mind (endowing it with a sense of distinction which girls don't have for their sexual organs) but it is the start of an implicit push towards putting it to use. From that comes the preoccupation with virility, which translates into male promiscuity, men's almost universal commitment to using their penises whenever possible. If circumcision is 'preparing the penis for action', which is tantamount to achieving manhood, then both parents have a healthy interest in their sons' activity reflecting that status. It is left to religious belief, when it exists, and the availability of willing partners to erect the only barriers against promiscuity.

Grandfather Aburish, a man of little religious attachment, had many an illicit affair with women tourists who stayed at his caravanserais, or when he was travelling. He had become a man when he was circumcised and his penis had to achieve its promise. Grandmother Rashedah knew of this, accepted the notion that his manhood demanded the use of his penis in a way he could brag about, and never complained. Whenever he got interested in another woman she would pray to have 'Allah dampen his sexual drive'; Allah seems to have listened and she outlived him by thirty years, never referring to him by any other term except the endearing 'my man'.

Promiscuity flourished in my father's generation because he and my uncles were also brought up to use their penises freely, because sex outside marriage became easier and also because they knew they would get away with it. Father and uncles Mahmoud and Ibrahim indulged and had mistresses, while the younger generation didn't simply because they couldn't afford it. My mother speaks of 'stupid loose girls' and asks, 'What did they expect to get out of it?' Salha Ibrahim says Ibrahim 'could do what he wanted to do as long as he came back at night'. Mirriam Mahmoud's present concern about her seventy-six-year-old husband centres around money : 'I just don't like him to spend too much on them – he gets carried away.'

All three women accepted the maxim of Rashedah's statement that her sons' penises were the envy of all the girls. Not only did they give their husbands unlimited freedom but they took visible pride in their sons' sexual prowess within and outside marriage and sided with the boy whenever a modern wife complained. In olden times celebrating a son's sexual adventures was part of tradition; nowadays – when a son is married – it is complicated by a mother's desire not to afford a daughter-in-law more than she herself was permitted. On seeing my married brother Rabah with a girl, my mother was far from disapproving and remarked with a smile that 'the girl was tall and pretty'.

The inevitable question is a comparative one: were we encouraged towards promiscuity in a way that doesn't exist in the west? The answer is 'yes', and it all started with circumcision and the obsession with virility that was set in motion by circumcision.

* * * *

Homosexuality deserves attention for two reasons: because of the existing image in western eyes that it is widespread in the Arab world and because of its relationship to courtship and marriage. Arab, Palestinian and indeed Bethany homosexual practices existed and exist at two levels. For the most part it is strictly a 'safe' avenue for sexual relief, one way to get the sexual urge out of one's system. The second type is where homosexuality is preferred.

Our concern is the first type, the one endemic in the Arab world: homosexuality as a relief from the restrictions of a social order which afforded no alternative. During my grandfather's and father's time, growing up in Bethany meant no sexual intercourse until marriage. Very few men escaped that dictum by going to illegal brothels in Jerusalem – but women were expected to remain virgins until marriage and losing one's virginity meant certain death. Killing a girl who lost her virginity outside marriage and brought shame to her family was accepted by all as an act aimed at restoring family honour. Murderers could become local heroes, although cases were few as honour demanded that the girl's family kill the male perpetrator as well and this acted as a deterrent. Even 'flirting' with a girl was unthinkable and I grew up hearing about a man who remained in hiding for eleven years after making advances to a girl from a decent family.

My parents and all my uncles and aunts were totally agreed that homosexuality existed only among men – lesbianism did not exist. When pressed as to why, two reasons were given: first women were afraid of the punishment they would receive if caught – men can punish women but not the opposite. Second, unlike men who could go to caves or order women to go somewhere else while they enjoyed themselves, they had no place to go. When no one mentioned the subject, I referred to traditional, cultural, 'compulsion'. The women finally agreed that, 'the men were supposed to have it but the women weren't'. In other words custom governed men's behaviour but strict rules regulated that of women.

It is obvious to me that homosexuality among men was quite widespread. It took place between people of the same age, usually teenagers, and was also practised by older men who seemed to fancy young, smooth-skinned boys. According to uncles Mousa and Mahmoud, homosexuality among the same age consisted of groups of young men going to the ruins of the old village and spending an afternoon rotating in teams of who did what to whom. More specific questions as to whether they themselves or other male members of the family ever took part in these sex parties produced a 'no' from Mahmoud and a statement from Mousa that 'I was never on the receiving end'. My father, when I questioned him, stated that it was all a filthy business for people who were 'badly brought up'.

My father's comments brought up the issue of the parental attitude towards children who participated in homosexual acts. There is unanimity here that grandfather Aburish would have proved most intolerant. It seems that every time he heard of this activity among the young men of Bethany he summoned his children and threatened to use the whip if they ever succumbed. Mousa's partial admission means he must have escaped his attention. However, much more telling is the fact that he needed to threaten his children in this manner – it confirms the activity.

In addition to boys performing homosexual acts with boys, there were elders who sought out willing boys. This, when it became known, caused a lot of trouble and was often the beginning of feuds, with the boy's family trying to punish the would-be perpetrator of the sexual attack, starting a cycle of violence which could accelerate to a serious level. Sometimes 'a proposition' would lead to that: when I was about ten years old an elderly neighbour invited me to go to his vineyard and when we got there he proceeded to expose himself. I ran home and told my mother who, in the absence of my father, told uncle Ali who gave the old man a black eye. No feud ensued because the old man didn't retaliate. Every male member of my generation appears to have had a similar experience, at one point or another.

What existed during my father's and uncle's youth existed to a lesser degree during the growing up years of my generation; it was there, but less prevalent because access to women was slightly easier. Khalil Ibrahim, Jamil Azzem and I were not allowed to go to the ruins of old Bethany with the boys because, in aunt Salha Ibrahim's words, 'Allah only knows what they do in the dark'. Not satisfied with that, grandmother Rashedah would quiz us with frightening directness: 'You are not playing with boys? Your father would be very upset and would punish you.'

As in all human activities trial makes converts. Khalil Ibrahim and Hilmi Ibrahim remember a boy who enjoyed the activity and became committed to it. Khalil says: 'I guess he became the local whore. Every time someone had the urge they took him to some cave and screwed him. I guess they bought him ice cream and gave him a shilling.' The man is still around and though married is suspected of being a committed homosexual. He represents the second type of homosexual, one who has chosen it out of preference rather than merely to relieve the sexual urge. This man became homosexual through trial and enjoyment and not because of the hate-of-one-parent and love-of-another syndrome as it exists in the west.

In Bethany's structured traditional society the male was supreme and the female secondary: that was the same for everyone and this notion was free of conflict. Of equal importance is the fact that this boy's activities were considered shameful for himself and his family. Nevertheless the rotation game in the old ruins was almost a routine.

There is less homosexuality in today's Bethany than during my father's and my time but it hasn't disappeared. In spite of my immediate family's forbidding attitude, homosexuality is an extension of an old tradition, as it is in Greece. Arab poets of the Ommayad and Abbassid Empires wrote of sodomizing pretty little boys with open glee, and it appears to continue to please.

The influence of circumcision on homosexuality is clear. It encourages promiscuity (whatever the direction) by attaching undue importance to the male's sexual organ and its use. Juvenile homosexual acts may not result in a commitment to homosexuality but have an influence on courtship and marriage. I asked fifteeen married males of my family whether they practised sodomy with their wives: nine refused to answer, three said no and three answered affirmatively. This hangover from traditional Arab and Bethany practices has caused at least one divorce and may be the one practice least subject to change. It has more to do with deep-rooted, transmitted inclinations and less with the demands of the world within which most of us now live.

5
Confusion before the storm

Palestine felt the influence of international thinking very early during the
Second World War. There were Polish and Greek refugees and soldiers
from many countries allied to the British. They all told us trouble was on
the way in Palestine once the war was over.

Mahmoud Aburish

If the 1930s were marked by the emergence of a unified
Palestinian identity then the early 1940s may be described as
the time when the Palestinian problem showed the first signs
of becoming a global issue. The British were preoccupied
with the Second World War; they had smashed the Palestinian nationalist movement, reducing twenty years of
struggle to naught and had served notice that Palestine and
its problems were on the back burner for the duration of
the conflict.

Impatient with British tactics and weary of Jewish plans,
the leader of the Palestinian Arabs, the Mufti of Jerusalem,
Haj Amin al-Husseini, fled to Iraq and from there to
Germany, to throw in his lot with the Axis powers, though
perhaps aware of the damaging consequences of such a move.
Blindly following their narrow-minded leader, most Palestinians, including Bethany and most Aburishs, suddenly if
indirectly placed their hopes in an Axis victory. Their leaders
told them that the Germans, Italians, and, to a lesser degree,
the Japanese, were friends who would help liberate them.
Fascism appealed to them because it was highly nationalistic
in nature and because it was the enemy of the Jews and
the British.

Not a single member of the Aburish family knew what

Germany, the leader of the Axis, stood for – certainly there
was no ideological basis for favouring them. There was no
appreciation whatsoever of Germany's racial policies nor, for
that matter, was there any real understanding of why
Germany was 'on the side of the Palestinians'. Having discovered that Germany was opposed to British rule and
Jewish plans, the Aburishs' attitude smacked of blind subscription to the age-old Arab maxim that 'the enemy of my
enemy is my friend'. This feeling was strengthened by the
fact that the Axis' early victories had managed to undermine
the once undisputed supremacy of the British Empire. Palestinian leadership made the most of this and an aura of 'super-
man' crept into the consciousness of Palestinians as
exemplified by Ali Aburish's refrain that 'our friends will
soon be here'.

Mahmoud, who in personal behaviour was the most Arab
member of the family, was an exception; he remained pro-
British. Years of exposure to British ways had endeared them
to him. Certainly he wanted an independent Arab Palestine,
but he had been indoctrinated: he had infinite faith in the justice of the British, and in their undoubted eventual victory. In
a way he was and is an excellent example of the success of
British efforts to win the allegiance of big and small chiefs in
their former colonies. He justifies his Second World War
attitude thus:

> I suppose I was brought up believing in the Empire. I kept telling
> myself the sheer weight of numbers would prevail. This favoured
> the British . . . it's that simple. As far as Palestine is concerned, I
> could still believe in the British sense of fairness. They would
> have found a solution but when the war was over it was the
> Americans who carried the weight.

Mahmoud is still an Anglophile.

Abu Said was on the other side: he supported the Mufti
and so, indirectly, Germany. He had returned to Palestine
from exile in Lebanon in November 1939, after he was
included in an amnesty decree by the British which, in an act

of appeasement, allowed Palestinian rebels to return home. He resumed his work at the Scotch Hospice unhindered, but soon left to become a partner in a taxi company, a more lucrative occupation. His anti-British revolutionary activities took a different, more sophisticated turn. Along with a number of nationalists, he began transmitting news via various secret channels to the Mufti in Berlin – their reports got to Berlin via Vichy-occupied Syria. An elaborate network of pro-Mufti sympathizers existed in the cities but only the chosen few came from villages, and it is clear that Abu Said was one of the Mufti's agents in the field. While there is considerable confusion about the importance of his role during this period – indeed, even the value of his anti-British reports and minor espionage activities – it is beyond doubt that some of the information he transmitted found its way to the Arabic language service of Radio Berlin. His reports dealt with pro-German and anti-British activities by followers of the Mufti and were exaggerated every step of the way to Berlin, so that the Radio Berlin Arabic service, using him and dozens of others, made it sound as if a full-scale rebellion was taking place in Palestine. In reality anti-British acts were few and far between.

There is nothing to suggest that Ibrahim adopted a particular stance. One thing is certain: like many of his kind he was among the chief beneficiaries of the large British wartime army stationed in Palestine whose presence contributed towards an improvement in the economic condition of the country. Any political feelings he may have had he managed to keep to himself. Instead he supplemented his salary from his job with the ministry of agriculture by, most illegally, selling British Army surplus goods at inflated prices, trading tinned foods, kerosene and even automobile tyres. Ibrahim's image and method of operation resembled that of the shady characters in the film 'Casablanca'.

Ali and Mousa sympathized with Abu Said, but, unlike him, were of no use to anyone. Despite their pro-German feelings, they too benefited from the British Army presence. Ali started a business supplying village labour and occasionally fresh food to the Royal Air Force, for the thousands of airmen in Palestine had to be accommodated and fed. He certainly didn't allow his political feelings to interfere with his work and thought nothing of bringing home dozens of British officers to parties which lasted until the early hours of the morning. The RAF men were a noisy, boisterous lot who appreciated the chance to escape the confinement of their barracks to places like Bethany, where they would sing barrack-room songs, imitate native dances and even shoot in the sky fiesta style. Mousa worked for Ali.

Daoud and Hassan were too young to have any political leanings. They stayed at school until 1943 when they too began working for Ali. The women followed their men. My mother's total inability to comprehend the complexities of the war didn't stop her from being distinctly pro-German, repeating everything my father and her father had told her and insisting that 'the Germans like us'. Equally, Mirriam Mahmoud's lack of knowledge didn't stop her from being pro-British: she borrowed Mahmoud's words and insisted the British were 'fair and gentle and very nice with us'.

At first neither the pro- nor anti-British Aburishs had any specific ideas on the war, certainly no clear comprehension of its possible consequences for the Arabs of Palestine. Fatmeh, in her usual way, offers an amusingly revealing account of the atmosphere of the time within the family: 'When your father said our friends, he meant the Germans; but when Mahmoud said our friends, he meant the British. We didn't know why they differed, but we tried to remember their allegiances to avoid offence through slips of the tongue.' So the differences in allegiance among the Aburish children produced no friction and they appear to have behaved towards each other in a totally traditional way.

Being for or against the British was seldom a sophisticated political decision, people followed their leaders, as in the case of Abu Said, or the people who directly influenced their lives, as with Ali and Mousa. The political position of other people was a reflection of their connections, or lack of it, with the British. Thinking and talking about the war took up a con-

siderable amount of people's time; they gathered in the coffee
house to listen to news bulletins and would argue about what
they meant, and whether a frigate was more important than a
destroyer or vice versa. But there were other more immediate
preoccupations, ones which directly reflected the social progress of the Aburishs, and undoubtedly many others in
similar circumstances.

Mahmoud, benefiting from an improved wartime economy
(over 100 Bethanites held service jobs with British firms) had
followed Abu Said's example in the area of personal comfort,
the Bethany yardstick of social progress, by converting one of
the rooms in *Hamweh* into a bathroom with two lavatories.
Ibrahim too incorporated a fully equipped bathroom in his
new house and bought a car. Mahmoud stopped wearing
native dress altogether, except on religious holidays and
special occasions, when his traditional role called for
ceremonial attire – perhaps at a *sulha* or a wedding. My
mother took the lead among women, and shed her native
dress in favour of western clothes, but continued to wear a
silk scarf over her head. All of the Aburish men began shaving
their beards daily as opposed to the two or three times a week
normal among their contemporaries. My mother started
gossip all over Bethany by wearing a gold watch which, along
with the RCA Victrola record-player my father had bought,
placed her way ahead of her time as an owner of much sought-
after western-made goods. Our house became a social centre,
where people came to listen to records and forget the war –we
had only six records of Arabic music which were played to
death. I remember the words of each song to this day.

Children, the third generation of Aburishs, continued to be
a centre of attention, for there was total subscription to the
Arab notion of 'he who breeds doesn't die'. My brothers Afif,
Wagih and Rabah were born in the early 1940s as were Hilmi
and Halima Ibrahim, Khalil and Wagiha Mahmoud, Amneh's
son Said and Fatmeh's son Jamil. Unlike our parents, our
dress was western from the start; shorts, shirts and mostly
sandals. The more western our dress, the more we liked it,
and the more other children envied us – another reflection of

implicit admiration for British ways. I owned a cap and a beret, something which caused as much Bethany talk as my mother's gold watch, while Wagiha Mahmoud's dresses were the envy of everyone. Because she looked like any western girl there were revealing comments such as 'she looks like a pretty English girl' or 'we ought to change her name to Elizabeth'. Changing to western dress and acquiring western habits was considered so elevating that my uncle Ali placed it ahead of obedience to religion and custom – which led him to exaggerate the number of bottles of whisky he kept at home. Ali and Mousa bragged about buying cake and chocolate in Jerusalem and took to complaining that *baklava* was too sweet.

Our totally western dress wasn't the only sign of our special position in Bethany: we were the first to go to boarding school and we went at an early age. Many in Bethany, including some of our mothers, thought that sending us away to school was an unnecessary act of cruelty. Another of the many new things we were exposed to was the cinema, and Khalil Ibrahim and I specialized in retelling the story of a film to our mothers and grandmother, squeezing every bit of drama out of films such as 'Tiger Woman and Tarzan'. Retelling those stories to my grandmother made me feel as if I were paying her back for some of the wonderful Arab tales she had told me. Once she inquired whether Tarzan had a family and how they dressed.

The rest of the villagers were moving towards western dress and ways but they were well behind the Aburish family. Sometimes their conversion was prompted by some generous British officer who gave them his old uniform. The height of advancement was the use of hair lotions which came from the British troops – some would overdo it and have greasy hair for weeks. Buying a new watch was almost a public event, and the news of such a purchase spread from the coffee house to the rest of the village. People would quarrel about who owned the best watch and very seldom took them off.

The local Greek Orthodox priest, Father Theodoseos, sums up the villagers' advances dramatically:

> You started seeing fewer one-eyed people in the forties; medical care was beginning to produce results. There were fewer maimed people too, because everyone had learned to cross streets without getting in the way of cars. Before, even though there were fewer cars, more people lost limbs because they couldn't judge distances and got themselves hurt. Many started using rude English words without knowing their full implication: they would tell each other to shut up and then laugh out loud.

Flavouring one's language by the use or abuse of an English word or two was the height of sophistication.

Most Aburish women occupied themselves with household chores and care for the young. While they themselves didn't suffer, because their husbands managed to get round the food and cigarette shortages, they spoke about others who were going without rice, sugar, coffee and grain, all of which were in short supply. Only those close to the British didn't feel the pinch. The women's meetings were taken up with gossip, and communal sessions of suckling their children, doubling for each other when one was busy or ran dry. My brother Wagih had no less than ten 'wet mothers' – which would have complicated his life had he been inclined towards marrying a Bethany girl, as in religous law, marrying a suckling sister is as much forbidden as marrying a real sister.

Besides household chores and children, the women talked about their clothes, native or western, and about their husbands' achievements, including such transgressions as hoarding food and buying clothes from British soldiers and officers. Amazingly, talk of their husbands' achievements included open discussions of their extra-marital affairs and, in the case of Salha, of Ibrahim's illegal activities; some took pride in their husband's affairs with western women, a Polish refugee or a waif, much as their husbands still took pride in working with Englishmen and having them as friends. Far

from being a source of anger, a husband's affair with an
English woman invested him with an aura of desirability.
Husbands not only told their wives about their affairs, some
like Ibrahim brought their English girl friends with them to
attend 'native' weddings and celebrations: little Salha
smiled approvingly.

The picture of life in Bethany in the early 1940s was a microcosm of Palestine, particularly the villages, which still
accounted for over fifty per cent of the population. People
were forced into a sudden acquaintance with the outside
world. Heetar (Hitler), Mussorini, Dunkirk, Hawaii and Crete
becoming household names. They continued to follow a
leadership in exile which demanded an independent Arab
Palestine, while they were still learning how to cross the
street without getting knocked down, and overtly and covertly
viewed the British as a superior race.

My father was involved at all levels. He was Bethany born
and bred, the leading local supporter of Palestinian aspirations to independence, and the man who moved farthest in
adopting western ways for himself and his wife. He recalls the
attitudes of the time, including the Arabs' inherent inferiority
complex towards the British:

> Yes, we lived at many different levels which were contradictory
> ... It was a love-hate relationship with the British. We admired
> their ways, acknowledged their superiority but at the same time
> wanted to be independent. These things are not mutually
> exclusive.
>
> The Jews were a bigger problem. Their claim to Palestine was
> serious indeed but don't forget the alien ideology they brought
> with them. The idea of a kibbutz threatened the fabric of Arab
> life, the attachment to family and tribe. It was a European idea
> implanted in the Middle East – it wasn't liked even by oriental
> Jews who like us championed traditional ways.
>
> I believe wanting to be independent, to run one's own affairs, is
> natural. Sure our leadership was followed blindly, but the basic
> instinct of the people was in their favour although the expected
> anti-British uprising never took place because people were

materially better off under the British. Remember, most people's term of reference was still the Turks, the previous rulers, and the British were much better.

We didn't know anything about German policies except that Germany supported the Arab claim to Palestine while Britain favoured the Jews. The Peel Commission's report proposing a divided Palestine confirmed our suspicions of the British. The Arab is a soft-hearted, kind person; there is no way any of us would have condoned concentration camps. We are hunters, fighters – the idea of killing people who are unable to defend themselves is against Arab thinking; it is dishonourable.

It is impossible for me to judge the Palestinian leadership of the time and its attitude toward the Germans. But if I had known then what I know now I wouldn't have done anything to help Germany.

The defeat of Nazi Germany brought an end to hopes of outside help towards the creation of an independent Arab Palestine. My father, like many other nationalists, knew the Arabs were in very deep trouble while a pro-British minority which included Mahmoud continued to hope. But in the 1940s Hitler's savagery, coupled with the Mufti's stupidity, brought world opinion solidly behind Jewish aspirations to create a national home in Palestine, and the Arabs lost support.

In 1945 every Palestinian Arab, however lowly and uneducated, accepted Germany's defeat as a defeat of Palestinian aspirations. The more educated followed the news of increased Jewish immigration to Palestine with fear of the consequences, while most Bethanites' hopes were kept unrealistically alive by a belief in the Houdini-like qualities of the Mufti. Against all evidence they believed Hitler was still alive, that the Mufti who had disappeared from Berlin was with him and that they were planning a surprise re-appearance equipped with secret weapons which would bring the British and the Jews to their knees. 'He [the Mufti] is cooking up something', was my uncle Ali's favourite explanation for Haj Amin's disappearance.

The daydreams of a Hitler–Mufti miracle were not shared by the elder Aburishs. My father had no doubt that an Arab–Jewish war was on the way, and kept repeating what a Jewish acquaintance had told him: 'If Britain wins then we will turn you into beasts of burden, but if Germany wins then you will have to protect me.' Mahmoud's belief in the justice of the British Empire started to waver when the newspapers began reporting the arrival of thousands of Jewish immigrants. Ibrahim was itching for things to get going so he might do some fighting. The younger Aburishs had no pronounced opinion on the subject but followed my father's lead.

One of the better ways to judge the atmosphere of a country is by looking at the way people speak to each other. After the Second World War people in Palestine began whispering and shaking their heads as a sign of dismay, while visitors to our house would pull their chairs closer to my father and speak in the hushed tones of conspirators. There was an atmosphere of gloom; fear of the unknown made people unhappy. They had no ideas about the future and no sense of political direction because the Mufti, who had presided over the Arab Higher Committee like a dictator, wasn't there to tell them what to do.

Then on 26 May 1946, news of the Mufti's return to Cairo to live under the protection of King Farouk of Egypt reached Palestine. His reappearance sent a shock wave throughout the country. True, many knowledgeable people still harboured strong doubts about the future, but, to people in places like Bethany, the 'father of the revolution' was back. Men smiled, shook hands and embraced each other while the women ululated and offered songs of praise; fires of celebration burnt in every courtyard of every village. Brooding despair gave way to a desire to fight, for the Mufti, with all his colossal faults, embodied the Palestinian Arabs' will to resist.

The first message to reach Bethany from the Mufti was for my father: he was asked to tell the people of the village 'to arm themselves and wait'. Ali Aburish and Ali Abu Zayyad spread the word, which once again was followed blindly;

Mahmoud stepped aside and did not interfere; events, namely the unchecked flow of Jewish immigrants to Palestine, proved him wrong and he knew it.

Suddenly, overnight there grew a black market in light armaments, mostly the type which were useless in actual combat. People used their own money to buy arms; uncle Ibrahim bought himself a Colt .45, Ali a Walther .38, Mousa an 8 mm. Beretta. The prices they paid were exorbitant, not only by the standards of 1946 and 1947, but even by today's. They handled their guns with affection, cleaning them too often, carrying them at their sides at all times when there was no danger of British patrols apprehending them, and going off into the hills together for target practice. There was no one to tell them that the war in the making would demand different arms, organized bodies of men and military training. Their conception of being armed was to own a gun, perhaps a small hand gun, and to be able to use it, not to prepare for war. Even their wives remembered the names of their guns and recited their husbands' exaggerated claims of their effectiveness.

One of the stranger aspects of this period was the fact that in economic terms Palestine continued to do well. The British still maintained a large army there; this time to keep the peace between the Arabs and the Jews. Exports of citrus fruits increased through the employment of modern transport methods, and there was some easing of war shortages. Even the breakneck pace of Jewish settlement contributed, since the Jews had to buy building materials from the Arabs and on occasions even employed Arab labour – despite frequent appeals not to participate in such activities.

For the Aburish family it was a period of marking time. No one knew what would happen next, so they continued in their various endeavours; they moved neither forward nor backward, except for Abu Said, who characteristically managed to broaden his circle of acquaintances among the rich and powerful aided by his special relationship with the Mufti.

One family happening temporarily took the minds of the Aburishs off their universal preoccupation with politics – the sudden and unforeseen return of Ahmad in 1946. A brief letter sent to Abu Said at an old address managed to reach him. In it Ahmad, in an act of supreme understatement, announced that he would be arriving in Haifa aboard a ship of American Export Lines late in October, 'along with three of my sons'.

As the letter had been posted in New York everyone in the family assumed that Ahmad had been living there and awaited his arrival with bated breath. There was a season of Ahmad stories with everyone recalling what they knew about him, and there was some uncertainty in Mahmoud's voice betraying a fear that Ahmad might be returning to assume his position as head of the family by virtue of being Khalil Aburish's eldest child. The fact that Ahmad's letter was addressed to Abu Said and not, as it should have been, to Mahmoud made matters worse.

All the Aburish brothers, with me as the sole representative of the new generation, travelled to Haifa to meet Ahmad. He disembarked from the ship taking long, easy steps followed by three boys whose colour betrayed a hint of black blood. There was a highly-charged emotional scene of hugs and kisses which included me and my three newly-discovered cousins, then our three-car convoy proceeded to Bethany at full speed to be met by an anxiously waiting throng of Aburish women and children and relatives.

The women in their best native dresses sang welcoming songs while the two relatives entrusted with firing their guns in the sky kept shooting until an exasperated Ahmad told them to 'stop the nonsense'. The women's show of affection was more emotional than the men's; even Ahmad's sisters-in-law became near hysterical although none of them knew him.

There followed two weeks of what felt like an endless dinner party given first by family members and then friends of the family, during which Ahmad regaled everyone with his adventures. It turned out that he went first to Chile, then Colombia and eventually Haiti where he had stayed for eighteen years, fathering four boys and eight girls.

Mahmoud, having determined that Ahmad's return was a mere visit, acted as a host for his elder brother and kept him company almost constantly. According to uncle Daoud: 'The difference between them was obvious, Mahmoud was a diplomat while Ahmad's directness didn't go down well in Bethany. It was alien.' Rashedah, while welcoming, viewed him distantly and no one recalls them having a great deal to say to each other. Daoud was blunt about this: 'Mother's relationship with Ahmad and Hamdah had been the one point of contention in an otherwise happy marriage to my father. Let's face it, they didn't like each other.'

I remember Ahmad as a blunt man: he had lost his Arab sentimentality so much that the mention of his father's pain over his disappearance would provoke the crude reply: 'He drove me to it along with my step mother – they made me leave.' He still didn't get along with my grandmother who, after the initial welcome period, said he was 'as miserable as ever'.

One aspect of Ahmad's return shed light on the character of his brothers: without prompting, he told Mahmoud that he had addressed the letter announcing his impending return to my father because 'Mohammad is reliable; I always depended on him whereas you and Ibrahim liked to play around'. Later he told my mother, 'I could have told you your husband would pull ahead . . . he is more single minded'.

Mahmoud swallowed Ahmad's remarks without comment for his half-brother was eleven years older and thus entitled to respect. By objecting to an elder's declarations he would have undermined his own personal position. My father saw in Ahmad's comments an attempt to interfere with the status quo; he viewed them as an expression of Ahmad's frustration at finding himself an outsider. Ibrahim enjoyed Ahmad as a sparring partner full of salty comments about the condition of Bethany, but no more than that. Being full brothers, Mahmoud, Mohammad and Ibrahim were naturally closer to each other, a closeness cemented by years of growing up together and sharing common experiences.

Ahmad stayed in Bethany six months, constantly complaining that there were no gambling casinos. At the end he went back to Haiti leaving his children behind to learn Arabic. The children, Khalil, Daoud and Suleiman, sixteen, fourteen and twelve years old, stayed with uncle Mahmoud another year managing to learn Arabic and endear themselves to kith and kin. Mahmoud's wife Mirriam and grandmother Rashedah cared for them, though these appealing youngsters were quite capable of looking after themselves, unlike their Arab counterparts. While their mastery of Arabic is far from complete they still speak an amusing, broken variety to this day.

As far as I can tell the children's mixed blood represented no problem whatsoever in Bethany, except for the outspoken Rashedah who attributed their occasional refusal to follow her old-fashioned ways to 'a surfacing of black blood'. Otherwise everyone took them to heart while silently condemning Ahmad for leaving them behind.

After his children returned to Haiti, Ahmad reverted to his isolation from the family, writing the occasional brief letter to indicate all was well. He died suddenly in 1963 to be mourned by all, particularly his full sister Hamdah. His children, who now live in many parts of the world, take pride in their Aburish name and shun their Haitian identity in favour of their Palestinian one. The elder, Khalil, is a committed Palestinian nationalist who devotes time and effort to the Palestinian cause.

*   *   *   *

Early in 1947 Mahmoud paid a routine visit to the Anglican Bishop of Jerusalem. The Bishop told him that things were going to be bad, that the British were getting tired of the uncompromising positions of the Arabs and the Jews and of American pressure on them which undermined their ability to adopt any sensible plan towards a solution. Mahmoud hurried back home to tell my father who, according to Mahmoud, squeezed his head between his hands and said resignedly: 'I know, I know, and we are not even prepared.

This is not 1936. Some of the Jews have been trained by the British – they served with the British Army. We are in trouble.'

The march towards the Arab–Israeli conflict accelerated. Palestine, a vague notion even to some of its original inhabitants, was to become a name synonymous with war and all the misery that short word contains. The Aburishs individually and collectively became involved every step of the sad, painful way.

6
Palestine in flames

We in Bethany knew trouble was on the way earlier than most people, in 1946 and early 1947. Truck loads of young Jews used to pass through the village to and from the Dead Sea where they received military training. They sang warlike songs and hurled insults at us as they drove through town. They weren't the Jews of old; they were a new alien group who obviously didn't like us.

Daoud Aburish

The 1948 Arab–Israeli conflict had a long and complex history. Before the outbreak of hostilities numerous commissions from Britain and other nations had studied the problem of the Jewish claim and Arab counter-claim to Palestine, hoping to reconcile the two. But they failed: the middle ground necessary for a solution was never found, for each side was convinced of the justice of its cause.

The Jews, burdened with thousands of years of abuse, would settle for nothing less than a safe national homeland where they reigned supreme, and because of undeniable historical and religious attachment they looked to Palestine as the place to establish a Jewish nation-state. The Arabs had occupied Palestine for centuries and believed it was theirs. Moreover, they recalled their historical generosity to the Jews and resented the west's attempt to make them pay for all the savage misdeeds of Hitler, the Christian churches, western kings and princelings and the ordinary every-day practitioners of anti-Semitism. After all, it was Saladin who brought the Jews back to Jerusalem after the Crusaders had driven them out, and even in far away Spain the Jews had received the conquering Arabs as liberators.

Both sides were right. In universal terms the historical mistreatment of the Jews made a convincing claim, while in more immediate regional terms, and judged by the Arabs' traditional behaviour towards the Jews, the Arabs had a right which was more compelling. The Arab case also had the distinct advantage of possession, for they held most of Palestine and accepting their claims to ownership would not have had any disruptive effects. It has become a classic case of two irreconcilable rights.

The natural arbiter between the two claimants was the British government, which had ruled Palestine since Turkey left at the end of the First World War. During their thirty-year rule in Palestine the British offered many solutions, all of which proved unacceptable to one or both sides. By the end of the Second World War the British were weary and near-bankrupt, totally unable to bear the cost of holding both contestants apart – a problem made worse by their inability to resist American pressure to accommodate the Jewish claim at Arab expense. The British knew that the best they could offer was a 'holding action'.

Violence, sectarian in nature and hence uglier than open warfare, returned to Palestine in 1947 in a more organized and intensified way than ever before. It began in isolated acts of assassination and bombings but quickly escalated into open conflict, first in areas of mixed populations and eventually throughout the country. Jerusalem, Jaffa, Haifa, Acre and other cities had both Arab and Jewish inhabitants, otherwise the Jews occupied small strips of land along the coastal plain and part of Galilee, while the Arabs had the rest of the country to themselves – at least seventy-five per cent of Palestine could be called Arab.

The Aburishs were to be immersed in this hideous conflict to a degree that could not have been foreseen or appreciated by any of them. This was not voluntary; it was a case of being enveloped in a war which forced itself on everyone, though it was very often beyond many participants' understanding. As a result some Aburishs fought and survived the war without having a clear idea of its nature and purpose, while others understood what was happening the more they became involved.

At the start of hostilities in 1947 my father was a partner in the Orient Taxi Company, the only telephone taxi company in Jerusalem – an inglorious business but highly lucrative. Uncle Mahmoud was the head of Bethany and the undisputed guardian of the welfare of its 3,000 citizens. Uncle Ibrahim had a position with the department of agriculture, while Ali worked for the Royal Air Force as a small contractor. Daoud worked for Mahmoud as his assistant, and Hassan, who had joined the Jordan Frontier Force, the regional equivalent of the Foreign Legion, had just been released and was seeking employment. Mousa had set up and ran a new coffee house in Bethany which replaced the old one as the main gathering place for the men of the village.

Fear filled the land. Armed Jewish gangs raided Arab quarters, terrorized the inhabitants by tossing hand grenades into crowded souks or shooting at innocent passers-by, then fled before the impotent British security forces could catch them. The Palestinians retaliated by ambushing Jewish buses, killing their passengers and blowing up Jewish buildings just because they were Jewish. Zionist terrorists blew up the King David Hotel (on 22 July 1946), killing ninety-one innocent civilians, and the Arabs hit back with equal lack of discrimination and flattened half of Ben Yehuda Street by detonating a truck full of explosives.

Sectarian conflicts are always close to the people and very difficult to avoid. They do not have the remoteness of organized wars with recognized theatres of battle. I was personally to experience the ugly results of random violence on the afternoon of 13 December 1947.

My brother Afif and I were in front of Damascus Gate, one of the seven gates of Old Jerusalem, waiting for a bus back to Bethany. Boarding schools had closed because of worry over students' safety and we were forced to make the journey from Bethany to Jerusalem and back every day. As always, the Damascus Gate was crowded, teeming with people waiting for buses and taxis, with fruit and vegetable vendors and many other people entering and leaving the old city. It was relatively far away from the Jewish parts of the city and was considered beyond the reach of would-be terrorists. The gate itself was at the bottom of a steep incline. I was looking up towards the main street, which was at the high point of the open square, and watched with horror as a black car stopped and the occupants rolled two cylinders with burning wicks into the milling crowd. Someone shouted 'bombs' and I instinctively pushed Afif down and threw myself on top of him, almost in time to avoid injury, but as I did so I raised my right leg and a fragment from one of the barrels of the crude home-made bombs hit me in the shin.

I felt no pain but as we stood up, Afif, eight-years old and in total panic, was screaming. He thought he was hurt because he was covered with blood. I was covered with my own blood and that of others but was too stunned to react. Soon my injury began to hurt and I remember trying to bandage it with my handkerchief. However, when the ambulances arrived and the first-aid people inspected the wounded, my injury was considered too light to be treated and we managed to get a taxi to Bethany. My mother was near to hysteria and initially she too thought Afif was the injured one. She eventually calmed down enough to administer first-aid to my right leg, and I carry the scar of the incident to this day.

Dramatic as my personal experience was at the age of thirteen, I recognized that sectarian conflicts generate other fears than the simple fear of injury in a regular war. The dominant worry was of the unknown or misunderstood, the overblown phantoms of war. Rumours flew around of the rape of little Arab girls by members of the Stern and Irgun gangs, two extremist Jewish organizations totally committed to violent means, and I have no doubt that equally sordid rumours were rampant on the Jewish side. Both sides were the victims of hysteria and hate, hate of people who until very recently had been their neighbours and friends. The wretched British were helpless and resented – even by the moderates of both sides – for their inability to stop the violence which was feeding on itself.

The inevitable butchery – Arabs refusing the surrender of occupants of a Jewish convoy and the Jewish killing of 284 innocent Arabs in Deir Yassin village – was at first far from us, in the mixed population centres. However, the overall battle for Palestine soon seeped through to sleepy places like Bethany. With the ignominious departure of the exhausted British on 14 May 1948, the Jews immediately announced the creation of the state of Israel without defining its boundaries. Emissaries of Haj Amin al-Husseini, the late Mufti of Jerusalem and head of the Higher Arab Committee, arrived in Bethany to 'organize the Arab forces', to arm and train the local population.

Their first task was to find a commander, a local leader and, as in all things Arab – particularly at that time – leaders were found in prominent families. This meant that they turned to uncle Mahmoud for help in choosing a militia chief, so he proudly and naturally nominated his brother, my uncle Ibrahim, to fill the post. Ibrahim was a tough guy who enjoyed a fight and the handling of firearms, so by the standards of the day the Aburish name and my father's connections with the Mufti were enough to qualify him as commander, I know that the idea of war intrigued Ibrahim more than the reasons for it, as he had no deep feelings about it all. In another age he might have been a mercenary, a soldier of fortune.

The local militia, which Ibrahim headed with obvious and considerable glee, was known throughout Palestine as the Holy Strugglers (al-Jihad al-Mukades). Their insignia, which they wore on their chosen headdress, whether beret, forage cap or an Arab *egal* (head band), was a badge incorporating reproductions of Muslim and Christian holy places – the Dome of the Rock and the Church of the Holy Sepulchre. This was a clever attempt by the Mufti to foster Muslim and Christian unity against 'Jewish intruders'. In that regard he was totally successful and Muslim and Christian Arabs were at one in their opposition to the Jews, and in their desire to create an independent Palestine governed by its indigenous population.

Ibrahim's first task was to select a deputy and that too followed family lines. Under normal circumstances the job should have gone to a member of the al-Khatib family, the second family in Bethany, but none of them showed any desire for combat after turning down petitions from a number of claimants the position was given to a member of the third most qualified family, the Aburumis.

After appointing Mohammad Awar, or 'one eyed', Aburumi as deputy, Ibrahim turned to the people of the village and asked for volunteers. Practically everyone offered their services, but Ibrahim had no uniforms for them let alone arms, and he had no clear idea of where their salaries would come from. Soon enough messengers from the Mufti, who was ensconced in the Semiramis Hotel in Cairo running his own long-distance holy war by proxy, arrived with answers to Ibrahim's requests for arms, money and uniforms in that order. They brought with them ill-fitting second-hand uniforms and rusty arms consisting of the discarded light equipment left behind in the Western Desert during the Second World War – Italian, German, British, American, Canadian and other makes. Ibrahim was also allocated a certain amount of cash each month, which he distributed to his volunteers more in line with the need than in accordance with rank or competence – in fact there were no ranks beyond commander and deputy commander. The pay was very small, but since the conflict had brought all economic activity to a standstill being a Holy Struggler was the only job to be had and everyone accepted the Mufti's meagre pay without complaint. Their salaries seldom arrived punctually, with the result there were often no rations and some Holy Strugglers went hungry for days at a time.

They were an odd, rag-tag army, the Holy Strugglers. Some of its members had to roll up their trouser legs to make them short enough to wear while others, normally attired in traditional Arab dress, used rope in place of belts. Some of them spent days at a time cleaning off the rust which jammed the bolts of the rifles or sub-machine guns issued to them, which had lain exposed in the Libyan desert for years. Even the ammunition was rusty and unreliable and there were several accidents resulting from explosions during cleaning. Ibrahim had his own way of treating his men. A person who was considered competent was given a British or German rifle, one deemed less able an Italian one, and so on. The smart uniforms went to the more skilled soldiers as well. Some Holy Strugglers would refuse Italian rifles issued to them because of the stigma attached and would refuse to show up for drill until Ibrahim issued them with another weapon or convinced them of the adequacy of the original one.

Uncle Hassan, because of his supposed experience with the Jordan Frontier Force, was issued with two British-made Mills hand grenades. This was a special honour since there were very few hand grenades to be had. The two grenades, like everything else, were rusty and needed cleaning, a job which he delegated to me because he wanted to spend the evening playing backgammon or dominoes with the boys at uncle Mousa's coffee house. It sends shudders through me to this day to remember that the grenades I cleaned were fused and could have blown me to smithereens, were it not for my skill in pulling out the spring and hammer before they snapped. I not only cleaned them but I put them back together ready for use, and Hassan was pleased enough with my efforts to pay me a whole shilling as compensation for my near suicidal effort.

There were no boots for Ibrahim's volunteers, only ordinary shoes, mostly second-hand. Footwear represented a special problem: when the shoes were too big the volunteers would pad the inside with cardboard until they more or less fitted, and when they were too small the soldiers would bend down the heels of the shoes and wear them like slippers. Naturally, this made marching or parading military-style almost impossible, because men would lose their shoes the moment a military march was attempted. In fact the Holy Strugglers' organisation was quite unsoldierly and informal; there was very little marching, but quite a bit of parading, done by the volunteers for the benefit of the women of the village, who enjoyed seeing their men with rifles and side-arms and used to greet their appearance with chants and

songs of praise of their bravery in battle: 'Your fire is destined for the heart of the enemy.' The same songs condemned
the 'cowardly' Jews.

The most colourful member of Bethany's Holy Strugglers
was 'one eyed' Aburumi, who had never worn western dress
until his elevation to deputy commander. He was a tall,
ungainly man, always in danger of losing his trousers, and he
had big feet unaccustomed to the confines of a pair of shoes
and so, like others, he improvised a slipper which he lost one
day while parading in front of some chanting women. He was
so embarrassed by the incident that he picked up his shoe
and threw it about fifty feet away screaming at his commander:
'Ibrahim, what the hell is the hurry? Let's just walk along
leisurely. The Jews are here today and they will be here
tomorrow and we'll get them sooner or later. So why do we
have to go through this military parading nonsense?' Such an
attitude and level of awareness was not unique to Aburumi;
most of the volunteers were illiterate *fellaheen* – villagers,
peasants who, until then, had learned how to use their guns
by trial and error. Some of them would sport a rifle for a
month or two before discovering it had a missing part and
could not be used – occasionally they continued to carry the
weapon symbolically because they couldn't get the spare part
or another rifle.

The original duty of the Holy Strugglers was to protect
Bethany against possible raids by Jewish terrorist organizations such as the Irgun and Stern gangs. Strategically,
Bethany was Jerusalem's back door, perched on the road to
Jericho, the link to Jordan and the eastern part of the Arab
world. The primary function of guarding the village was
achieved when Ibrahim, after considerable difficulty, managed
to develop a rota system whereby guards were posted at certain points leading to the village, the approaches most likely
to be used by would-be attackers. As strict military discipline
did not exist, a few of the volunteers who had money (their
meagre savings) and who were supposed to be on guard duty,
would pay a colleague a few piastres to fill in for them, often

putting their attachment to a card game in the local coffee house above their military duty – in fact, they sometimes played cards to determine who would go on duty. When uncle Hassan was on guard duty he very often took me with him and let me carry his rifle, something which made me proud and even my mother approved. I remember being with him as he and other Holy Strugglers sat behind barrels full of stones which they used as road blocks and chatted away, totally oblivious and certainly unprepared for any attack that might take place.

Incidents portraying the confusion of the times deserve recall. One evening during the autumn of 1947 the two sentries posted at the northern approaches to Bethany, about two miles from the Hebrew University, decided that they had seen intruders and began shooting at the dark shadows facing them. Every man in the village grabbed his gun and ran out in the direction of the shooting, most of them firing at random. A deafening level of noise, made up of intermittent gunfire, children's screams and people running around in all directions, created the impression of a Bethany of 3,000 people completely out of control. Any idea of an organized militia capable of facing an enemy vanished into thin air.

Uncle Ibrahim's canny ear led him to Barutcha, the actual scene of the incident, to investigate. Meanwhile, people from across the valley, from Abu Dis, the nearest village, were arriving in Bethany on foot, with rifles, pistols and sub-machine guns in hand, wondering what had caused the mayhem and asking what they could do to help. By then the scene of the incident had been established and the news had even reached my mother, who told me to stand at the corner where the Abu Dis relief force was arriving to direct them to the field of battle. So, clad in a pair of undershorts and nothing else, I stood at the spot connecting Bethany with Abu Dis and started shouting at the top of my voice: 'People of Abu Dis, the attack is at Barutcha, go to Barutcha . . . that's where the fighting is!'

My improvised act as a troop dispatcher is remembered by most of the older people of Bethany to this day. During my latest visit to the village an old lady looked at me and mumbled 'to Barutcha', and we both doubled up with laughter. This came up again when I turned to another old lady whom I hadn't seen in over twenty years and asked her whether she remembered who I was. She snickered and said: 'Ah, of course, I do, you are the fellow who sent the people of Abu Dis to Barutcha'. With hindsight I am extremely doubtful that the sentries in Barutcha did anything but imagine the attack, perhaps from fear of the dark. It was an odd place for would-be attackers to choose; there were more natural, easier approaches which the organized and knowledgeable Jewish organizations would have used, and attacking Bethany from the north made no military sense.

Soon the whole attack – if that is what it was – turned into a party, with Bethany playing host to their Abu Dis helpers in an all-night affair which included hundreds of cups of Turkish coffee and endless recitations of Arabic heroics. My mother remembers an elderly Abu Dis man lamenting his late arrival: 'If only I had arrived earlier, they would never have got away.' One of the sentries who started the shooting insisted he had wounded one of the intruders because he had heard his victim moan when the bullet hit him.

My memories of the Barutcha affair are corroborated by Father Theodoseos of the local Greek Orthodox monastery. The good father had spent time in the Greek countryside during the German occupation in the Second World War, so upon hearing the shooting in Barutcha he climbed the church tower and began ringing the bells in an attempt to signal the impending attack, just as the Greeks had announced the arrival of German troops during his youth. Unacquainted with this signal denoting impending danger, the fighters of Bethany decided that Theodoseos was sending 'a message to the enemy'. Some were so incensed that they directed their fire towards the church tower and Father Theodoseos slid down the rope of the bell tower in a hurry, lacerating the palms of both hands. His good intentions were eventually explained and he continues to reside in Bethany as a pillar of the community.

Another incident vividly demonstrates how corrupting the prevailing atmosphere of 1948 was. Ibrahim and I were close, and like the rest of my uncles, he took pride in his eldest nephew and, like Hassan, though less frequently, he used to take me with him to places unusual for a teenager. One day he asked me to accompany him to witness what he described as 'something very special'. He was equipped with a pair of binoculars and a .45 pistol which he wore tied to his right leg cowboy style. We went to the western approaches to Bethany and hid ourselves behind a big rock with Ibrahim using the binoculars to watch the road from Jerusalem. He asked me if anything special happened at that particular time of day, about four in the afternoon, and I pleased him by telling him about the convoy of British soldiers which usually passed through the town.

Ibrahim handed me the binoculars and told me to look toward Jerusalem and there they were: three half-trucks led by one Bren gun carrier making their scheduled daily journey through Bethany to Jericho to demonstrate to the local population the continued (though impotent) British presence in the country. Within a few minutes they were in front of us, about 200 yards away, and out of nowhere, from behind rocks, fences and from small caves, ran about twelve people, their arms at the ready, screaming at the British to surrender or they would shoot. The major commanding the British convoy was in the Bren gun carrier: he stood up, raised his hand and stepped out of the vehicle. The rest of his soldiers followed suit and while I could not make out the details of what the major said, the British troops proceeded to throw down their arms, led by the major, who discarded his revolver. Soon they stood in file and marched back towards Jerusalem. The Holy Strugglers jumped into the Bren gun carrier and trucks and drove east towards Bethany, while Ibrahim laughed uncontrollably, still watching the scene through his binoculars.

Ibrahim and I sneaked away from behind our rock when the British troops were out of sight, went to his house to collect his car and drove to a small olive orchard behind the local

Greek Orthodox monastery where he was greeted by his
troops, who hugged and kissed him and howled cries of joy.
Some of the troops were busy trying to learn how to drive the
Bren gun carrier and the three half-trucks. You would have
thought Bethany had just acquired a mechanized force.
It wasn't until years later that Ibrahim told me about the
conspiracy. He had bribed the British major with £400 of the
Mufti's money, so what looked like the fastest surrender in
British military history could take place without any violence.
Wily Ibrahim managed to do the same thing with the UN
armistice troops two years later.

Ibrahim, a man of keen natural intelligence, did more than
conspire with the British Army major to prepare his troops
for war. He sent some of them to Damascus, where a welcoming Syria trained them, and others to Trans-Jordan to be
instructed by Glubb Pasha's Arab Legion. After the British
left Palestine in 1948 the Arab armies marched into Palestine, and Bethany and Jerusalem were within the part of
Palestine occupied by the Arab Legion. (Jordan, in a case of
liberator turned occupier, eventually annexed the part of
Palestine not conquered by the Jews without any deference
to the wishes of the local inhabitants.) Co-operation between
the Legion and the Holy Strugglers then took place on a more
regular, though often strained, basis, with the Strugglers
gaining from the experience of the best fighting force in the
whole of the Middle East.

The co-operation was marred by several incidents reflecting the incipient inter-Arab conflict. The Mufti, who had
spent the Second World War in exile in Germany, dreamed of
a revolutionary Palestine from which he would export anti-
British, American and Jewish ideas much like Khomeini in
today's Iran. On the other hand, King Abdallah of Jordan was
staunchly pro-British and wanted to annex Palestine or some
part of it to his domain, Trans-Jordan, the Jordan of today.
Their feuding over the non-existent spoils began early in the
game while they were fighting the Israelis, and affected
Palestinian–Jordanian relations at all levels.

Ibrahim and his Holy Strugglers were envious of the

better-equipped Arab Legionnaires and maintained that with their equipment they would 'finish the job' and, in the words of one commander, 'throw the Jews into the sea'. Their bitter refrain gained momentum every time they ran out of ammunition, which was often. Once, without their commander's sanction, Ibrahim's men raided a supply convoy of Arab Legion trucks passing through Bethany in order to steal ammunition. This started a street battle which lasted for forty-five minutes and in which the Legionnaires gained the upper hand, wounding six of Ibrahim's soldiers including my first cousin Mohammad Hirmas, Hamdah's son. The consequences of this incident were temporary and it was forgotten after Ibrahim and the local commander of the Arab Legionnaires met, promised each other closer co-operation in the future and kissed each other on both cheeks to seal their agreement.

Three months later the Holy Strugglers got their own back, when they intercepted a truck full of furniture leaving Jerusalem for Jordan. The driver and two other occupants were armed Jordanian irregulars, close cousins and relatives of the Legionnaires. On being interrogated by Ibrahim they insisted that the furniture was Jewish and was *kassibah* (profit). Ibrahim's sense of humour was tickled and he insisted on knowing the difference between Jewish furniture and Arab furniture.

Well, it appears that our Jordanian 'brothers' were convinced that Jerusalem Arabs lived in basements and that the Jews always lived on the floors above. As they had looted this furniture from a third-floor flat they automatically assumed it was 'Jewish furniture'. As if that wasn't enough, the furniture turned out to be very Arab indeed: it belonged to one Anwar Nusseibah, a leader of the Arab community who had lost his right leg fighting for an Arab Jerusalem and Palestine. Ibrahim handcuffed the men and delivered them to his Arab Legion counterpart and then returned the nondescript furniture to a thankful Anwar Nusseibah; once again the two Arab commanders kissed and made up.

There were innumerable incidents of violence between the

Palestinians and Jordanians, for the Palestinians thought the Jordanians crude bedouin mercenaries in the service of a corrupt government. They joked about their dialect, their homosexual tendencies and their demands in restaurants that green salad should be heated up. On the other hand, the Jordanians resented the Palestinians and would secretly say that they deserved everything they got because they had sold land to the Jews.

By Palestinian standards Ibrahim's force somehow became a model one; not only was he able to afford Bethany protection, but fifteen of his troops were despatched to Jerusalem every night to do duty there. This was when the tide was running in favour of the Arabs and they were mounting an attack against the virtually surrounded Jewish part of Jerusalem. Arab spirits had already been lifted by the fall and surrender of the inhabitants of the Jewish quarter in the old city of Jerusalem on 28 May 1948.

I remember the battle of Jerusalem vividly. My friends Naji Sinnawi, Mahmoud Yusef al-Khatib and Munir Hass'an and I used to walk about a mile to the top of the Mount of Olives to watch the fighting. We couldn't see clearly, but bullets whizzed by or fell near us without causing the slightest stir or fright, for in our mid-teens we had grown accustomed to the sound of battle and the sight of blood and were unmoved by exposure to danger. We would lie on our bellies and argue endlessly about the sound of the machine-gun which had just been used, each convinced of his infallible ability to recognize a gun by its particular firing pattern. After all, a German Schmizer sounded different from a Browning, a Hotchkiss from a Bren Gun, a Thompson from a Sten Gun, and Italian Beretta from a French Mitrailleuse and a Czech or Belgian machine-gun from the rest. Some machine-guns made an intermittent clapping sound, others thundered loudly, a third type chugged repeatedly and a fourth type would fire non-stop like a water hose until it had used up all the ammunition in its magazine. I think I can distinguish the sound of those different machine-guns and rifles to this day, but, unlike then, the sound of a firecracker exploding near me now is most unwelcome and likely to send me running.

The Arab Legion wasn't the only Arab force which came to Jerusalem after the British departed. Coming to Jerusalem meant coming to Bethany as well and the most notable new arrivals next to the Legionnaires were troops of a specially-formed army of volunteers called the Liberation Army. This army was financed by the Arab League, the regional alliance of Arab states, who declared war on Israel, and it was made up of Syrians, Iraqis, Yemenis and other Arabs who came to free Palestine from 'Zionist encroachment'. At the time mysterious legend surrounded the commander of the Liberation Army, one Fawzi al-Kawkji, but years later he was exposed as a hopeless drunk with few military skills. His reputation was based on an inglorious stint as an officer in the German Army.

Unlike the proud Arab Legionnaires of the famous Glubb Pasha, the troops of the Liberation Army were totally disorganized. They arrived in Bethany on foot or in trucks with no idea of where to stay and no equipment or semblance of logistical support to keep them alive. They didn't even have tents and their arms and uniforms were variable. The officers were for the most part invited in to the houses of local families – Mahmoud got stuck with four, Father Theodoseos with six – while the NCOs and ordinary soldiers improvised encampments and waited for orders and supplies to come: though how, from where and from whom these things were to come Allah only knew. They certainly didn't. The battle for Jerusalem raged while the ramshackle Liberation Army lounged around refusing to participate because, in the words of its mostly Iraqi officers, 'There are no orders' (makoo awamer). Not only were there no orders but most of the time there was almost no food, only occasional truckloads getting through, their contents donated by an Arab country which felt generous enough to send provisions for the poor volunteers of this force.

One day a contingent of Liberation Army troops was sighted marching towards Bethany from the direction of Jericho. After establishing its identity Ibrahim's Holy

Strugglers ran down a valley to greet them and there were
wild scenes of jubilation mixed with the customary volleys of
gunfire towards the sky. They were all oblivious of their position
under the overhead telephone lines connecting the Arab
command in Jerusalem with the outside world and they
managed to cut the lines in an unintended demonstration of
sharp shooting. The Arab command in Jerusalem was incommunicado for two days – no one had bothered to report
the incident.

The presence of non-Palestinian Arabs, the Arab Legion
and the Liberation Army changed Bethany irrevocably.
There was an immediate difficulty in understanding dialects,
as the foot soldiers came from peasant backgrounds where
regional dialects are strongest, and there was a need to
understand what the various Arab guests were trying to say,
and vice versa. There were also less immediate problems,
such as different tastes in food: the Yemenis used totally different spices and the Iraqis had their own variety of rice
which they preferred to all others – it was called rashidi. None
the less, despite everything, the most overwhelming discovery was the apparent kinship which bound the people of
Bethany to this odd collection of Arab arrivals, the common
religion and the similarity in their day-to-day behaviour.

Politically, this bond was explained in many different ways.
The more educated officers from within the ranks of the Arab
Legion or the Liberation Army, citing clear historical links,
said that the Arabs were one people. To them differences
between Palestinian and other Arabs were an imperialist fab-
rication perpetuated by the British and French in accordance
with a 'divide and rule' policy. Others explained their close
relationship to us by saying that they came to fight for
Jerusalem on strictly religious grounds, and some of these
carried an 'immunity scroll', an inscription of Koranic verse
guaranteeing them passage to heaven in case of martyrdom.
A much smaller group said that the Jews must be eliminated
because they had been trouble-makers from time immemorial,
as the Bible and the Koran attested.

Thus Bethany changed. Not only was acquaintance with

other Arabs increasing but there were outsiders too, the few
pro-Arab anti-Jewish Britons who deserted their army and
joined the Arabs, or volunteer Yugoslav Muslims who also
came to fight and had their own peculiarities. Soon the
everyday behaviour of our guests permeated our lives: the
people of Bethany began making coffee the way the Yemenis
did because the Yemenis grew coffee in the southern part of
their country and supposedly knew more about it, while
Ibrahim's men began to imitate the Iraqi military step, thinking it the most soldierly step in the Arab world. The cumula-
tive effect of this enforced if brief integration was to provide a
background which answered the most important single question about the relationship between us and other Arabs: why
were these men prepared to fight and die for Palestine?
There is no doubt about the answer: it was because, for some
reasons which are intelligible and others which are not, they
considered themselves bound to us as fellow Arabs and considered Palestine, Jerusalem and Bethany part of the
Arab world.

Variations on these ideas flourished locally and Palestinians began to feel more Arab than ever. This two-way traffic
in brotherhood moved Bethany out of its limited role of being
a village adjunct of Jerusalem and hurled it into the turmoil of
a much larger Arab world. Before, we were Arabs because we
lived and behaved like Arabs; after 1948 this identity was
sealed through a conscious adoption of that label.

The Aburish family stood right in the middle of all this.
Ibrahim was drilling and training his troops day and night,
overcoming the resistance of Awar Aburumi, who was committed to the idea that field combat was the only training
necessary and would argue his case openly in the presence of
the troops. Mahmoud was trying to hold the village together
by working with international relief agencies, attempting to
help the influx of refugees from coastal areas overrun by
Jewish forces. Ali, Daoud and Hassan were part of Ibrahim's
troops, while Mousa continued to run the local coffee house –
though he joined the Holy Strugglers part-time when the
spirit moved him. My father ran what remained of his taxi

company and also acted as a secret Mufti public relations man with members of the foreign press corps who used his company's services – he was always predicting an impending Arab victory. The women's subordinate position didn't allow for direct participation in the decisions of war, yet Salha Ibrahim took visible pride in her husband's position, Mirriam Mahmoud lived up to her husband's expectations and ran an almost permanent open house for Arab and foreign visitors as well as helping with refugee work, and Munira Hassan saw to it that her husband's uniform was so clean and starched that it provoked jokes from his comrades. The others, my mother included, carried on stoically.

When the orders finally came, the Liberation Army, the Arab Legion and the Holy Strugglers began squeezing the Jewish-held part of Jerusalem of three sides. Only the western road to Tel Aviv remained open, which ran through a narrow defile called Bab al-Wad, door of the valley. Israeli convoys from Tel Aviv, daring to negotiate the Bab al-Wad route to relieve their beleaguered compatriots in Jerusalem, were exposed to Arab fire for a brutal stretch extending for over a mile. Most relief efforts failed to break through, some of them suffering sixty per cent casualties, so that everyone, the Israelis included, expected Jerusalem to fall to the Arabs.

When the Arabs failed to completely close the Bab al-Wad they tried to move on Jewish Jerusalem from the east. The most difficult obstacle in the way of the Arab forces advancing from this direction was a strategic hill on top of which were the Church of Notre Dame and the French Hospital. The Israelis held on to these two buildings, in spite of repeated Arab Legion shelling by twenty-five pounder artillery and continued night attacks by the best of the combined Arab forces. These two buildings became the focus of the battle for the city and on the third day a frontal commando attack to dislodge the Israelis was undertaken, supported by uncle Ibrahim's Bethany forces, all of whom left Bethany unprotected to join the battle. They managed to enter both buildings, moving forward slowly and bloodily through the endless maze of corridors in the church and the hospital. And it was there that uncle Ali was killed. Characteristically, he was leading the assault on an Israeli stronghold in the eastern wing of the hospital, single-handedly carrying an overweight anti-tank rifle with which he tried to knock down doors and walls. He was shot in the head and died instantly.

I heard of uncle Ali's death at the family house, while sitting on the verandah with uncle Mahmoud, who was trying to listen to the news on the radio and make out the positions of the various combatants. Uncle Ibrahim marched toward Mahmoud solemnly and, unusually, saluted him military style and declared: 'May you live long. Ali has been martyred. We lost him with others in the battle for Notre Dame.' I was stunned and speechless. Mahmoud rose heavily, grabbed Ibrahim by the shoulder and kissed him on both cheeks, answering: 'Our heads will always stand high in his honour. Father would have been proud. I will tell mother.' My grandmother and Ali's wife, my aunt Nafisa, who was then eight months pregnant, were told by Mahmoud. Grandmother's grief was not open: to outsiders she showed no emotion, but relations could detect a slowness in her step and a wandering, sad look in her eyes. Upon hearing the news she opened her hands towards heaven, recited something from the Koran, spread her little rug towards Mecca and prayed. Her only question to Ibrahim was whether 'my child' suffered. Nafisa, on the other hand, became hysterical and a doctor had to be summoned to administer a sedative.

The burial took place before sunset on the same day. All members of the family appeared and my father gave me a Luger pistol, telling me to use it to salute my dead soldier uncle when the time came. The funeral was improvised, almost spontaneous, a mixture of chaos and bravado. About 2,000 people tried to attend and those who walked behind Ali's body included Holy Strugglers, comrades, friends and family, wailing women and children, delegates from the Arab Legion and the Liberation Army. In this wave of humanity no one knew what to do or where to go. When the coffin was lowered, and after the sermon the vengeance-seeking speeches were over, I saw a group of men with their rifles turned skywards and I rushed over and stood next to them. I thought, rightly, that they were the guard of honour and I cocked my Luger and fired one shot in the air. It jammed and I couldn't shoot any more; I also couldn't see any more, for tears were rolling down my cheeks and I was sobbing like a baby. Ali had been my favourite uncle.

Family legend blossomed around Ali's heroic achievements. In truth the only confirmed fact is that he had been fighting for three days and nights without sleep and that he was indeed a fearless leader of men, always in the forefront of battle, inspiring his fellow soldiers in action.

The Aburish women did not wear the customary black to mourn Ali because his death bestowed honour on us all. Instead, attention was focused on his widow, on meeting her financial needs and her wait for the unborn baby. Members of the family, chiefly Mahmoud, Ibrahim and my father, assigned Nafisa a modest income, and soon, to the joy of all concerned, Nafisa gave birth to a boy who was given the name of Ali after his father. Because of his father's heroic status he became the darling of his family and the whole village. He was always introduced as 'son of . . .'.

On 11 June 1948 there was a month's cease-fire, after which the fighting resumed, but the tide had by then turned in favour of the Israelis, who were rejuvenated by better leadership and modern arms. Besides, the inspirational leader of the Holy Strugglers, a first cousin of the Mufti, Abel Kader al-Husseini, had already been killed and his loss was calamitous. The Arab troops became demoralized by bad leadership and unending quarrels, and Israeli convoys and reinforcements were breaching the Arab blockade of Jerusalem, allowing the Israelis to take the offensive for the first time in months. With every Israeli success the battle was moving close and closer to Bethany, moving south towards us from the Hebrew University east of Jerusalem, crawling east from al-Baka' and the King David area, and inching nearer to Government House – only a mile away from our home. Even my mother joined in trying to identify the sounds of battle, though to her everything thunderous was German.

The loss of initiative by the Arabs produced calls for more fighters, and in response Bethany's troops continued to do double duty, guarding the village and helping to defend Jerusalem. Once, when a particularly persistent Israeli attack threatened the New Gate of the old city, thirty of Ibrahim's now famous fighters were dispatched to stem the tide of battle. They crept towards the New Gate under heavy fire but took time off to beat up a middle-aged Arab Jerusalemite. It appears that the poor man was ineptly shooting in the direction of the attackers with a 5 mm. hand-gun by sticking his hand out of the door of his house and firing at random. He greeted the arrival of Ibrahim's men with: 'Now I can rest, the *fellaheen* are here.' Rightly, they didn't appreciate his haughty, townsmen's attitude towards them, in spite of the implied compliment to their fighting prowess.

Mahmoud, Ibrahim, Hassan, Daoud and even Mousa continued as before. My father, his taxi company closed after its offices were destroyed, found himself a job working with O. D. Gallagher of the London *Daily Mail* reporting on the Arab side of the battle. He made notes in Arabic then orally translated them to O.D., who wrote them down and transmitted them to the *Daily Mail* in London. Because of my father's connection with the Mufti, the *Daily Mail* was willing to accept this tortuous method of working – Abu Said could not write his own dispatches, but the value of the material he was offering overcame this obvious handicap: his reports were from the inside, not available to the run-of-the-mill reporter, and he and O. D. Gallagher became a famous Fleet Street duo. Stories about their exploits are recalled by older Fleet Street colleagues to this day.

The Arab lines were beginning to break under the relentless and well-organized Israeli attacks, and in an ironic twist of events the Arab garrison in the al-Katamoun district of new Jerusalem, led by one Ibrahim Abu Dayeh, was surrounded on all sides except for a stretch of road less than 100 yards long which was exposed to Israeli machine-gun fire. The

Israelis tried to reach the road and complete the encircle-
ment of the garrison but the Arabs held on to it as stubbornly
as the Israelis had held on to Notre Dame and the French
Hospital. However, as Abu Dayeh's only connection with the
outside lay completely open to Israeli fire it was difficult to
get any supplies to his troops. Yet when reports filtered out
that the Abu Dayeh garrison was running out of ammunition a
number of volunteers took it upon themselves to risk fate and
carry supplies to their compatriots. Among them was my
father.

It was Radio Jerusalem which told the story of how Abu
Said loaded his own car with whatever ammunition he could
gather from the various forces and ran the seige fourteen
times, exposing himself to near death every journey. Not only
was this a demonstration of my father's commitment to the
Arab cause but also Abu Dayeh was a personal friend, and no
one could dissuade him from undertaking what he considered
to be his holy mission. His car was hit in thirty-six different
places and became a show-piece; its body was riddled with
holes, some as big as half a fist, but luckily the engine, the
driver and the load escaped harm.

Throughout this period my maternal grandfather, Mousa
Shahine, a member of the Arab Higher Committee, was in
Cairo with the Mufti. It was the members of this Arab Higher
Committee who liaised with the various Arab governments
which sent their armies into Palestine after the departure of
the British and ran and financed the Holy Strugglers
throughout the country. When news of the deteriorating
situation in Jerusalem reached him, my grandfather sent
word to my grandmother to leave Bethany as soon as possible
and to bring with her as many members of the family as
she could.

Grandmother Mirriam Shahine arranged for a four-car
convoy to make the trip to Cairo, taking with her my young
maternal uncles and aunts, and offering space to all
grandchildren whose parents allowed them to join her. Her
route was to take her from Jerusalem to Bethlehem, then
Hebron, on to Bersheba, through the Sinai Peninsula and

eventually to Cairo. There was no organized way to make this frightful trip and there was no specific plan on how to reach Cairo.

Our house was on grandmother's way, on the western edge of Bethany near the roads to Jerusalem and Bethlehem, and she stopped her convoy there at 8.00 a.m. to ask my mother to allow me and my brothers to accompany her to Cairo and exile. As my father was away and because of the traditional Arab responsibility invested in the eldest son, I refused to leave, insisting on keeping my mother company. I had kept the Luger my father had given me the day of Ali's funeral and sported it dagger-style under the belt of my short trousers and wandered around Bethany proudly pretending I was capable of using it. On the other hand, my brothers Afif and Wagih, only half awake at that time of the morning and still in their nightshirts, followed my mother's orders and jumped into one of grandmother's cars. By then they were nine and eight years old. They left without changing clothes and with my mother throwing belongings after them through the window of the moving car, as black smoke rose up from Jerusalem burning in the background. The sound of battle accompanying my grandmother's departure was unforgettable: the thud of artillery, the clip-clap of machine-gun fire, the occasional single shot of a sniper. Smoke, most of it black and ominous, rose from the rubble of crumbling buildings in that holy city.

There was no way of knowing whether my grandmother would ever make it to Cairo since telephone, telegraph and postal communications had ceased to exist and her planned escape route was one long war zone, where the dividing line between the enemies changed daily. My personal experience tells me that if there is agony in war then uncertainty claims the top of the list. We did not know whether Afif and Wagih and my grandmother had reached Cairo safely until six months later, well after we ourselves had abandoned Jerusalem and moved to Beirut. We assumed their safe arrival, but I remember my mother with her teary far-away looks and I, too, often cried myself to sleep thinking about my young playmates and

what had happened to them. Even my usually imperturbable
father took to biting his lower lip. As it turned out, my
grandmother and the rest were interned in a disused POW
camp for three weeks and then joined my grandfather in
Cairo.
However great our pains and misfortunes, they were
neither unique nor isolated. There were others in Bethany
who lost loved ones, and divided families became the order of
the day, while refugees arriving in Bethany were in an even
worse condition, like the child of five who came from nowhere
having lost both parents and two brothers. The local Jesuits
adopted him. None of this compared with the anxiety common to all Arabs: the dread of what would happen to us if the
Israelis overran Jerusalem.
Now uncle Mahmoud ruled absolute in Bethany; he had no
central authority to hold him to account, for any semblance of
organized government had departed with the British.
Because of this unusual position Mahmoud is an excellent
eyewitness to life in the shadow of impending Israeli victory
and, luckily, his account is a clear, vivid one.

People were frightened. They didn't want to live under a vic-
torious Jewish army. Many wanted to run away but, contrary to
legend, the Holy Strugglers tried to stop them. In Bethany there
was a small committee called the Black Hand, which had the task
of forcing people to stay. A lot of frightening rumours were
exaggerations, but then some were true. One must remember
that the Israelis themselves weren't clear as to what they wanted
and certainly they had problems with their hot-heads, Begin and
company – the ones who annihilated Deir Yassin. Secretly, Arab
fears had as much to do with Arab attitudes as anything else. We
knew we wouldn't be kind to them if we had won, so why should
they be kind to us?
Some people were hungry so they stole, other people stole
every time they went into Jerusalem because it was easy: there
was no one to keep discipline. Every time a group of refugees
arrived in Bethany I sought out a leader, armed him and told him
he was responsible for the behaviour of his bunch. We did shoot

some people, but then how else could one keep them in order? It worked.

It was a war without rules. One's only hope lay in the other side's humanity, and there wasn't much of that – the Jews were determined to win. We had places to which we could go in other Arab countries and they didn't. Of course, we were afraid, but so were they, and one can't trust the behaviour of frightened people.

Besides the awareness of other Arabs as blood and cultural relations and a certain feeling of unity which resulted from that, the social stresses caused by the 1947–8 war brought to the surface the inner thinking of society, much as personal stress exposes our inner fabric. In this case, the level of social awareness can be judged by the explanations offered by the people of Bethany and members of my immediate family of the causes of the war that was consuming them.

Grandmother Rashedah blamed the whole war on the British. Being an old-fashioned Muslim woman she stated, with an emphasis that left little room for discussion, that Turkey, the previous occupier of Palestine, would never have done this to us. Setting aside her previous admiration for the British, she even recited songs praising Turkey and condemning Britain: 'They use us like beasts of burden so Mustafa Kemal please come back and help us.' (*Hamalouna hmal waja'louna bgal Mustafa Kemal ashfi' fina ho*). Rashedah's refrain had more than a measure of truth in it for Turkey had never denied the Arabism of Palestine or the ownership of land.

To the younger women, my aunts, my mother and her contemporaries, it was all a plot against the Jews, and against all odds they continued to preach that one should not despair. Their theory was that the British didn't want the Jews in their own country because they didn't like them, so they and other Europeans were sending them to Palestine to get rid of them. Secretly, they averred, the British hoped the Arabs would win and rid the world of the Jewish problem. They took the conspiracy theory a step beyond that and stated categorically that a certain point in time the British would help the Arabs rid the world of the Jews.

The thinking of the men was varied and a little more sophisticated. People like Mahmoud were aware of the Balfour Declaration (the statement by the British Foreign Secretary which had promised the Jews a homeland in Palestine after the First World War) and the deliberations at the end of the Second World War which led the UN to sanction the establishment of a Jewish state. But he was at a loss to know what was in store for the Palestinian Arabs, and confused as to what would happen to him personally. He understood what was happening in terms of the Jewish claim, though he did not accept it; his inability to cope with its results as they affected Palestine and himself remain with him to this day.

My younger uncles were not as sophisticated and they saw the whole thing strictly in tribal terms: to them the Jewish tribe wanted what the Arab tribe had – Palestine. Honour demanded refusal even if this meant a fight to the death against odds made unfavourable by American and other support for Israel. After all, 'the Jews ran America' and this is why they were helping the Israelis. The American–Jewish connection, they thought, made it a losing battle, but they were determined to fight.

My uncle Ibrahim was a different matter – he was in his element. I don't think he was interested in analysing the situation. Like members of the Maquis in France during the Second World War his motivation was a reflection of his character. Being tough was part of his make-up and his new role suited him down to the ground: he was a totally fearless and, in many ways, irreverent man, not only with regard to the Israelis but in his relationship with other Arabs, including some of his superiors, some of the Mufti's effete emissaries. I remember hearing him complain to one of them about the lack of funds and ammunition from which his men were suffering. He finally looked the man straight in the eye and shouted: 'Tell him [meaning the Mufti] we are having a hell of a time, but please do it in the afternoon after he takes his nap.

I wouldn't want him to accuse me of disturbing him. After all, he is our leading actor.' (In Arabic actor and representative are one and the same word.)

The person whose appreciation of the Arab–Israeli conflict saddled him with the greatest mental anguish was my father. He was a Mufti man through and through, and a totally committed Arab. Not only that, he had indirectly worked for the Germans during the Second World War, accepting the Palestinian leaders' claims of eventual victory and their simple logic of joining forces with 'the enemy of my enemy'. His action in helping Abu Dayeh was evidence enough of his commitment to the Arab cause, yet his work with the taxi company, the *Daily Mail* and his previous direct contacts with Jewish people, all went to form his overall attitude. He never used the word Jew in a disparaging way, nor would he allow it to be used by us or anyone else while he was present. If he was talking to strangers and they assumed that my father harboured unreasoning anti-Jewish feelings he always defused the situation by saying: 'Well, I guess they are people like other people. They have ones they love just as we do, and they mourn their dead just as much as we do.'

The book *O Jerusalem* by Collins and Lapierre documents how Abu Said saved many an innocent Jew from the Mufti's more militant toughs, while also crediting him with being one of the organizers of an Arab raid on Jewish Jerusalem which led to the blowing up of the building housing the *Palestine Post* newspaper – one of the more celebrated exploits of that war. Abu Said refuses to go into the matter in greater detail.

*   *   *   *

We as children were exposed to the war and to this kaleidoscope of interpretations of what was happening, and we changed. The war did more to us than it did to our elders. The third generation of the Aburishs – I was the eldest but still not old enough to develop sophisticated thoughts on the subject – was rushed into a world beyond our years and will.

In a way, when I now think of myself and my brothers, I lament the fact that we were never young: distinguishing the sound of one machine-gun from another is not normal children's play and to this day I do not relate to children's games, be they Arab or western. Beyond that, what mattered was what was done to our minds, the indelible impressions that were to find expression in the way we conducted our future lives.

To me, my memories of Arab disorganization during the war has permanently coloured my judgement of the Arabs' ability to manage groups, organizations or armies. I remember the Liberation Army not knowing where it was going to sleep and I remember Ali's funeral and the mayhem surrounding it. I also remember the first time the artillery of the Liberation Army fired from Bethany, when the people thought it was a local explosion and ran in different directions screaming and wailing and not knowing what to do. I worry about the Arab ability to act collectively. The Arabs are believers in individual genius and leadership: the Holy Strugglers' command disintegrated after the death of their leader, Abdel Kader al-Husseini and his replacement by an incompetent first cousin by the name of Khalid, who lived in Bethany drinking whisky, well away from the fighting. Like all Arabs, the Mufti had to keep it in the family.

My cousin Khalil, son of local commander Ibrahim, took his explanations and attitudes from his father. He was left with the impression that: 'Given arms and training, the Arab soldier would have done his job. We were sold down the river by stupid leadership which never properly supported its fighting men.' My maternal uncle Majid Shahine, nine months older than I am, is now an atomic scientist living in Paris. He incorporated his 1947–8 experience into his later education and now believes: 'You are as good as your weakest point and your weakest point was the illiterate peasant who couldn't even read instructions on how to use a gun. How can you win a war that way?' My brother Wagih offers a simpler, more poignant point of view: 'The Arabs had no plan to win.'

The youngest descendants of Khalil Aburish have developed

instinctive reactions to 1948. Aunt Amneh's son Said is committed to working for the PLO 'to erase the shame of defeat. It is possible'. My brother Munif, born in 1946, was a member of the command of a militant Palestine Liberation Front. To him, 'the gun is the only answer. Otherwise, the Israelis will claim Baghdad and Mecca as their historical rights. What would the world do if the Arabs occupied Spain because it was once Arab?' My daughter Charla's view is towards persuasion: 'I can't believe that anyone who knows the facts would be anything but pro-Arab.' It would be less than honest to pretend that defeatist attitudes do not exist. I have two cousins who have developed a loathing for Arab ways. One says: 'When two million Jews defeat over a hundred million Arabs, then the Jews are better people.' The other is 'ashamed of the Arabs . . . they are backward'.

*　*　*　*

The year 1948 was the beginning of a sudden and lasting awareness. We got to know fellow Arabs and recognized our relationship to them, became acquainted with simple pieces of military hardware and the sounds they made, witnessed people who are tribal and individual by nature being subjected to rigid military training, suffered the loss of dear ones, noted the change of human behaviour under pressure and, for the first and last time, we were dispatched to different Arab countries to start a new life. This was the beginning of the dissolution of the family, the start of forced migration. Bethany would never be the same again after 1948, and the Aburish family would never again know a wedding or circumcision ceremony like the ones they had known in the past, the ones integral to old Bethany and its ways.

Taking stock of the physical impact on the Aburishs is simple: my father moved to Beirut after a final truce was declared and continued to work with the *Daily Mail*. Ibrahim got a job managing the largest Arab refugee camp in the Middle East, housing 30,000 people, a job demanding as much toughness as his military command. Hassan and Daoud worked for the United Nations in minor relief jobs. Mahmoud continued to run a Bethany swollen to three times its former size by refugees and with at least ten times its previous problems. Mousa stayed to run his coffee house. The most important change of all concerned their collective perception of Bethany; the dramatic events which enveloped it detached them – it no longer represented a cosy little home.

So, like the rest of the Palestinians, we were defeated and scattered, though if one believed the propaganda directed at us from the various Arab countries, we could live for a while on the illusion of going back. Details of our reasons and reaction to the defeat have been given and they differ, but a single response came out of it: educate, educate, educate.

Without exception the Aburishs reasoned that the Israelis beat the Arabs because they were better educated. Mahmoud always compared their hospitals to Arab hospitals and concluded that 'they were ahead'. Ibrahim spoke of their military co-ordination being superior to that of the Arabs. My father referred to their developed sense of community. In other words, the Israelis were better organized, could handle the gun better, command groups of men better and altogether manage the element of planning and execution better. On this everyone agreed, and this was the beginning of another phase.

7
A generation joins the modern world

As uncle Mousa was listening to the radio one day he suddenly ran out and knocked at the door of the outhouse: 'They're going to play that favourite song of yours', he told my grandmother. 'Right,' she said, 'I'll be out in a minute, so don't turn the wireless on till then.'

That incident, apocryphal or not, was supposed to have taken place in 1936, and was a fair reflection of the education of girls of Rashedah's time. When she was young, in the last part of the nineteenth century, women's education was seen as being tantamount to corruption, so she was brought up as an ignorant bedouin. The universal maxim of 'what you don't know can't hurt you' was reduced to 'ignorance is bliss'. Knowledge for women would have threatened their traditional roles as housekeepers and child-bearers, so to say that women's education was discouraged would be to overstate the case by suggesting that it was even a matter for consideration: it wasn't. The facilities were not there, and even if they were, the male decision-makers were totally against educating their womenfolk, with the result that women were excluded from taking part in anything except household chores and helping with farming, thus perpetuating their state of ignorance.

In fact, men's education was only a short step ahead. Most people in the Palestine countryside lived off the land, and therefore had no need of education. They were preoccupied with making a living farming their small family plots of one to three acres, a task made all the more difficult because of the primitive methods used. For most people there were no newspapers to be read, letters to be written or legal documents to be examined. Besides, there was usually a single educated person in the village who was called upon to do the reading and writing for the whole community, and was paid for his services, the modern equivalent of the scribe of Biblical times.

That was the system under Turkish rule, when education and religion were inseparable, with one man in each village responsible for both, much as priests acted in Europe in the Middle Ages. This one man would lead the people in prayer every Friday, the Muslim Sabbath, and during the rest of the week would teach the boys of the community. So according to the importance each individual gave to the separate functions, the man would be known as 'istaz', the teacher, 'Sheikh Madrassah', the head of the school, or simply as 'Sheikh', a term of respect for a religious leader. More mundanely, the teacher would also keep the records, entering details of births and deaths and land transfers on the rare occasions when such things were formally noted.

Until 1917 in villages the size of Bethany, the local school was a one-room affair, which was usually part of the local mosque. Instruction was limited in more ways than one: first the school was the exclusive domain of the boys of the village and the girls, whose traditional roles did not require even the most basic forms of literacy, were denied access to it; the second limitation had to do with the curriculum, which was restricted to the four Rs, the three traditional ones plus religion. Particular emphasis was placed on the reading of the Koran, both as the masterpiece of the Arabic language and as the religious document governing a person's future conduct. These were church schools in the classic sense, with the level of education attainable dependant on the uneven degree of scholarship of the local teachers and not on the need and potential of the students. Within that limitation, and given there was only one room to accommodate the whole school, each student was viewed as a separate entity entitled to progress in accordance with his ability and age, which normally spanned the years five to twelve. Schooling was not mandatory and the most generous estimate suggests that the number of boys attending school did not exceed ten per cent of those eligible.

The school day started with a recitation from the Koran which was concluded by thanks to the Almighty for his generosity, with the only other regular daily feature being the reading of ancient Arabic epic poetry which had sufficient praise for Arab heroics in it to be nationalistic in character. These two imperatives, of attachment to the Koran and to Arab legend, can be seen as forming the basis of a cultural identity, though there were of course no tributes to Palestine or to the Arabs as a nation state, but merely to the idea of a distinct culture represented by the Koran and poetry. Failure to master either meant being subjected to the care of the *istaz*, who appears to have administered punishment with the total acquiescence of parents – perhaps their way of demonstrating a basic interest in having their young acquire some rudimentary education. Just as in European schools, a lesser punishment called for copying the Koranic sura or a poem twenty to forty times, an obvious attempt at force-feeding knowledge.

The only textbook was the Koran, with probably only one, possibly two or three copies available, which would be passed round with priority assigned to 'achievers'. A student who read right through the Koran went back to the beginning and did it again and again, up to six or seven times. Beyond that students who could afford it had a writing pad and pencil which the poor ones had to do without altogether; the paper was crude and grainy, murky white, while pencils were of poor quality and broke under the slightest pressure. The blackboard was the teacher's only aid, using local chalk or limestone. Many of the pupils came to school barefoot and sat on straw mats which were too thin to protect them against the cold of winter, when an ancient coal burner attempted to heat the schoolroom.

The girls weren't even that lucky. Their education consisted of going to the home of a woman called *Haja*, an honorific entitled to be used by any woman who had performed the pilgrimage to Mecca but in fact bestowed on any woman who could read the Koran and write, regardless of whether she had in fact been to Mecca. Very few people concerned themselves with girls' education and the *Haja*'s school accommodated less than one-tenth the number of male students, less than one per cent of eligible girls, who visited her house and paid her for tuition in accordance with what they could afford rather than a fixed fee. In the *Haja*'s school instruction was strictly oral, and a girl's progress was judged by her ability to read the Koran aloud. There wasn't even a blackboard. As with boys, girls often absented themselves to help with the household chores or the harvesting season, things which were accepted as legitimate excuses, which even the *Sheikh Madrassah* or the *Haja* agreed were more important than mere learning. Aunt Suha Ibrahim's irregular attendance record meant it took her three years to recite the Koran. Says she: 'I kept having to start all over again like a beginner.'

These were the most common methods and levels of education, though Egypt and the Levant, Syria, Palestine and Lebanon, had had mission schools of every type since the beginning of the nineteenth century, French Jesuit, Russian Orthodox, Italian Catholic and even pioneering Quaker schools. These institutions had a number of basic advantages which included division into classes in accordance with age and competence, the teaching of the language of the school's country of origin, second to Arabic, and dealing with the sciences in a straightforward way – the Arabs who had introduced the words alchemy, algebra and alcohol to the world had neglected the sciences for centuries and many teachings had come to be considered against the Koran. But the mission schools were few in number and the missionaries were usually found only in major cities such as Jerusalem and Haifa. Also, one of the primary aims of missionary schools was the conversion of Muslim students to Christianity so that very few Muslim families took advantage of their presence and they were literally relegated to preaching to the converted, the local Christians.

It was the British who brought an end to the monopoly of religion – Muslim or otherwise – in institutions of education, as one of their first moves after the 1917 occupation of Palestine was the enactment of laws promising free public education to all. A department of education was set up, dealing first with cities and afterwards villages, so that Bethany had its first secular school in 1921. This calculated British move was aimed at freeing the population from the restraints of Koranic learning and paving the way towards the attainment of 'higher education' without offending the native Muslims by subjecting them to alien religious teachings, though for unknown reasons they stopped short of ordering mandatory attendance in places where it could have been done, and chose to allow Mosque schools to continue for fear of offending Muslim sensibilities.

However well-intentioned the British were, a shortage of money, of qualified people and of time limited what could be done. In any case, villages like Bethany were at the bottom of the list and, in the end, all that could be provided there was a three-room boys' school with three teachers, which meant a youngster could go no further than the third grade. Women's education played no part in original British planning, and there is good reason to believe that this was another conscious decision aimed at avoiding conflict with traditional Muslim values. The British Government's conservative attitude stood in sharp contrast to that of the zealous missionaries who placed their 'civilizing' purpose above sensitivity to local feelings.

Much to their father's satisfaction the elder Aburish boys, Mahmoud, Mohammad and Ibrahim had completed the Bethany school around 1922. Mahmoud and Mohammad were average students while Ibrahim was always near the top of the class. Afterwards Khalil Aburish took advantage of his connections with the various Christian churches to place his children in their schools – unlike others, he had overcome the common fear of conversion to Christianity or adoption of Christian ways.

For reasons which remain unexplained to this day, the boys

were sent to different schools in Jerusalem. Mahmoud went to Terra Sancta (Italian Catholic), Mohammad to Frères College (French Jesuit) and Ibrahim to St George's (Anglican). Their schooling was as varied as the background of their educators, undoubtedly leading to a stimulating atmosphere outside the schools, when the boys would compete over who knew the meaning of an Arabic word in Italian, French or English. They visited the neighbouring monasteries in Bethany to exercise their newly-acquired linguistic prowess with the generous and accommodating local priests. It is endearing to note the lasting esteem and affection which they retained for their schools and teachers and their religious neighbours throughout their lives. My father becomes an unreasoning, intolerant man at the slightest criticism of the Jesuit Order. To him the Jesuits are 'great educators. . . . They tried to help and I don't remember one instance when they tried to convert me.'

The Aburish boys were day students, trekking on foot from Bethany to Jerusalem and back, following the path taken by Christ, over the Mount of Olives, down to Gethsemane and then on to Jerusalem's Damascus Gate, which they reached in about an hour, at 8.30 in the morning. There they branched out in different directions, to meet again at 4.00 in the afternoon for the journey back home. The two-mile trip was too dangerous to be undertaken by any of them on their own; the barren hillside still sheltered the occasional wolf and hyena, as well as bandits. The devotion to schooling of Khalil Aburish and his children appears to have overcome all these difficulties; they accepted the two-hour daily journey without complaint. To my father, 'the difficulty of the trip particularly in the winter when it was wet and windy, gave us a sense that we were doing something important. We enjoyed it.'

They absorbed everything their schools had to offer, Ibrahim becoming a star soccer player and Mohammad a boy scout leader, and they reached a fair scholastic level, though still somewhat lower than a western secondary school education. Their thirst for education was never completely satisfied, as their schools stopped at the second or third year of high school and there were no universities in Palestine which they could attend. Much to his children's chagrin, Khalil Aburish was reluctant to send them to a foreign country, not even to nearby Egypt or Syria. His unhappy experience with his first son Ahmad had left an ineradicable sadness in him, against which no one dared to argue, for his fear was not that they would be 'corrupted' but simply that they would not return at all.

The younger boys, Ali, Mousa, Daoud and Hassan, followed in their elder brothers' footsteps, with the full encouragement of their father and brothers. Ali and Daoud succeeded, Mousa proved ineducable and Hassan, though extremely intelligent, became a problem student; his bad behaviour was in part attributable to the lack of a father figure, as his Jerusalem schooling began after my grandfather died in 1936. It may be that the absence of a father and his discipline, plus the fact that his mother gave in to him too much, produced that rowdy, unmanageable boy.

This commitment to education, predictably, did not extend to the girls. Hamdah, Khalil Aburish's daughter by his first marriage, was of the same generation as grandmother Rashedah and suffered the same fate. Amneh and Fatmeh were considerably younger but education for girls had not improved by the 1930s; both testify to their father's desire to educate them though they do not recall specific discussions on the subject because 'they were too young to be consulted'. The practical barriers to their education appear to have been the absence of a Bethany girls' school and the problem of sending them to Jerusalem – apart from the physically dangerous journey it was a potentially morally corrupting influence, and hence out of the question. Their only schooling consisted of intermittent trips to the *Haja*'s house for about two years, a situation which they lament with hindsight, but which was not an issue for discussion at the time.

By the 1940s, what started as a pioneering effort by Khalil Aburish had become the accepted norm for his grandchildren, and the boys were expected to attend the local and Jerusalem schools, though fathers alone made the decisions concerning sons' and daughters' education, as they made all decisions involving finances. Mothers' positions fell short of participating in such weighty matters: they became the guardians of traditional values, gently cautioning against the erosion of religious attachment by book learning. Like my grandmother before them, they prodded their husbands into attempting to instil religious belief which they felt was threatened by the new schools. Even around 1950 aunt Salha Ibrahim was known to couple her morning goodbye to her school-bound children with the refrain, 'Don't forget your religion', and whenever one of aunt Amneh's children spoke of his or her achievements, their mother would ask if they had mastered any of the Koran and would make them read passages out loud.

So my generation took for granted what the previous generation had considered a rare privilege. Our parents were determined to give us the best education in Palestine, and this was facilitated by the early 1940s, because almost everyone then accepted the benefits of missionary education. Except among a few diehards, there was no stigma attached to missionary education when I grew up, though eventually private schools run by Palestinians who tried to strike a balance between the traditionalists and missionaries did make an appearance.

At the outbreak of the 1948 war no less than fifteen grandsons of Khalil Aburish were attending schools in Jerusalem. The value of education was hammered into us by our parents every day; my father used to do it by example, repeating the names of successful people in the country and attributing their achievements to their learning – my maternal grandfather Shahine, a judge of the High Islamic Court, was his prime example. Uncle Ibrahim used to get carried away and tell his children that any of them who failed school would be 'thrown out of the house at night to be eaten by wolves', while aunt Amneh used gentle persuasion with both daughters and sons, pushing them every inch of the way; Fatmeh laid down a rule that every child had to spend so many hours a day with his or her books and made sure she was obeyed. Mahmoud's eldest children were daughters, but he unflinchingly decided in favour of their schooling and sent them to Bethany's newly-founded girls' school demanding that they match the performance of their male cousins.

It was more than an ordinary case of caring and wishing your children to be educated: it went beyond that and became an obsession. There were incessant enquiries about our grades, our ability to negotiate a foreign language and our involvement in all that a school had to offer – we had to play games, take part in school plays and join the boy scouts. Every time I ran into a relative I hadn't seen for a while, I was given a scholastic test on the spot. After the 1948 war, performance in school became the sole topic of conversation, for in Mahmoud's words, 'this is the only way we are going to equal the Israelis and eventually beat them'. This simplistic refrain became the slogan of the whole family – indeed it appears to have been universally adopted by Palestinians, one of the few side benefits of an otherwise destructive conflict. When I recently asked a Bethany lady about her son, she answered: 'He has two university degrees. He's alright.'

So the 1948 war-induced rush towards education was an Aburish, Bethany and Palestine phenomenon which touched everyone and carried with it a blind faith that in education lay the answer to the ultimate question: how to understand and correct the roots of Palestinian defeat. Within my own family special pejoratives were used to describe poor school performers: a bad male student was called *tanbal* (thick) or *baghi* (mule), and even girls got the occasional *hmara* (female jackass) when they didn't meet expectations. The resort to abusive language was not a reflection of harshness peculiar to the members of the family, it came instead from frustration. Because our education was galloping ahead of the level they had reached they found it very difficult to help us with our homework and therefore their only standard of judgement on our performance was our grade score. The result was that unduly harsh labels were assigned to poor students to make them work harder. Moreover, though no member of my father's generation will admit it, adults were competing with each other through the scholastic achievements of their children.

My father put his money where his mouth was and his exhortations to us to read were accompanied by the opening of an account for us at a local bookshop near our boarding school in Jerusalem. This was our first experience of charge accounts, yet he really did permit us to buy all the books we wanted on the assumption that we would read them. Nor did it stop there. He hired tutors to help us with our English after deciding the school curriculum 'was not enough'; his personal interest extended to encouraging us to read poetry out loud and there was visible happiness on his face when I obliged one day by reciting Arabic poetry by heart. His commitment to our schooling was total so that, to us, and indeed to all our cousins, the fact that we were university-bound was beyond question. This was made plain to us from a very early age, and though my father shied away from steering us towards a particular course of study, he read about British and American universities and talked to people about them so that he would be able to give us advice if necessary, or if one of us showed a particular inclination about which he knew little. Later he learned about the universities we were attending and would regale any willing listener with stories about our superior institutions of higher learning.

Ibrahim's strict discipline was effective when it came to his children's education: a child's pocket money was increased, reduced or cancelled altogether depending on the grade score, and he often resorted to the cane. His son Khalil fondly remembers the 'bonuses' he received every time his grade justified them. Considering that he had twelve children, this simple bonus system was an exceptional act of generosity, though as he said: 'I'll beg, steal and even murder to get you kids to the university but the work must be done by you.' When he heard that one of his sons at university was neglecting his studies and spending a lot of time with his girlfriend, Ibrahim crudely threatened to 'fly over and chop your thing off. Study now – you can screw later.'

When Amneh's husband complained about the cost of his children's education she took exception to his attitude and threatened to leave him, an unheard-of act of courage for her generation of women. Eventually she sold her few pieces of jewellery and prevailed upon him to give up his forays to the local coffee house and use his money for a nobler purpose, a decision she lived to celebrate, as has her ever-reluctant husband.

Fatmeh, according to my mother, is so shy 'she has never looked anyone in the eye', but this did not stop her from hounding Mahmoud about her need for money for her children's education until he apportioned a certain amount of her modest inheritance towards that purpose. Her own joyous comment was: 'I was willing to go without food to educate them. It was that simple.' Mousa followed Fatmeh's example and sold his share in the inheritance to Mahmoud, using the money to pay for schooling. Daoud's children, quiet and studious, earned scholarships from the age of twelve until they finished universities. Everyone joined the march to academe and for the most part they succeeded.

We children prided ourselves on our scholastic achievements, and knowledge for its own sake became an obsession with us; we derived secret satisfaction from being more knowledgeable than our parents and certainly our grandparents. I remember at seven or eight regaling grandmother Rashedah with stories about the eskimos, their life-style and snow houses, whereupon grandmother looked at me askance and said something like, 'that's fine, dear . . . just don't tell the neighbours about the snow houses'. Aunt Nafisa Ali warily listened to her son Ali recite Shakespeare and then confided in uncle Ibrahim her fear that this type of from-the-bottom-of-the-stomach reading 'might give him haemorrhoids'. Whenever Jesuit-educated Khalil Ibrahim disagreed with his mother he answered her in French, to which she always said: 'That's all fine, now answer me in plain Arabic.' Then he would preface his Arabic translation to her by the coquettish, 'ma belle petite'. Both of them were having a good time and knew it.

As Mahmoud's actions showed, the education epidemic enveloping my generation spread to include girls, though it was a few years after the boys, in the late 1940s, when Bethany girls began going to school in Jerusalem and the Aburishs were in the forefront of this effort. Some girls who were not scholastically inclined sought sanctuary in the traditional role of the Arab female to avoid going to school, but happily no one listened to them. Mahmoud snorted at one of them: 'Nobody marries an uneducated girl any more.' She relented.

The daughters of Mahmoud, Ibrahim, Amneh and Fatmeh were the pioneers of the girls' education, taking the bus instead of walking to Jerusalem and back. And though aunt Mirriam stopped her daughters from using any language at home but the Arabic she knew because she would not know 'what they were up to', she was totally supportive of the effort to educate them. At the same time she did not want them indulging in activities of which she did not approve; using a foreign language meant 'naughtiness', an indication of the lingering suspicion that girls' education could lead to corruption.

Recognizable landmarks in the field of education were occasions for celebrations almost as important as wedding and circumcision ceremonies. Graduating from high school justified a party in which all age groups took part. The certificate of graduation was shown to everyone and was eventually framed and hung on a wall occupying a place of honour in the house of the graduate's parents. Congratulations and presents were very much in order and many parents and graduates were offended when uncles and aunts ignored such happy events, for congratulations to the parents of the graduate were a recognition of the success of their efforts. The family would place announcements in Jerusalem newspapers congratulating a graduate on his or her fine achievement, often accompanied by a picture. The most commonly heard phrase was, 'May Allah keep him [or her] for you to help you in your old age'.

Going to a university, in addition to its novelty, was a more complicated proposition. The most immediate difficulty was that there were not enough places available, and the second was the physical location of most universities. The other Arab countries, relatively free from disruptive conflicts, were ahead of the West Bank (the part of Palestine annexed to Jordan) in the field of higher education and naturally gave priority to their own nationals. Even Jordan discriminated against its Palestinian-born citizens.

These two restrictions of limited availability and discrimination compelled us and our fellow countrymen to go to western universities where, in addition, there was always a greater chance of a scholarship or some other form of financial aid. Certainly, part-time work to complement parental support was available in the United States, Canada, Germany and other places and was not frowned upon as it would have been in the Middle East – a young Aburish would think it beneath his dignity to be a bellboy in Damascus, but not in New York. These two financial factors very often determined the university one attended, and scholastic inclination was often subordinated to monetary needs.

There was universal awareness of our parents' sacrifices to educate us, as when Mahmoud's wife sold her jewellery to pay one of her sons' school fees. Somewhere along the way my father and my uncles made the decision to deny children who couldn't cope with university discipline the privilege of attending one, which meant that money would be saved and re-channeled towards the education of those better-suited to a university curriculum.

This *ad hoc* system produced an incredible mixture in our educational backgrounds. The western universities and colleges attended by descendants of Khalil Aburish include Princeton, the Sorbonne, the University of California, the University of Berlin, McGill University in Canada, the University of Houston, Austin College, Swarthmore College in Pennsylvania, New York University, the University of South Dakota, The University of Oregon, the American University in Washington, Knox College and other places including Bucharest. This is not to mention the regional universities such as the Beirut College for Women, the American University of Beirut, Damascus and Baghdad universities, the Arab College in Jerusalem. In all, Khalil Aburish's grandchildren and great-grandchildren hold between eighty and ninety university degrees – a fact which finally forced my mother to stop her degree-framing activity. When Khalil Aburish died in 1936 there was one college graduate in the whole of Bethany, my other grandfather, Mousa Shahine; at present there are twenty-six Aburish descendants attending universities, including the University of Moscow.

Most of our education was in the field of the arts but a few read the sciences. Not only was there a built-in traditional fear of the sciences but they demanded a greater, more exact, mastery of a foreign language, which wasn't always possible. Among members of the family there are lawyers, economists, historians, teachers, professional revolutionaries, a writer, a pharmacist, an atomic scientist and dozens whose education falls under the nondescript heading of liberal arts. I wrote a thesis on Fitzgerald and Hemingway, cousin Khalil Ibrahim read French, my brother Wagih has a Master's Degree in communications, while cousin Daoud Ahmad studied finance and is a banker. Cousin Fathi Ibrahim studied sociology and is a special assistant to the minister of education in Qatar. Cousin Samih Ibrahim studied hotel management and is the manager of a major hotel in Washington D.C.; Said Hamad, aunt Amneh's son, studied sociology and is now a revolutionary. Interestingly, there isn't a single doctor of medicine in the family, normally the benchmark of educational success in developing societies, though there are two Ph.D.s including that of my brother Munif, prompting an on-the-spot comment by my mother that, 'Ph.D.s are much more important. I know'.

For the girls the choice was narrower. There was an inherent reluctance to send them to other countries to attend universities until my sister Mona broke the mould in 1964 by attending the ultra-liberal New School for Social Research in New York. The other confining factor was the continuing idea that girls do not work and are destined to be housewives, so that there was no pressure on girls to attend a university. Even when a girl acquired the necessary expertise she was not allowed to use it. My sister Mona is an accomplished linguist but she remains a housewife in Portugal; similarly sister Alia attended university for three years and then gave it up to become a housewife in Houston. Ibrahim's, Mahmoud's, Mousa's and Hassan's daughters attended university, and two now teach at a girls' school where they are considered safe from the corrupting exposure associated with working women.

However, time has caught up with the reluctance to allow the girls to work, though it has taken a generation to do so: my daughter Charla Josephine, aged twenty-six, B.A., M.B.A., has worked since the age of twenty-one and the thought of her not earning a living fills me with utter financial fear. The barriers are falling and Charla's generation, Khalil Aburish's great-granddaughters of which she is the eldest, will undoubtedly earn their own way. Every member of the family I interviewed accepts this eventuality without reservation: Esther, daughter of cousin Hilmi Ibrahim is an excellent student who wants to be a doctor of medicine. Hilmi is proud and when I pointedly enquired about her eventually having to examine nude men, he shrugged his shoulders and said, 'a doctor is a doctor'; and when Hilmi's mother was asked about her granddaughter's inclination she gave the same answer. Cousin Ali's daughter is top of her class, and wants to study agriculture.

The greatest number of Aburishs to attend college and universities did so in the United States and there was no question about our determination to succeed. During our university years book learning and loneliness were the most obvious factors affecting our lives, but there were other cultural elements which were immediate, amusing, often embarrassing, and in the end melted into the body of knowledge which each of us acquired and which represented our total education. These things belonged to our mode of living and behaviour outside the classroom, the area of informal education, the osmosis of knowledge. I remember the first time I tried to eat pumpkin pie in the Middle West; to me it was 'sweet mud' and I couldn't swallow it. About fifteen years later in Roumania in the 1970s cousin Hassan Ahmad suffered the same fate: this time the food on his plate was blood sausage. He was a guest at the home of a Roumanian family and he just looked at the hostess and declared that he simply could not eat it. Cousin Khalil Ibrahim recalls how he used to pass the serving plates on a table to the right instead of to the left and suffer the stares of all around.

My sister Mona was so impressed by her acceptance at the new School for Social Research in New York that she attended her first class covered with rings and jewellery, and dressed as if attending an Arab celebration. It took her only one day to change her ways. Cousin Daoud Ahmad tells me that for two years his American classmates thought he was Jewish, and when I declared that Arabs and Jews looked alike, he said that had nothing to do with it: it was because he cracked his knuckles all the time, a trait his classmates attributed to Jews. One of my female cousins was shocked when her roommate in an American university suggested to her that she use Tampax. She was totally convinced that using it was a substitute for 'the real thing' and that sanitary considerations were an excuse. For many who moved directly from Bethany to a cosmopolitan New York or London, what they learned outside school was as important as what they learned within it. Certainly it contributed to their cultural make-up, to being comfortable with the idea of permanent exile.

Wherever we went and whatever we became, the immediacy of what we experienced in our years at university remained with us. However, one single, unvarying familial attitude remained unaffected and untarnished: it was the attachment to Palestine and everything Palestinian, the state of mind instilled in all of us by our parents and one of the reasons we were being educated. So while individual experiences differed there was a common commitment to use our education to speak on behalf of the unlucky Palestinians. In a strange way it was not limiting, for in the provincial United States and elsewhere we became more than students, we became energetic spokesmen for the Palestinian cause. I remember addressing a Women's Auxiliary Group in the B'nai Brith in Chicago about the problems of the Middle East. My mere presence there would support the contention that I am a liberal, reasonable person, but when I finished a kindly, elderly Jewish lady approached me and said: 'You know so much about it, you ought to join the State Department.' 'Madam,' I replied with the harshness of the inexperienced young, 'your State Department killed my uncle and took away my land. I can't and won't join them.' She walked away hurt and confused, for which I've never forgiven myself.

My brother Munif carried the obsession with Palestine to extremes and tried to fashion a mutual co-operation agreement between the PLO and the Black Panthers, so the FBI deported him from the USA. Later he obtained a Ph.D. in economics from the Sorbonne. Daoud Ahmad, a prickly character at the best of times, introduced an element of unease at dinner parties by refusing to say Israel and resorting to the slogan 'occupied Palestine'. If our education was our parents' obsession, the national identity they had acquired found its expression in us.

Our education should be viewed in terms beyond what happened to us as a family, as an extension of the craving of the Palestinian people for an answer to their unending tragedy. We, as a component of this misfortune, had education pushed down our throats to a greater degree than Arabs in other countries: we had to be better – just as the Jews had to be better to compensate for the absence of equal opportunity due to prejudice in western countries – and we felt unique, just as the Jews do. In the process our horizons were broadened and so it is in more ways than one that we cannot return to Bethany or Palestine. In my sister Mona's rather disagreeable words: 'What am I going to do in a place like Bethany? It has stood still since the stone age.' This doesn't stop her from tirelessly lecturing any willing listener about the 'rightness of the Palestinian cause'. The conflicting statements don't seem to bother her.

To each of us, Palestinian rights were a holy cause, for there is a lack of dignity in being a displaced refugee, and that's what we are; circumstances, not least the patronizing attitude of other Arabs, wouldn't let us forget it. Education loosened the family identification, the attachment to Bethany, and replaced it by a bigger Palestinian one. Fathi Ibrahim and I, though not lacking in commitment, are exceptions, being spared the blind nationalistic fervour enveloping other family members. Even my daughter Charla, the eldest representative of the new generation, a person who speaks no Arabic, has it: the commitment to Palestine is being transmitted by determined people to a new generation. As cousin Khalil Ibrahim says: 'I haven't been able to do much but my son might. If he doesn't, his son will.'

8
The people and the state

You don't want our problems – Bethany's – solved by outsiders from the government. They don't know us. To them our problems are the same as others and they don't take into consideration the long history of relationships within the community.

Khalil Aburish

When Khalil Aburish, towards the end of his days, was passing on his philosophy of local government to his heir, Mahmoud, he was reflecting an attitude towards the state rooted in generations of experience. Yet at the turn of the century a small settled community like Bethany, in the Turkish colony of Palestine, had little or no direct relationship to the state, the government of Turkey or its official representatives. Communities the size of Bethany communicated with the state through their chiefs, in this case through Khalil Aburish, for though his ascent to power may have been unusual, his functions were typical of his kind, the local chiefs of villages. The fact that most of them had inherited their positions from their fathers while he had created his did not limit his influence.

Governing Bethany then, or more appropriately allowing it to function, to continue in its lazy, traditional way, meant the application of both tribal and civil laws which, for the most part, dealt with the two perennial conflicts affecting people's everyday lives: on the one hand land and property, and on the other 'honour'. The ownership of land, even that surrounding a single olive tree, could be contested and cause trouble, for the records on ownership were seldom clear, and the local chief of the village had to decide who used what in accordance with the legend of the village and what seemed fair and equitable. 'Honour' was an even more troublesome and elusive issue, for until the late 1930s a problem of honour could arise from innumerable day-to-day happenings including how a boy eyed a girl, indirect responsibility for another person's accidental death, spreading false rumour, including slurs on one's ancestry and accusations of theft – and all of these were present in abundance. A mythically proud and intemperate person, the semi-bedouin Arab was in an almost constant state of 'honour war' aimed at maintaining individual integrity.

In all such cases, and despite the existence of civil courts, tribal law prevailed and problems of land and honour were settled by means of a *sulha*, a gathering of concerned families where a settlement was announced and accepted. Arranging a *sulha* was one of the functions of the head of Bethany, and Khalil Aburish was very good at it; problems would reach the civil courts only when Aburish failed to resolve them, a prospect which he viewed as shameful, while the British, like the Turks before them, were happy to leave these local matters to Aburish and his kind.

The most obvious limitation on his judicial activity, apart from his ability to solve problems, appears to have been instances of capital crime, as both Turkey and Britain chose to apply stern civil laws in such cases to stop a blood feud from beginning and then perpetuating itself. However, even in cases of capital crime, the civil (governmental) courts took into consideration whether a tribal settlement (*sulha*) had been reached or not; in other words, civil law came into effect in pure form only when tribal law failed. With capital crime if a *sulha* had been reached and the feuding families chose to bury the hatchet, then civil law complemented rather than replaced tribal law and differences in jail and other punitive sentences reflected the existence or absence of a *sulha*. No death sentences were ever passed after a *sulha* had been reached, and prison terms tended to be short.

Khalil Aburish's first step in settling a dispute was to contain it. Upon hearing of a problem he would serve notice to the disputants that they should stop whatever hostile acts they were planning against each other, that the matter was in his hands: 'I pledge my honour between the feuding parties that both will be satisfied.' After that they would be summoned separately to voice their grievances, and it was the seriousness of the case and the strength of feeling surrounding it which influenced him in deciding whether to continue his attempts at separate mediation or to bring the feuding parties together. This was a most delicate affair, for Arab quarrels are accompanied by a lot of empty noise, some of which could lead to injury. Eventually, both parties had to be present when Aburish proclaimed the terms of settlement and the concerned parties had to give their agreement to it and promise to make their kin adhere to its terms. Everyone from each side had to be involved, because blood feuds threatened not only the life of a killer but his relations, all of whom were considered equally liable.

If the dispute was serious and there was danger of reprisal and counter-reprisal, Aburish would place the threatened party under his direct protection to guarantee their safety, often inviting them to stay with him. In one instance where someone died after accidentally falling in an empty water well, the family of the victim thought the owners of the well were responsible and there was talk of vengeance. Aburish hurriedly placed the family owning the well 'under his protection' which stopped the victim's family from taking hasty action, as after that it was Aburish's honour which was at stake, and any precipitate reprisal meant they would have had to contend with him. As death was involved, this particular case came under both tribal and civil law; tribal law, exemplified by Aburish, called for compensation to be paid to the family of the victim, even though the civil law threw the case out of court, saying that it was an accident pure and simple. Aburish took the financial condition of the feuding families into consideration, including the position of the deceased as the sole provider of his immediate family, and the ability of the owners of the well to pay; if civil law alone had been followed a blood feud would have ensued.

Once a young man learned to play a double reed wind instrument and took to doing so out loud; his neighbours worried about their young women, exaggerated his motives and threatened to put a violent end to his 'musicals'. Luckily for the young man Aburish heard about this misunderstanding, demanded a private recital to determine 'the provocative nature' of the tunes and, with a smile of appreciation, strongly counselled the young man to cease his seductive practice. He was permitted to play his instrument only in far away olive groves where no sexual interpretation could be attached to it.

Again, this was a case resolved locally where civil law would have been impossible to apply. The intercession of Khalil Aburish prevented what could have turned into an ugly honour feud. He solved a problem at community level before it developed enough to deserve the attention of the civil court.

There were a few other areas which fell within the jurisdiction of civil courts, in addition to capital crimes – mainly problems which extended beyond the physical and structural limits of a small, settled community such as Bethany. Difficulties between Bethany and other villages were mostly for the civil courts, unless Aburish and his counterpart in the other community avoided such arbitration by settling them locally, something in which both had a vested interest. If they did go to court Aburish represented Bethany and his counterpart spoke for the other village. Avoidance of obligations to the central government was treated the same way: government officials would go to Aburish to find out why someone had not answered a summons to serve in the army or gendarmerie, or to pay land tax, on the very rare occasions either was demanded. They also went to him when people built little huts without prior registration with the government, or when a government vehicle ran over someone from Bethany.

So Khalil Aburish was not only the arbiter of the local disputes of his community, he was also the power broker, the accepted representative of his community to the central government, a role enhanced by the attitude of the govern-

ment which allowed him, whenever possible, to represent
Bethany in dealing with other communities.

It is against this background that the present attitude
towards the state of the people of Bethany, and their like, has
been developed. The state, the government, was almost
instinctively seen as presenting problems: it restricted
individual freedom in such matters as where one could build
a hut and it interfered in major problems such as capital
crime; it was the power which conscripted young men to fight
wars and the one which levied the occasional tax.

Because the people of Bethany believed that Khalil
Aburish (and his predecessors for many generations) had a
better understanding of their problems and resolved them in
a more traditional way, made no claim on the lives of their
young men and taxed them only in an indirect, subtle way
which they didn't perceive, they preferred his ways to those
of the central government. Besides, 'his law' extended
beyond actual problems to eliminating their causes, as in the
case of our local musician. He preserved and extended
bedouin custom which championed individual heroism and
dignity and which had been in existence for centuries, and
was now in direct conflict with the restrictive nature of central governments which sought to make a community subservient to the notion of a country – an idea inimical to the free
bedouin spirit.

When the British arrived in 1917 they at first both accommodated and enlarged the power of the Khalil Aburishs of
this world. They knew they could not superimpose a modern
judiciary on a traditional society and were happy, in most
situations, to leave the fate of the people of Bethany to Khalil
Aburish, whilst remaining wary of the potential for abuse of
position by a headman – such as the possibility of buying all
the village land or making all the villagers his shepherds.

Instinctively, Khalil Aburish favoured limiting Bethany's
development, and so keeping the people from identifying
with the state and its laws; it was a way of safeguarding his
position and perpetuating it through his eldest son. He wanted
to stop Bethany from joining the larger governmental system

which was already at work in the cities, where problems of land and honour were less frequent. Also, he realized there was no advantage in the emergence of any direct relationship between his followers and the government, for that would have eliminated his role. The idea of a nation state, in this case Palestine, with uniform laws guaranteeing the equality of its citizens did not interest him.

There were a good number of cases demonstrating Aburish's determination to protect what he considered his prerogatives. Most dealt with land or honour problems which traditionally went to him but which could, after the mid-twenties, have gone to the civil courts. In one case when a landowner sued another in a civil court, disputing the line of demarcation between their lands, Aburish felt threatened enough to testify for the defendant and even bribed the judge to obtain a punishing award against the plaintiff. The local rebel suffered considerably for his attempt at direct dealing with the central government – in reality the judge himself appears to have favoured Aburish's law.

In another case a family attempted to negotiate directly with the people of another village to settle a blood feud. When Khalil Aburish heard of this he served notice on the head of the other village that any settlement would not be accepted by him because the 'interests and honour of Bethany' were at stake, and any agreement reached without satisfying that risked reprisal by people who weren't directly related to the feud but considered themselves equally aggrieved. Again, Aburish found an ally in the other village chief and had his way: fearful that a *sulha* without Aburish would not last, the people of the other village, through their chief, dropped direct negotiations and settled with Aburish, and the Bethany family involved in direct negotiations was also forced to relent.

In settling disputes he acted speedily, bringing into play not only the facts of the matter but recalling all the conditions that had a bearing on a settlement, mostly the financial position of a family and/or their history as trouble-makers. A government couldn't put anyone under its protection to stop trouble from spreading, but he could; a local government wouldn't feed a hungry family while they tried to recover their land, but he would: his justice worked because it had a distinctly human, traditional face to it and he was a master of his craft. When a man being fed by Aburish appeared to refuse the terms of a *sulha*, Aburish embarrassed him into acceptance by accusing him of being a layabout who didn't want to work.

So there were obvious cultural reasons why his system was preferred to the imported system of the central government, European in origin. These reasons were exaggerated by Khalil Aburish and his like and have done much to inhibit the development of a relationship between 'the people' and 'the state', regardless of whether that state was Turkey, Britain, Jordan or Israel – the countries which have governed Bethany during the twentieth century.

Four elements worked directly in Aburish's favour: the first was that his was the traditional way that people were accustomed to. The second was the tentative nature of his decisions; he brought both sides in a dispute together in what was often a protracted affair of give and take until an acceptable compromise was reached. The danger of his ruling not being acceptable to either party and thus leading to more trouble was eliminated because of the disputants' participation in the decision-making process; it was a negotiated settlement under the guidance of Aburish and not an abstract judgment by an outsider. The third element was language and literacy: people shied away from formal use of Turkish and English, and even classical Arabic, and distrusted paperwork because they couldn't read or write. The final element was the absence of the idea of statehood: people certainly believed in their family, perhaps their village and tribe, and, naturally enough, in Arab legend and in Allah; they did not believe in Palestine as a government – they did not know what that was. The few Palestinians who gained representation to the Turkish parliament represented a city bourgeois minority who had more in common with the Turks than their own people. Their status was more symbolic than real.

The circumstances of the people of the village made it impossible for them to relate to the state, and to a great extent that is still true. In poor, small places like Bethany, meeting the demands of everyday life, eking out a livelihood, is still an immediate matter, a preoccupation which precludes the development of a community spirit. There was no energy, money or time that could be diverted from the needs of one's immediate family to the community. The only communal functions were weddings and funerals because they did not demand sacrifices; all other community problems belonged to the chief. If there was any loyalty beyond that to one's own family and village then it didn't reach far, and loyalty and identification with a country didn't exist. The idea of a country, a central government, was alien.

The government made occasional, and by outside standards, small demands, but put together they amounted to interference in the affairs of a small self-contained community. In the 1920s this included more than conscription and small taxes, for the British Government attempted to send roving doctors to examine the people of the villages, women included, for obvious, prevalent diseases such as bilharzia and eye infections; it was a sensible and useful campaign but when it involved women it conflicted with prevailing Islamic custom. Aburish advised them to make the medical examination optional – to deal only with the women willing to be examined. The government also tried to make everyone register births, deaths and marriages, which some people thought both unnecessary and a further intrusion in their affairs.

Even when its motives were humanitarian and crystal clear, the single name given to the acts of the government was interference. Around 1921, the British began an attempt to change matters which had remained unaltered for centuries; among other things licences were needed for shops, and health standards applied to butchers. Acting alone or with Aburish as a front, the British became the disturbers of the peace and of traditions, and the British administration was referred to as 'they'. The Turks had been 'they' because 'they' took young people away to fight in far-away wars which no one understood or supported – even Acre was considered far away – and 'they' levied taxes. The British became 'they' because people spoke of their determination to organize shops and abbatoirs, to interfere by regulating and improving the use of land and water, and by introducing new varieties of citrus fruit which sometimes demanded special skills which were difficult to master.

In 1922, 'they', the British, thought of rejuvenating the system of *mukhtars* – village headmen – to govern local affairs, to act as recorders of weddings and deaths and overall Notaries Public. After five years of 'enlightened' occupation using a single chief, it was time to move towards a semblance of representative government, time to get rid of Aburish. Three people were to be elected *mukhtars*, and Khalil Aburish's old powers would be divided into three parts. Aburish refused to stand for office, to acquiesce in the division of his powers, and three *mukhtars* including his own brother-in-law Shehadeh al-Khatib were elected, though few people chose to vote. A direct, unavoidable confrontation developed between the legally-elected representatives of the people and Bethany's popular chief.

In due course Aburish got the upper hand. Rightly, he persuaded Bethany people that the *mukhtars* were an extension of the central government, the organizing enemy, the usurpers of freedom, the perpetrators of rigid inhuman laws. He shifted his role from that of final arbiter of people's disputes to that of spokesman, while remaining the guardian of traditional values. Time and again he confronted the *mukhtars* with a *fait accompli*; he pre-empted them when they tried to settle disputes and led many a rebellion against the building of roads through the centre of the town, and against having children go to school when their parents wanted them to help with planting or harvesting.

When Khalil Aburish died in 1936, Bethany had three ineffective *mukhtars* and a rebellious reactionary chief, for though he had not eliminated the *mukhtars*, he had neutralized them. Everyone in town owed him a favour while the *mukhtars* were owed nothing. The central government was associated with a long list of negatives, while little was said of its contributions in the field of education, the introduction of new citrus trees and strains of grain, the increase in the number of much needed water wells and the use of disinfectants to purify water. The absence of a community spirit and the attachment to custom and freedom nevertheless meant that the concept of 'they' was universal in all places the size of Bethany, and this attitude was confirmed beyond doubt when the villagers began using Mahmoud Aburish to continue his father's role in undermining the *mukhtars*.

Mahmoud Aburish lacked his father's wiles and authority, but Khalil Aburish had succeeded in attaching an aura of leadership to the family name sufficient to guarantee a smooth 'accession' for his twenty-six-year-old son. But the institution of the *mukhtars* was perpetuating itself and the central government was doing everything possible to transfer authority to them. Mahmoud tried, without success, to hold the line against the central government, but even the smallest of feuds was dealt with by a civil court on top of *sulhas*, whose importance was minimized. Health standards were being applied universally, until they even included the ancient way in which olive oil was made; and the early successful introduction of pears, plums and peaches was producing results which did nothing to help Mahmoud's stance.

Mahmoud's first move was to try harder, to assume in full the role of the local 'Mr Fix It', to compete with the *mukhtars*. He ingratiated himself with people by successfully lobbying against the *mukhtars'* Notary Public fees and by finding lawyers to defend local criminals being tried in civil courts. He even devised an elaborate system to allow children to absent themselves from school at harvest time, and later make up for lost time by putting the onus on the teacher. In many instances he would act as a protector of the poor, a champion of the oppressed, a glib, roving advocate of the rights of Bethany people – all in a determined attempt to recover his father's position of supremacy.

The continuing pressure to reconcile tribal ways with civil

authority came to a head in 1951, when Bethany was annexed to Jordan and became known as the West Bank. Jordan continued the efforts begun by the British to eliminate the growing divergence between tribal, traditional ways and the demands of a modern state, and drew up a new plan calling for the creation of a town council, headed by a proper mayor, to replace the *mukhtars*. There was such pressure on people to take part that each of the twelve families in the village elected a representative to the council. This meant Mahmoud Aburish couldn't count on the loyalty of the people against the council the way he could against the *mukhtars*; some people were beginning to accept the benefits of health care and crop rotation, and anyway they wouldn't go against their own relations. It was a clever move, a merger of old and new ways, a clear, brave attempt at representative government incorporating the all-important, accepted family ties as a base. Mahmoud Aburish felt challenged and responded by standing for the office of mayor, which was to go to the councillor who received the highest number of votes.

Hcw do you campaign for office in a town of 6,000 people which had never known an election? What issues were there to discuss that people would understand, and what methods were to be used? Do you open wide the floodgates of democracy and speak to one and all about the real issues of the day, or do you pay tribute to the all-binding family ties and speak to the heads of families in the way Khalil Aburish did, asking them to 'direct' their relatives? Mahmoud decided to avoid controversy, to deal exclusively with the heads of families, while allowing the village tough, his brother Ibrahim, to take the low road by making life difficult for the opposition.

When he spoke to the heads of families, Mahmoud dwelt on the relationship which bound them to the Aburishs: he would recall how the Aburishs protected them from their enemies, how Khalil Aburish and now he, Mahmoud, continued to represent them in spite of the *mukhtars*. In one case Mahmoud whispered to the head of a family that his thieving son would still be wanted for crimes were it not for a fabricated Aburish cover-up; in another instance he made it plain that the man's family were not entitled to their water supply but that he would continue to look the other way as long as they voted for him. He appealed to each family in accordance with the extent of their relationship with the Aburishs.

Mahmoud's classic give-and-take was accompanied by Ibrahim's unabashed bravado. Citing the frequent visits of government officials to Mahmoud's house, he told everyone in the village that the results of the election were a foregone conclusion and woe to him who opposed the Aburishs; there were hints of physical violence, but more importantly there were references to the results of enmity with the most powerful local family which could result in claims upon their unregistered land, denial of grazing rights, lack of protection in case of disputes and many other matters which could turn a simple, semi-primitive life into sheer hell. Nor did Ibrahim shy from calling on their nationalistic feelings by reminding them that the Aburishs 'fought and died for their country'.

When the election results were announced Mahmoud Aburish received ninety per cent of the vote. His opponent, and second cousin on his mother's side, received ten per cent and, as arranged, the twelve representatives on the town council came from Bethany's twelve families: the merger of tribal and representative government was complete and 'they' claimed the local tribal head as their own and he became an official of the state directly responsible to its higher authority and entrusted with the task of amalgamating the old with the new.

Happy as he was with the results of the election, Mahmoud recognized its major problems, for instead of appearing to deal with the possible and blaming all unacceptable decisions on 'them', he himself as 'they' would have to say no once in a while.

*   *   *   *

Mahmoud Aburish's first election to the office of mayor of Bethany in 1952 coincided with government plans to alter the life of such villages through the introduction of electricity, running water and rigid sanitary rules covering the disposal of waste and use of septic tanks. But to the people of Bethany, the most appealing of these newly-available services was the telephone: it bestowed status on the owner and appeared harmless: it was fun, it was a toy, so, naturally enough, Mahmoud obtained the first 'phone, with the easy number of 222, and the expense of installing this instrument of communication was borne by the town council. This created what was tantamount to a local scandal, for the people of the village did not accept the principle of a free telephone for its mayor. This claim on their money lacked the subtlety of some of Khalil's and Mahmoud's previous doings, with some councillors going so far as to accuse Mahmoud of spending his telephone time flirting with women in Jerusalem, while others damned the instrument because it allowed him to report wrong-doings to the police without time for the old revered system of 'containing' problems before they came under civil law. It took years before the notion of the mayor having a free telephone was accepted.

Electricity and running water were even more complex matters. The mere act of connecting both was costly but the building of the inner works was even more so, and few could afford to incorporate them into their houses as often the building was totally unsuitable. Again, there were no properly-trained electricians and wires were often left bare and dangerous. Little use was made of electricity beyond providing light to replace the old kerosene lamps, for in 1951 there were no vacuum cleaners, irons, heaters or water tanks to be used – just a dangling light bulb, annoyingly glaring at the end of two dangerously loose wires. The electricity meter was an instrument of wonder with which everyone tried to tamper.

The problems solved by having running water rather than transporting it from wells, some of which were centuries old, were obvious, but again the use of running water was limited by old habits and most houses ran a simple pipe and one tap which provided water for drinking, washing, bathing, cleaning the house and all other uses. But the most difficult single

aspect of bringing modern ways to Bethany was the introduction of basic sanitary rules: this, more than anything else,
caused Mahmoud problems because, unlike water and electricity, its application was mandatory. Yet most Bethany people
had no outhouses, they went to ancient caves or dug holes in
the ground which they used for a week or two at a time then
covered with earth. There was a cost involved in building a
septic tank, and, to most, the benefits were not readily
apparent. A protesting member of the community bluntly
told Mahmoud: 'I am shitting in my back yard and not on anyone's head. What damage can that do?' Another equated the
use of septic tanks with 'effete city folk'.

If the mere act of creating a lavatory was difficult then the
disposal of refuse was well nigh impossible to explain, for
Bethany people threw their rubbish into the middle of any
unused land. The only possible element of restraint was
whether the land was being used for farming, so when
Mahmoud insisted the issue was a sanitary one rather than
whether the land was farmed or not, a villager accused him of
the ulterior motive of wanting to buy the land used as a rubbish dump. When Mahmoud used the example of the local
monasteries and how they buried their refuse and eventually
used it as compost, the protestor shot back: 'I am not a Christian and don't want to live like one.'

Mahmoud's new duties were a simple case of the poacher
turned gamekeeper. There was no sense of public spirit or
responsibility to help with the introduction of communal
ways, even waste disposal, so Mahmoud was seen as restrict-
ing the freedom of his citizens. When someone was elec-
trocuted or even suffered an electric shock, Mahmoud, the
man who introduced electricity, bore implicit responsibility
for the mishap, and when a normal interruption in water supply
took place, again it was Mahmoud's mistake and people
would stop paying their water rates. Above and beyond that,
because he was mayor, responsible for collecting the taxes
needed to instal these systems and the fees for their use, he
became known as a 'taker', or tax collector, the ugliest
expression of the nation which produced 'they'.

A people accustomed to viewing authority, government or

any restriction on their traditional behaviour as alien and unacceptable, viewed the representative of these manifestations in an even dimmer light. Mahmoud Aburish, the second of a family which championed the freedom of a small community against the inevitable hegemony of the state, was now the representative of that state and the instrument of its designs on the community. He had become 'they' before the 1967 Israeli occupation of the West Bank – the fourth time an alien power had moved in to govern Palestinian Arabs this century. Since the arrival of the Israelis the mayors position has become even more precarious, complicated by the fact that the civil authority is now an enemy occupier state.

Mahmoud Aburish continues to be elected major, though by an ever-decreasing majority, and as Bethany has increased in size, so too have its problems. Its present population is nearly 17,000 people, due to a very high birthrate amongst the original inhabitants and an influx of refugees from the parts of Palestine overrun by Israel in 1948. It has now changed from a small society where tribal law predominated, but which civil law complemented, to one where Israeli-administered civil law predominates and tribal law complements. The people and the local council give no support to the local leader because he is the mayor and as such is the representative of external authority and must obey its law.

All disputes now go to the appropriate civil court, and tribal justice is used only in a complementary sense. For example, a court might send a murderer to jail but tribal law is still used to avoid feuds through payment of compensation to the family of the victim, depending on their need. Land and property disputes are very few because property deeds are the order of the day, so Khalil and Mahmoud Aburish's old functions of deciding ownership have all but vanished. Problems of 'honour' have to be more overt than eyeing a girl or playing a musical instrument because society is infinitely more permissive; today a question of honour would have to involve elopement, open, unchecked flirtation, or illicit affairs. All are the domain of civil and tribal laws, in that order.

The old problems appear to have succumbed to change but

new ones have arisen, perhaps not as basic to everyday life but equally troublesome. Mahmoud maintains that the biggest difficulty facing the town council is that of collecting money: 'I can't order anyone's electricity to be cut off for non-payment because he'd never forgive me and his family would vote against me in the next election. I either cancel the bill or accept payment by instalments.' The same is true of water bills and direct taxes; the people know this and act accordingly.

More complicated is Mahmoud's relationship to the Israeli-controlled courts. His function used to be to keep 'his criminals' out of court; now he has to report them to an alien police who have them tried, and the only protection available is that same police. Since the 1970s, the people, aware that they elect the mayor, no long sing his praises; on the contrary, they expect him to court them to protect his diminishing share of the vote.

The one element least affected by change is the overall relationship of man to the state. Khalil and Mahmoud Aburish didn't invent the idea of alienation from the state, but championed it as long as possible until Mahmoud decided that 'if you can't beat it, join it'. The state is there and daily becoming more intrusive, as everyone knows, but its acceptance by the people is still only skin deep, because it didn't evolve from tradition but was superimposed from outside.

While the abhorrence of the idea of the state is due to the fact that it has always been alien (Turkey, Britain, Jordan and Israel in this century alone) in that the Palestinians have never known a central government made up of their own people responsive to local custom and need, the degree of estrangement from the occupying powers has differed substantially. Turkey was Muslim and religiously accommodating; Britain was mostly a caretaker regime sanctioned by the League of Nations; and Jordan, though unpopular, was Arab and Muslim; but Israel is a conqueror with a radically different culture and a claim on the very source of existence of the people, their land.

Mahmoud Aburish's very important but vain attempt to

merge the old with the new has succumbed to the 'they' of Israeli occupation, temporarily. The antipathy towards this more callous and instrusive 'they' is likely to be with us for a while.

9
The clan is brought down

No picture is ever perfect. Allah in his infinite wisdom sees to that. For the Aburish family things were perfect until Allah reminded us that we were mortal, vulnerable, always at his mercy.

Mirriam Mahmoud Aburish

The years following the 1948 Arab–Israeli war were good ones for the Aburishs. While Jordan annexed what was left of Palestine in 1949, and with it Bethany, the Aburishs prospered, and their performance in the 1948 war added to their prestige. Even Ali's death fighting for Jerusalem, except for the sense of personal loss, appeared to have added to their upward mobility.

Mahmoud now ran a much larger Bethany and presided over the refugee relief work of the various churches who were trying to help Palestinians displaced by the recent fighting – both positions added to his local and now national status. Ibrahim worked for the United Nations Relief and Work Agency: he ran Aqbat Jabr, the largest single Palestinian refugee camp in the Middle East, near Jericho, which housed over 30,000. The United Nations had decided, rightly, that it needed a tough administrator with unquestionable credentials as a Palestinian nationalist to be the manager. Abu Said's odd but valuable position as news correspondent was established beyond question – he moved to Beirut in 1949 because that was the centre of the foreign press corps covering the Arab world. He left the *Daily Mail* for the *New York Times* and finally *Time Magazine*. His genius seemed to lie in creating an image of a reliable, trustworthy man who through western press contacts was needed by local politicians. Mousa ran his coffee house and doubled as an assistant to Mahmoud, and gentle, quiet Daoud had a minor position with UNRWA. The youngest, Hassan, with a wife, son and daughter, changed jobs frequently, and though Mahmoud saw to it that he was gainfully employed, he was a trouble-maker much as Ibrahim had been when young, but without Ibrahim's charm and toughness. The Aburish boys also saw to it that their brothers-in-law, Amneh's and Fatmeh's husbands, had decent jobs.

The Aburish name was in the ascendant, with Mahmoud giving legendary parties for local leaders, diplomats, government officials, church dignitaries and everyone around Jerusalem who seemed to matter. His jobs as mayor, supervisor of refugee aid programmes, owner of a Jerusalem tourist agency and marble factory, land and other real estate, and his continuing position on a larger scale as a regional 'Mr Fix It' earned him a lot of money and expanded his influence – and like his father, he enjoyed money and what money could buy. His leadership of Bethany was undisputed, for now he acquired a new following made up of destitute refugees, job and office seekers – even people running for parliament needed him. Slowly he had moved up into a much larger sphere of influence than the constituency he had inherited; even the central government treated him as someone with whom to reckon, and King Hussein saw fit to give him a gold watch as a present.

Ibrahim too was running his own little kingdom. The United Nations was committed to 'maintaining' the Arab refugees but had problems dealing with their day-to-day needs, so surrendering this difficult function in their largest camp to Ibrahim served them well and satisfied Ibrahim's ego. He was the right man in the right job, often employing methods of outright intimidation to subdue his restive flock. An example of Ibrahim's native ability to overcome problems had to do with food and clothes distribution to his 30,000 wards. As each refugee had a ration card entitling him or her to a share of food and other benefits, reporting a person's death meant loss of these benefits to the family, so some refugees took to burying their dead secretly at night in order to avoid this loss. The UN, always pressed for funds and aware of this cheating scheme, looked to Ibrahim for a solution: his response was to decree that any family which failed to report a death would be punished through denial of benefits to the whole family, and complemented this by hiring a number of informers to report 'secret deaths'. Suddenly the number of inhabitants of his camp fell by seventeen per cent in one week – which produced from him the comment: 'I know the camp is located below the Mount of Temptation but nobody is going to live for ever while I am around.'

Abu Said's value to the news organizations he served increased in proportion to the growing importance of the Middle East, then as now one of the world's major trouble spots. He managed to endear himself to every Arab king, president, political leader and, in the words of one of his former colleagues, 'everyone who appears to know anything which matters'. Operating under the name of Abu Said – very few knew or know his first name – he not only extracted news from people who mattered, he became their friend, confidant and advisor because he was their channel to the foreign press corps and by observing strict rules of behaviour in reporting personal views and meticulous fairness in other reporting areas. Also, he was the 'Mr Clean' of the press, never accepting money, even presents from his acquaintances. King Hussein of Jordan remembered his anniversaries, the late King Saud of Saudi Arabia sent him special invitations to visit him in Riyadh, and no less a person than Gamal Abdel Nasser, the leading Arab politician of this century, sent him special emissaries seeking his help in advancing the idea of Arab unity by promoting its benefits among foreign journalists. His name became so well known that someone advised by *Time Magazine* to contact him in Beirut foolishly wired: 'Abu Said, Beirut', mistaking his name for a cable address. The cablegram was safely received at the famous St George's Hotel which he used as his headquarters.

Mahmoud's, Mohammad's and Ibrahim's achievements

well exceeded those of their younger brothers, and the name Aburish became well known in Lebanon, Syria and all of Jordan. By 1956, it looked as if a new clan was coming to the fore, as the members of the new generation, with me in the lead, were attending universities, full of optimism about our position in life and what awaited us. One of my uncle Mahmoud's letters to me spoke of 'returning to assume your natural role. I think we can get you a seat in the Jordanian Parliament.' It wasn't the first mention of this prospect – an aide to King Hussein had already advised my father that His Majesty's Government 'would look with favour upon [my] eventual candidacy'.

The women made much of their husbands' successes, hired maids and went to hairdressers and manicured and polished their nails for the first time – some would bite them to determine whether the polish was permanent. Mousa, Daoud and Hassan built houses which allowed for all the modern amenities, while people reluctant to approach Mahmoud directly to ask favours would do so using Amneh and Fatmeh as intermediaries – because of his busy life Mahmoud couldn't see everyone who asked a favour. Rashedah took pride in her children, thanking Allah for his bounty every day of the year, and for 'having lived long enough to see my boys prosper'. The children of the family were distinguishable by their expensive western dress and some began adopting arrogant attitudes towards their local playmates. They all had a car and Mahmoud and Ibrahim had chauffeurs.

This rosy picture of success feeding on itself was to be shattered with paralyzing suddenness on 6 August 1956. On that date Hassan Aburish's Bethany house was surrounded by a contingent of Jordanian special force troops and he was arrested and whisked away to Amman in an army pick-up truck accompanied by two armoured personnel carriers. Nobody could conceive of anything Hassan might have done to justify what resembled a small military operation; after all, Hassan was the family's perennial under-achiever. Mahmoud Aburish telephoned the deputy prime minister, Akef Pasha al-Fayez, to enquire about 'the unthinkable reason behind Hassan's arrest' and Ibrahim, true to character, declared that 'unless those sons of bitches release my kid brother I'll take forty armed men and get him out of jail'.

Ibrahim's histrionics notwithstanding, Hassan was kept incommunicado with not the slightest explanation in answer to his family's incessant enquiries, and then on the third day after his arrest Radio Amman, the Jordan State Radio, announced that a major spy network operating on behalf of the Israelis and headed by one Hassan Aburish had been uncovered and that its members would soon be tried.

Mahmoud journeyed to Amman and requested an audience with King Hussein but was turned down. Ibrahim screamed that it was 'a bloody lie and whoever is behind it will be punished'. Abu Said heard the news in Beirut, and when he telephoned King Hussein's chief military aide-de-camp for clarification was icily told: 'Matters of national security are for the law courts, in this case a military court, and I have no comment to make.' The family's relationship to the state, forever the measure of any family's importance, was completely shattered, and without it they were suddenly bereft of power or influence.

None of the brothers believed what they heard, but even more bewildering was the sudden silence with which they were met everywhere. For this was a case of treason: Israel was the enemy and Nasser, then at the height of his powers, was the new Arab Messiah promising salvation from Israel, 'the cancer implanted in our midst'. Hassan's arrest took place in a Middle East inflamed by Nasser's rhetoric, a time when blind nationalism consumed everything which stood in its way; it was the period immediately before the Suez War when Arabs everywhere believed in Nasser and hated those opposed to him, and spies, by the nature of the act, were the number one enemy.

By the time Hassan's case came for trial, the Suez War was part of history, and the feelings of the Arab masses against Israel were stronger than ever. Recalling this painful period uncle Mahmoud says: 'All of a sudden I had no friends. Even my own employees seemed to eye me funnily, or so I thought, and things got worse with time. All the frustration caused by Egypt's defeat in the Suez War found its relief in hate against us.' Ibrahim, persistently declaring Hassan's innocence, began carrying a gun when entering the refugee camp which he managed, afraid for his own life. My father went into a deeply reflective mood and told my mother: 'Something is wrong... Hassan is of no value to anyone as a spy. He has no information to transmit nor could he write a report if his life depended on it. But there is nothing to do – no one in power will listen to us, the atmosphere doesn't allow for reason.'

The Aburish women, full of shame, stayed indoors; they all speak of crying their eyes out. Their laments, which always accompany Arab tears, recalled Ali's heroism and indirectly denied Hassan's possible guilt through his brother's sacrifice. My grandmother Rashedah was seventy-nine and Hassan, always a trouble-maker, remained to her the youngest boy and the apple of her eye; as with Ali, her concern was that he shouldn't suffer. Hassan's wife, Munira, along with her three-year-old son and two-year-old daughter, moved to Mahmoud's house because she found living alone intolerable.

The Aburishs, without exception, moved into a world surrounded by hate and rejection, their bonds with acquaintances, friends, community and the state cut off. And as Hassan Aburish's predicament was complicated, unexplained except in the most general way, the family was helpless, surrounded by a singular evil, the air of treason. Their achievements in life were an extension of what they had inherited from their father, a man capable of rationalizing disputes and feuds and representing a way of life which no longer existed. They had improved upon his legacy through hard work, but now, overnight, their liberty and success were being challenged by the law of the state which accused one of them of being a traitor and through that sought to destroy them.

Their initial response to their devastating dilemma was unanimous: to try to 'fix' the situation – still ignorant of the details of the accusation against Hassan and what lay behind it, they fell back on their inherited instincts, which meant an attempt to circumvent the laws of the land. Mahmoud did appoint one of the leading lawyers of the country to defend Hassan – his only intelligent action to meet the situation; more in line with his traditional thinking, he eventually managed to contact a minister in the Jordanian cabinet and put him on a 'secret retainer to do what is necessary'. The retainer was high and what was necessary was to bribe the minister so the charges against Hassan could be dropped; His Excellency's belief in Hassan's guilt or innocence didn't matter.

Ibrahim visited comrades from the days of the Holy Strugglers and solicited testimonials of Hassan's bravery in fighting for the Arab cause and his naturally nationalistic bent. There were a few cases where personal loyalty prevailed and some of his former comrades signed petitions asking for Hassan's release – again, without the slightest reference to the merits of the case against him. This was an instance of the tribe defending its own.

Abu Said, his emotions eventually overriding his original rational analysis, appealed to his friend, the founder of Time Inc., the late Henry Luce, to intervene – still labouring under the notion that westerners are superior. He suffered from a belief that King Hussein couldn't possibly ignore the wishes of the world's leading magazine publisher.

Hassan was still in a military jail and was not allowed visitors, so a crippling despondency enveloped his family; compared to Hassan's problems everything in life was secondary and set aside, and his fate became their only business. Mahmoud sold his marble factory because no one would buy its products, as the churches and their aid branches saw fit to distance themselves from him lest they themselves became suspected of anti-Arab activity. Ibrahim gave up his rough-and-ready ways and began courting the refugees in his camp to the extent of allowing the dead to stay alive. My mother insists, and others support her, that my father's hair turned grey in three months. Fatmeh speaks of going for days on end 'without sleeping a wink' and poor Amneh suffered the

humiliation of being stoned by children in the street for being
'the sister of a traitor'. My grandmother said: 'Allah is testing
us . . . we don't deserve what is happening to us, but we know
our friends – if we have any.'

Mahmoud's, Ibrahim's and Abu Said's efforts could not
eliminate the fanfare leading to the trial. Henry Luce cabled
King Hussein pleading for clemency but the king said that
could only be considered after judgment was passed. The
days when the wishes of influential westerners became
automatic commands were long gone; Hussein knew his people
would never forgive him for pardoning a man accused of spy-
ing for Israel. Meanwhile Mahmoud's cabinet minister and
others took money, offered promises and did nothing.

Hassan's trial, along with seven supposed conspirators,
began in March 1957. It was the first time any member of the
family had seen him since his arrest, and he looked as if he
had lost 50 lbs; his wrists were bandaged and he appeared to
be absent-minded and disinterested: clearly he had been tortured. He was accused of 'knowingly aiding and abetting the
enemy'. This, the prosecution alleged, comprised reporting
on the movements, encampments and armaments of the
Jordanian Army to an Israeli officer who paid him for his
information. Hassan was supposed to have created a spy ring,
the members of which supplied him with material for his
reports.

In a trial which lasted four months, Hassan refused to testify on his own or anyone else's behalf, while his co-
defendants did not confirm or deny the allegations against
him. A confession obtained from him while in jail admitted to
knowing the other defendants socially, but even that was
questioned by the court-appointed handwriting expert who
stated: 'If this is his handwriting then he was, for reasons the
court can discover and I can not, unable to use a pen properly.' The defence lawyer alleged torture, demanded that the
'confession' be thrown out of court and said that the whole
case had no foundation since the mere act of knowing someone could not be translated into a conspiracy. The lawyer
claimed that the government was conspiring against an hon-

est man 'who is neither a spy nor capable of being one'. His
eloquent defence was that of a committed man, but Anwar
Nusseibeh (of Jewish furniture fame), a hero of the 1948 war
and once a Jordanian minister of defence who aspired to the
premiership, was to pay dearly for questioning the methods
used in this case by the government: King Hussein never
forgave him, and he never held office again, in spite of being
popular and eminently qualified.

King Hussein was under considerable pressure from
within and outside his country not to appear lenient in a matter of treason because it would reflect poorly on his anti-
Israeli credentials, and of course the king viewed his
government's reputation as being more important than the
merits of Hassan's case. So Hassan Khalil Aburish, in his
thirty-second year, was condemned to death and executed by
hanging by a government who viewed a fair trial as an unaffor-
dable luxury.

Reviewing Hassan's case took half as much time as
researching the rest of this book. I began by paying an almost
perfunctory visit to the late Anwar Nusseibeh, Hassan's
lawyer, and was driven to investigate the matter in depth
after he looked me straight in the eyes and announced, 'Said,
my word of honour: he was innocent. But there was nothing to
be done. He was a problem the king wanted out of the
way.'

I have interviewed sixty-two people and read 3,000 pages
of court records covering Hassan and his co-defendents' trial,
and Nusseibeh was right. Hassan was the victim of two
things: a Byzantine plot and, more importantly and dis-
tressingly, the failure of members of his family to understand
the workings of a modern state and its judicial system.

The whole affair had its apparently innocent beginnings
with the Anglican Bishop of Jerusalem, who in the 1950s was
a kindly old man by the name of Stewart; devout, with a deep
concern for humanity and little understanding of politics,
Bishop Stewart wanted to do whatever he could to help the
refugees of the 1948 War, and his first action in this direction
was to open a refugee relief centre in Bethany. Distributing

food and clothes was done with the local chief's, Mahmoud's, blessing, and was followed by a very modest resettlement scheme for the refugees in land east of Bethany.

Resettling Arab refugees was much more complex than feeding and clothing them, for a resettled refugee was someone who accepted a new home, and hence renounced his claim to the old – in other words he accepted Israeli occupation of his former home. Arab policy rested on reclaiming lost land rather than settling in new areas, so the bishop's efforts were against basic, universally accepted Arab policy. This political attitude, if recognized, concerned the bishop less than improving the lot of a few hundred refugees, and he was determined to follow his plan with his ready and able ally, Mahmoud Aburish.

There was no law on the books against refugees building homes and settling down – only the 'attitude' of the government, but the Anglican Bishop was beyond the reach of those who opposed the resettlement scheme. This was a god-sent opportunity to local politicians who resented the growth of Mahmouds' power, particularly the local member of parliament Kamel Irekat. Pretending opposition to resettlement plans, they conspired to undermine Mahmoud Aburish for he, through helping the bishop, was the one who went against Arab thinking. They claimed it was he, as an Arab, who should be stopped. In addition, there is evidence suggesting Mahmoud reaped financial benefits by broking the sale of land for the resettlement scheme and that he did not heed several warnings that he was playing with fire. Like his father before him, he did not believe in vetos and thought he was comfortable in his relationship with the government: obviously he misjudged the gravity of his actions.

Nevertheless, Mahmoud was a local notable beyond reproach, a popular leader made more so by the undeniable contributions he and his brothers made to their community. Hassan, on the other hand, was an easy target, uneducated and impetuous; he was the most likely Aburish to break down under torture, and to accept an accusation that would reflect on the whole family. If a government spurred to action by

most of Jerusalem's politicians got at the Aburish through
Hassan, then Bishop Stewart's and Mahmoud's resettlement
programme would stop and others would not copy it. The
foundations of this bizarre plot are almost too simple, but
then there is no denying that Hassan, in my father's words,
'couldn't be of any use to anyone as a spy. Half of the time I
didn't trust him to post a letter.'

That Hassan was tortured beyond human endurance is
now a matter of fact. The late Adnan al-Kassem, one of the
army officers who arrested and interrogated him, confirmed
this to me a few years ago in Beirut:

> He was a hell of a man – never confessed, not really. It was the
> army as well as a few politicians who wanted the resettlement
> programme stopped but they were wrong when they thought he
> would break down. The king knew he was innocent but couldn't
> oppose the army, not on such an issue. He wouldn't get anything
> out of pardoning Hassan but a lot from appearing tough on
> Israel.

The second part of the Hassan disaster was the behaviour
of all of his brothers who mattered; they bribed people, who
then ran away with the money, and they had no way of
recovering it; they induced people near and far to intercede
on behalf of their brother, and in one instance Ibrahim
threatened to harm the family of one of Hassan's co-
defendants when the latter appeared about to incriminate
Hassan. Mahmoud tried to see all members of the cabinet
and Abu Said had an audience with the king's mother,
Dowager Queen Zein, when she passed through Beirut.

Every single step they took – bar the appointment of
Hassan's able lawyer – testified to their lack of faith in the
due process of law. Certainly the charges against Hassan
were false, put together by a group of misguided army
officers and politicians trying to win votes, who themselves
failed to use the law to stop Mahmoud. But the Aburishs
fought them on equally baseless assumptions which called
for bending the law rather than using it. Had they refrained

from doing what they did – things which suggested Hassan's guilt – he might have escaped the hangman's noose. He personally behaved with honour, and deserves sympathy: he refused to appeal against the verdict, and when sentenced criticized the judge for making him wait so long. On the other hand his brothers' behaviour was a confirmation that their view of the state and its laws had not been altered by their advancement: under pressure they wrongly thought that they could buy and manipulate their way out of the reach of the legal system. Little did they know that the more they spent, the more they confirmed their brother's guilt. The affair showed their relationship to the state had not changed since the days of their father; the state was still the mysterious 'they' which abandoned them in their hour of need. 'They', according to Mahmoud, 'will never be trusted'.

10
A new generation in a new war

Come back to Jordan, to your country, to visit us. Let us forget about the painful past which we cannot change and concentrate on the future.

A message from King Hussein to Abu Said

For the Aburishs, the situation in the early 1960s was an extension of the 1950s, a painful period of readjustment when they lived in the shadow of Hassan's execution and the shame it brought upon them. It wasn't a time to grow and advance: it was difficult enough to maintain what they had, to contain the results of the disaster. Mahmoud, because of his position as head of the family and his responsibility for organizing Hassan's defence, was the most vulnerable; besides, as mayor, he was an elected public official and hence the most likely focus of people's direct disapproval. For the first time since Khalil Aburish established the family's primary position early in the century mutterings against them could be heard in Bethany, and indeed in other places as well. Mahmoud contemplated resigning his office but after long thought chose to continue. To him resigning would have been tantamount to accepting the notion of guilt by association, surrendering sixty years of his and his father's work. So he decided to fight in order to maintain the family's local position of supremacy; he knew it would not be easy but he felt honour bound to try, a feeling strengthened by his total belief in Hassan's innocence.

After deciding against resigning, one of Mahmoud's first moves was to curtail his social activities, so the non-stop party-giving came to an end as well as his attendance at other people's parties. Other signs of financial well-being had to be trimmed to the new sobriety, so he followed the sale of his marble factory by the sale of the travel agency, and a little later by giving up one of his three cars. He stopped visiting the tailor as often as before and gave clear instructions to family members to 'watch their step', to refrain from any activity which could lead to misinterpretation. It was a state of semi-seclusion aimed at weathering the crisis.

Mahmoud's behaviour towards the people of the village changed as well: he became more available, more conscientious in his treatment of their complaints, he attended more of their weddings, funerals and circumcision ceremonies than ever before, and would stay longer than the previous five minutes he accorded these occasions in the past. He visited the sick, gave a little money to the needy – more would have been suspect – and congratulated school graduates. He went as far as impressing upon members of the village council the need for open, free debate, something which he had previously opposed, and adopted some of their suggestions and proposals whenever possible. Clearly, he was in the business of pleasing his constituents, of remoulding his image to avoid loss of position.

When elections were held at the end of 1962, Mahmoud received seventy-two per cent of the vote, considerably lower than his previous record but still a comfortable majority. His hard work was rewarded and most people of Bethany confirmed that they still put local allegiances and attachment to traditional leadership ahead of matters dealing with 'national issues', with the central government. At the same time, their vote of confidence in Mahmoud confirmed a suspected diminution in the importance attached to blood relationships, a remarkable departure from the concept of general family and tribal liability. Many Bethany people said openly that Mahmoud shouldn't be punished for Hassan's supposed deeds, even those who thought Hassan was guilty.

My father's problems were different from Mahmoud's. Still, his normal work for *Time Magazine* required travel to the various Arab countries and meeting Arab leaders and politicians, and Hassan's trial had been highly publicized by Jordan State Radio in a clear attempt to confirm the government's solid anti-Israeli policies, so everybody had heard of it. King Hussein, the man who confirmed Hassan's death sentence and a friend of long-standing, at first took to avoiding him – naturally enough, members of Hussein's government did as well. Prince Talal bin Abdel Aziz, then Saudi Arabia's Minister of Finance, told him: 'Too bad the traitor in Jordan bears your name. I am sure he is no relation to you.' People whom *Time Magazine* had criticized tried to get their own back and openly accused him of treason as did many a jealous colleague.

Essentially, Abu Said followed Mahmoud's approach: he did the minimum amount of work, shied away from controversial issues and waited for the storm to die down. But this wasn't enough; it didn't work. Being the brother of a 'traitor' means that you are an easy target, that the protection due to you by law and by virtue of a position has been stripped away.

On New Year's Day 1963 two officers of the Lebanese Army, unhappy about the political direction the country was taking, attempted a *coup d'état*: the country was in a state of confusion for forty-eight hours, long enough for some of my father's enemies to do some evil whispering in the ears of officers belonging to an army faction which remained loyal to the government. Abu Said was arrested, interrogated regarding his possible complicity in the plot to overthrow the government and then tortured. He had nothing to confess. Barely able to walk, he was released after three days when a deputy, Raymond Edde, rose in Parliament to condemn 'the crime committed against an innocent man, a pillar of the community, a person whose presence within us is a source of honour'. Abu Said survived the ordeal with no lasting physical or psychological damage and refused to press charges against his tormentors, saying 'there are times when doing nothing is equal to winning'. The officer responsible for his arrest and torture was compelled to apologize.

In some ways Ibrahim had the biggest problem, certainly the most immediate and dangerous one. He was managing the largest Palestinian refugee camp in the Middle East, inhabited by people who were displaced by the Israelis in 1948, and so harboured feelings of unmitigated hate towards Israel and everyone connected with it. The refugees were not like the people of Bethany who remembered Khalil's and Mahmoud's good deeds and felt they had obligations to them. The refugees owed the Aburishs nothing, so the likelihood of an attempt on Ibrahim's life, organized by a zealous anti-Israeli group or individual, was real.

Anyone but Ibrahim would have fled from the Akbat Jabr refugee camp, but he didn't; instead he continued to wear a gun for protection, and went out of his way to please the camp's inhabitants and any others with whom he had to deal. His position precluded withdrawal; he had to be visible in order to manage the refugee camp. Characteristically, he manipulated the situation well and eventually managed to bribe, browbeat, isolate and neutralize the voices raised against him, through increasing their rations, helping their sons and daughters obtain scholarships and the like. He even placated a local refugee leader by arranging his marriage to a pretty girl twenty-five years his junior.

However, the pressure of the situation, including the pain of being reduced from a hero of the 1948 war to a blemished brother of a traitor, took its toll and Ibrahim suffered considerable mental anguish which found its outlet in heavy drinking and bitter refrains about having to kow-tow to cowards who did nothing in 1948.

Mousa's welfare was subsidiary to Mahmoud's. For two to three years Bethany's people stayed away from his coffee house, but they came back after Mahmoud rode out the storm, some of them openly admitting that they had feared being 'associated with the Aburishs'. Daoud, still a minor UN official, went his own unassuming way and was not involved except for the occasional direct or implied insult aimed at him by resentful people. In all cases he pretended not to hear. Rashedah, her daughters Amneh and Fatmeh and her daughters-in-law, including Hassan's wife, followed the men's line and kept to themselves. Rashedah's only excursions out of Mahmoud's house were daily visits to the graves of Ali and Hassan, a routine which she followed for the rest of her life. Fatmeh speaks of a neighbour who wouldn't answer her greetings for about a year 'and then she changed her mind and we both pretended nothing had happened'.

The atmosphere created by Hassan's execution did dominate the lives of his family for a few years but eventually time took care of that and the whole thing receded into a piece of unhappy history. The developments in the 1960s which were to have more lasting effects were the coming of age of the third generation of Aburishs, the first batch of university graduates, and the simultaneous emergence of an external economy, the new employment opportunities brought about by the oil wealth in other Arab countries, which affected the Aburishs and their contemporaries in Bethany and the West Bank.

The 1960s produced the solid results of the Aburishs' commitment to education. Being older, I finished university a little earlier, in 1957, while Khalil Ibrahim and his brother Fathi finished in the 1960s as did my brothers Wagih and Munif, cousin Jamil Azzem, Fatmeh's son, and Said Hamad, Amneh's son. Twenty-one other descendants of Khalil Aburish were attending institutions of higher education.

Our attitudes, outlook and ambitions, indeed our concept of Palestine, the world and our place in it, differed from that of our parents. Stung by Hassan's legacy, I decided to remain in America to avoid any possibility of hindrances and problems, as the thought of being identified as the relative of a 'traitor' was beyond bearing.

Upon receiving his Master's degree, my brother Wagih, too, decided that: 'There is no place for me to go to. Nobody in the Middle East wants me . . . it's bad enough to be a Palestinian, Hassan made it impossible.'

Cousin Fathi Ibrahim bravely returned to the Middle East, not to Bethany and shame but to Qatar which was a safer place because it was further away where Hassan's infamy was known to few if any people. There his job was to screen the outside world for the Qatari Minister of Health and Education; he remains in the shadow of His Excellency and his position and influence have grown with time.

Jamil Azzem, Fatmeh's son, was educated in Jordan and had no contacts in other countries and hence no option but to work for a bank in Amman. As Hassan's nephew, and sitting in the nerve centre of his uncles' downfall, Jamil felt a marked man who had to keep a low profile and take special care in how he handled people.

Khalil Ibrahim, a bookish man who is happier with the printed word than with people, taught high school French in Washington DC while studying for his doctoral degree. Confronted by the Hassan problem he decided to stay in the USA, and taught French at university level, still in Washington DC. To him the safety of Washington was preferable to the uncertainty of the Arab World.

My brother Munif obtained two degrees from Californian universities and a doctorate from the Sorbonne. He superimposed the 1960s University of California revolutionary atmosphere on his Palestinian background and became a committed revolutionary, French style; turtle neck sweaters, a weakness for pretty girls and a commitment to righting the wrongs of a world of which he didn't approve. He returned to Beirut to spread the revolutionary gospel and, impelled to outdo fellow revolutionaries so as to overcome Hassan's stigma, he eventually joined the radical Popular Front for the Liberation of Palestine, becoming part of its command for eight years of totally mysterious activity before resigning to go into business. When with the PFLP Munif adopted the nom de guerre of Mufid Shahine, and blunted all suspicion of his Aburish background by always volunteering for the most dangerous assignments. He says, 'I can't recall the number of times I risked my neck because of Hassan'.

Said Hamad, Amneh's son, is another ordained revolutionary, though he differs from Munif in outlook, being more of a Palestinian nationalist than an international revolutionary idealogue. His explanation for his devotion to the PLO is the same as that of my brother Munif: 'We'll show them what we are made of ... we'll overcome the Hassan disaster by doing more.'

The moves away from Bethany were the result of lack of opportunities there; most of them would have happened even if the Hassan disaster hadn't struck. But the migrations to the west and other far-away places instead of neighbouring Arab countries was the direct result of Hassan's execution. Among others my brother Wagih and cousin Khalil Ibrahim turned down lucrative jobs in the oil-producing countries and opted for lesser positions in America to avoid the Hassan label.

As important as our diverse inclinations was the sudden emergence of new opportunities away from Bethany in the oil-rich countries of the Middle East. These countries needed professionals: teachers, lawyers, bankers, doctors, experts of every type to meet the demands of economies growing at unimaginable speeds. Arabic-speaking people from Lebanon, Syria, Egypt and the West Bank of Jordan, including Bethany, were natural recruits and this included some Aburishs and their relatives. My brother Afif left Beirut for brighter prospects in Kuwait in 1964, found himself a minor job with Kuwait Airways and ended up an officer of the airline. Rabah my third brother, followed Afif to Kuwait, moved on to Amman and eventually settled in Cairo.

So in one form or another, the 'external economy' claimed Afif, Rabah, Fathi Ibrahim and eventually Munif – who in 1980 gave up 'the revolution' to run a $60 million Saudi Corporation – and two of Mahmoud's sons-in-law. Other near and distant relatives went to oil-producing countries from where remittances to Bethany helped not only their families but the local economy in general, and the combined remittances of similar people helped the economy of the whole country. Had they stayed in Bethany they would have had to settle for considerably less.

Looking back it is apparent that clear divisions were taking place within the new generation. A few stayed in Bethany, others went to oil-producing countries, a third group stayed in the west and a small number joined various political organizations. Overall, our careers were determined by the limited opportunities which existed in our place of birth, set against the opportunities made possible by our education and family situation and an awareness of the favourable circumstances in other places, particularly the oil-producing countries. Our career objectives were less open-ended than our parents, shaped by our educational background and the more exact requirements of would-be employers everywhere. Whatever professions we followed even the most aware of our parents thought we were moving too fast, and we had a difficult time explaining ourselves. What we did and how we lived were completely new to them and so they felt they were losing touch with us.

Uncle Ibrahim always lamented the fact that his son Khalil taught French: Khalil loved his job but Ibrahim, judging Khalil's work solely by a monetary yardstick, and unable to appreciate the non-financial rewards of teaching, complained that Khalil wasn't paid enough. When I joined Ted Bates Advertising, becoming a young vice president in two short years, my father was bothered by the fact that I managed the Mars Chocolate advertising account. He sadly asked if there wasn't 'something more substantial' to advertise. One of our Bethany relations approached cousin Jamil Azzem to borrow money, and when Jamil said he didn't have any, the disappointed relative mumbled something about thinking he was a banker. Invoking the rights of a blood relation, practically everyone expected Afif to give them free airline tickets and sulked when he couldn't and didn't. Hilmi's overuse of credit cards caused a lot of talk in Bethany and led aunt Amneh to warn: 'They will catch up with him sooner or later. He will have to pay.' Hearing about Wagih's work with John Mecom, a Texas oil billionaire trying to prospect for oil in the Middle East, grandmother Rashedah told a neighbour with great pride that there 'wouldn't be oil in Saudi Arabia except for Wagih's efforts'. The communication gap between us, our parents and our grandparents was widening.

If this gap produced amusing intra-family incidents, then our lives outside were still more droll. Often people didn't understand us: one of Mecom's Texans couldn't say Wagih (Wa-jeeh) and insisted on calling my brother Wahoo Aburish. When one of Khalil Ibrahim's American students thought he was French, Khalil said his name was Abu Reesh, not Richabeau. Hilmi, on a US trip drumming up business for his travel agency, tried his best to tell an American counterpart that a Palestinian was Arab but 'an Arab isn't necessarily Palestinian', like a Texan is American but an American isn't necessarily Texan. The man listened then decided the whole thing was too complicated for him because he couldn't tell 'one camel jockey from another'. When Samih Ibrahim applied for a job with the Hyatt Hotel chain, one of the questions on his application for employment was whether any member of the family had been in the hotel business. He shamelessly wrote that grandfather Aburish had owned two hotels, al-Houd and al-Khan.

There is an inherent grin-and-bear-it element in being the centre, even if not the victim, of a funny story. Wagih's correct demeanor would preclude an Arab calling him Wahoo and Hilmi did not appreciate being referred to as a camel jockey but, with a twinge of pain, both laughed with their well-meaning tormentors. On the other hand Samih capitalized on the ignorance of his would-be employers and used it to make fun of them.

Those of us who stayed in America did not adopt the America-is-the-greatest attitude of earlier generations of immigrants. Nevertheless we did want to belong and that desire revealed itself in our adoption of American names. Sy was not my invention and I always found it unattractive, but my brother Wagih became Bill; cousin Ghaleb Ibrahim adopted Steve, while Samih Ibrahim resorted to a more natural diminutive and uses Sam.

Our encounters with down-to-earth provincial Americans produced a treasure trove of anecdotes which promise to be with us for a long time. When my advertising agency tried to solicit the account of a farm equipment manufacturer, they sent me to Iowa with a representative of the company to study the workings of a farm implement dealership. I arrived

at the store one sunny afternoon to find the owner himself
there, one arm resting on a tractor, a big hat on his head and a
straw in his mouth, looking into the sunset. I was introduced
to him.

'John, this here is Sy Aburish.'

'Howdy, Sy.'

'Howdy, John', with difficulty.

'Sy Aburish, is that your name?' The straw in the mouth
was moved by his tongue from one tooth to another.

'Yes, Sir.'

'Sy Aburish, hah.'

'Yes, sir, that's my name.'

'Sy Aburish you said.' Another move of the straw in his
mouth.

'That's indeed my name.'

Then he pushed his hat up with his finger and stared
squarely in my face.

'Sy, you Jew boy by chance?'

'Yes, sir, but don't tell uncle Mahmoud.'

He didn't know what I was talking about, but it made me
feel better.

Overall, by the mid-1960s the world was once again smiling
upon the Aburish family, for time had reduced Hassan's
episode to nothing more than an ugly memory. Miraculously,
Mahmoud, Ibrahim and my father managed to hold on to
what they had, and Mahmoud's management of Bethany's
affairs now extended to trips to Europe and the USA to raise
money for schools and a clinic. My father's role as an entreé
to influence in America led to tête-à-têtes with the once
elusive King Hussein and scoop after scoop with Arafat, King
Feisal and others. Ibrahim's refugees appeared to follow him
wherever he directed them and so he was courted by both the
PLO and Jordan, who vied for their support. In addition,
Mahmoud, Mohammad and Ibrahim, with their brothers and
sisters, took pride in celebrating their children's successful
emergence as fully-fledged actors on a much larger stage.
Despite the widening generation gap, the qualities of self-
reliance, improvisation and fearlessness implanted in the

family by Khalil Aburish appeared to have taken root. In the words of the irrepressible Hilmi, son of the irrepressible Ibrahim: 'If we see it and want it, we'll get it. We are gunmen.'

Our lifestyles showed as much development and change as did our occupations. My Park Avenue apartment looked like a small art gallery, full of Picasso, Miro and Matisse lithographs, which grandfather Khalil would not have understood, but which had now become part of my march away from Bethany.

The most important room in Khalil Ibrahim's Washington DC house was his study. Afif developed an eye for oriental rugs and began collecting them, but not as a child of the East. He was now like any other western collector basking in the discovery of a remote culture. Hilmi Ibrahim, at that time still a single man, got his satisfaction from driving a huge Cadillac because, among other things, 'girls like Cadillacs'. Fathi Ibrahim's house in far away Qatar has a huge marble bathroom which he shows to all visitors; Wagih joined an exclusive Houston country club to be with his own type and Jamil Azzem wouldn't think of wearing anything but superbly tailored suits. The new generation of girls donned western dress, some down to their French-made silk underwear: many went to hairdressers, visited New York, London and Paris on holiday, accompanied their husbands to night clubs and demanded help with their household chores. They read Dr Spock, helped with their children's school homework and cooked steaks and chops.

We began to worry about diets, to play tennis and squash, go to the theatre, and tell bi-lingual and tri-lingual jokes. We ate pasta and andouillete and drank eau-de-vie, and some of us started wine cellars. Our women, American, Irish, English, Belgian, Palestinian and Egyptian added to the broadening of horizons by contributing bits of their backgrounds to our lives, something which was copied by others, American imitating Belgian, Irish imitating Egyptian and so on. Hedonism, long a family trait, stayed with us, but in forms distant from our roots.

We did all of these things avidly and well. But whether it was collecting western lithographs or 'oriental' rugs, going to the theatre or enjoying a game of squash, and regardless of the levels of interest and pleasure, a deep feeling in us hankered for things which had been part of our make up but weren't available to us anymore. Despite our rejection of the place, the distant shadow of Bethany continued to beckon to something inside all of us.

*   *   *   *

When the ugly shadow of war and conflict reappeared, a new experience for some, a recurring nightmare for others, these doubts about our identity reached boiling point. The year was 1967 and Nasser was president of Egypt and leader of the Arab world, formulating policies and setting the pace for all Arab countries. Other Arab governments followed him because he was popular with their masses, and opposing his policies would be a luxury their leaders could not afford because their own people would have toppled them. So Nasser, a little dizzy with success strengthened rather than diminished by his Suez War defeat, decided it was time for a settlement of accounts with Israel, time to reclaim lost Arab dignity and honour, time to correct injustices. He applied pressure on Israel to come to terms with the Palestinians; his efforts were supported by King Hussein of Jordan, Prime Minister Bitar of Syria and the budding Palestinian political movement which had exaggerated the strength of its various military and paramilitary branches.

Israel, using the closure of the Straits of Tiran as an excuse, sought to break Nasser's hegemony over the Arab world and launched the Six Day War to occupy Jerusalem and the west of Palestine which it had always wanted. Using their superior technology, the Israelis unleashed surprise air attacks which destroyed the Egyptian and Syrian Air Forces on the ground, leaving their armies critically and hopelessly exposed and vulnerable. Except for Nasser, Arab leaders, civilian and military, panicked, leaving their foot soldiers to fight a lonely, losing battle. The Israelis were successful beyond their most optimistic expectations: they followed their overwhelming aerial success with gains on land, occupying the Sinai Peninsula, the Golan Heights in Syria and the West Bank of Jordan including Jerusalem and Bethany, all in six short days. Bethany and the West Bank came under a new rule for the fourth time in forty years.

In Bethany, Mahmoud went all six days of the war without sleep other than exhaustion-forced naps. He expected the war to last longer, the Arab forces to do better: he had dreamt of an Arab victory; instead there was a shameful defeat, so he locked himself indoors, listened to the news of Arab humiliation on the radio, wept until 'my eyes literally ran dry'. Still, he made a clear, brave decision about whether to remain in Bethany or to flee: 'We will not leave Bethany. If we do they will never let us back. Look at what happened to the '48 refugees.'

Ibrahim's refugee camp was full of Palestinian irregulars, commandos, and the Israelis knew it. Israeli planes roamed the skies at will, going for specific targets within the camp and scoring direct hits; yet without air cover the commandos were helpless, as were thousands of innocent civilians who suffered just as much. Ibrahim sneaked his family across the River Jordan and told them to go to Amman, but returned to his camp himself to direct ambulances, calm people, save children. He too went days without sleep; he too didn't believe possible the collapse of the Arab armies.

In Beirut, Abu Said worked around the clock. He was all right until the fighting stopped, then he looked at his colleague Lee Griggs and said, 'Lee, they've got Jerusalem' and cried his heart out.

None of us knew what had happened to poor Mousa who had put all members of his immediate family in a pick-up truck and headed towards Amman and safety, joining a sea of humanity of over 300,000 people trying to do the same thing. A lone Israeli fighter bomber circled above a long convoy of trucks including Mousa's, then dived to attack, strafing and dropping bombs. Mousa was seriously wounded by shrapnel,

hit in the right side of his head. The driver carried on to
Amman while Mousa's head bled, lolling in the lap of his
weeping wife in full view of his children who stared silently,
gripped by the utter terror of the moment.

Amneh and Fatmeh, with their husbands and children, fled
to Amman with no clothes, no money and very little idea of
what they were doing. So did Hamdah's two sons and their
families. Along with Mousa and his family, they all went to the
only place they knew, Daoud's house – he had been
transferred to Amman by the UN. Mousa, unconscious, was
put in the French hospital, while in Daoud's five-room house
(in Daoud's words):

How can a five-room house accommodate forty-two people?
There was not enough floor space, let alone beds and food – hell,
everyone in Amman was hoarding . . . none of them had any money,
the price of food went up a few hundred per cent – I had no
money. Never did.

I'll never know how we managed. It was an absolute miracle.
Mousa was in the hospital for forty days and then they released
him to die at home! Well, I got him into another hospital. He was
there for six months and had two operations. They saved his life
but he's impotent and incontinent, poor man.

People started going back to Bethany two weeks after the fighting stopped. The Israelis let them back after determining they
belonged there. Mousa and his family went back a long time after
he was released for good.

I remember everything, everything. Nobody had any clothes,
and they took to wandering around my house half naked. The
place reeked of unclean humanity. My number one worry was
that the lavatory would break down, but it didn't. We talked
about the war, what happened to other people. Everybody
became an expert comparing '67 with '56 and '48 – the young
children wanted to hear about the old wars. From the mouths of
babes . . . one of the kids reacted to all of this by saying: 'The
Arabs haven't come very far, have they?'

My children remember everything too. How can you forget
something like that? In '48 I had a rifle in my hand, in '67 there
was no glory. It only took six days but we fought for a year in '48.

What's the use, you remember '48 don't you? It was fun in a way. I
don't know, I don't know.

The refrain demands silence; Daoud is glassy-eyed and
far away.

Mousa remembers 1967 but at first he refused to discuss it
with me, and Khadija, his normally chatty wife was also silent.
Belatedly I changed my approach to the interview and told
Mousa that I didn't want his recollections of the incident
when he was injured, just his feelings on Israel. He accepted
the challenge and was more lucid than I had expected: 'The
Israelis will lose in the end – they don't know the Arabs. We
believe in revenge; it will take a hundred years, maybe more,
but they will lose.' I looked at his wife. She nodded agreement; her semi-invalid husband stared into the distance.

Two days after my initial interview with Mousa in August
1985 I returned to see him again. I had a specific question I
wanted to ask him: was it true that he and Mahmoud had
been feuding, and was the reason for whatever misunderstanding existed between them political? Mousa, after the
usual Arab expressions of respect for his eldest brother,
admitted that his relations with Mahmoud were 'cool' and
confirmed that the reason was their different attitude to the
Israeli occupation. His eyes filled with tears as he continued:

This is probably the first time we have a quarrel in the family – a
sorry state of affairs indeed, but then we have to stand up and be
counted, we must resist. Mahmoud has lost the will to resist; he
believes firmly that our destiny is in the hands of other people,
that our wishes don't matter. Perhaps he has seen too much.

The experiences of Khalil Aburish's children in 1967 were
immediate and simple. In 1948 they'd felt defeat, with the
loss of brother Ali, and in the 1950s they suffered with
Hassan: the Suez War had less impact on them – it was not as
close to home, there was no fighting on the West Bank.
Besides, there was more to it than Palestine; it dealt with
many other issues, such as colonialism and the leadership of

the Arab world. So to the Aburishs the Six Day War was the most crippling catastrophe because what they lost was their home, Bethany and Jerusalem. Because of that and because they had come to despair of even the barest Arab successes, they became bitter and disillusioned.

To most members of my generation the Six Day War was a new experience. Dismissing 1948 and its humiliating consequences was easy; we blamed that on the old, uneducated generation, while the Suez War too was a conspiracy which could be explained away. But the 1967 War was our war, we were grown up, capable of contributing, even fighting. We had to accept that no one was to blame except ourselves – unless it was 'they'.

My personal torment was fed by the fact that I had long discarded the notion of the separateness of the individual and the government, and I fully accepted individual responsibility. To me there was no 'they' to blame, so I blamed myself. What was I doing selling Mars chocolate bars when I should have been fighting for my country? Were my moderate attitudes towards the Arab–Israeli conflict true or were they an excuse to opt out, to escape responsibility? I was, spiritually and intellectually, thousands of miles away from Bethany but it was my only home and I had always related to the image of Khalil Aburish and adored his legend. Was it time to divorce myself from New York's posh '21' Club, the apartment on Park Avenue, Mars bars which 'melt in your mouth not in your hands', and return home? But in that case, where was home? All the members of my generation asked the same questions.

In the middle of my agony, three days after the fighting had stopped, I received a telephone call which determined my attitude for that moment and forever. My 'phone rang at 9.00 a.m. one Saturday morning. I answered it rather drowsily and a voice said: 'My name is Yahuda Hellman, we met at Pamela Powers' party two weeks ago. I am the Israeli with whom you argued all night long.'

'Oh, yes, I remember', with rather an edge.

'Mr Aburish, I am very sorry about what happened. War is

war I am afraid. Is there anything I can do for your family in Jerusalem, have you heard from them? I am an employee of the Israeli government, I am a good friend of Golda Meier and the others.'

'Mr Hellman, Mr Hellman, I haven't heard anything from my family but I'd rather they die than solicit your help. Mr Hellman, we *are* at war.'

'I am sorry.'

'So am I – goodbye.'

Half an hour after I telephoned Pamela Powers and told her what happened: 'Pamela', I said, 'Please call him and thank him, but tell him I'm sorry I can't accept his offer of help. He is a nice man but I just can't.' And with that I broke down and joined the sobbing sons of Araby.

Khalil Ibrahim was teaching at a school in Washington DC, so I telephoned him from New York to enquire about his welfare. He said that 'they' had sold us down the river. Impatiently I told him off and hung up. Khalil's brother Hilmi was in the USA promoting his Jerusalem travel agency, and the war left him stranded with $400 to his name. The whole issue was beyond his understanding and it took a long time to convince him he couldn't return to Bethany and Jerusalem. When he finally understood, he started a travel agency in Washington with borrowed money.

My brother Wagih, always a definite, uncompromising man, resigned from the employment of John Mecom to go and 'fight for my beliefs', but the war ended before he could manage to get back and he had no problem reclaiming his job with Mecom. Wagih has the blunt ways of a Texan, and the assessment he gave to people around him at that time is one he still reiterates: 'How the hell did the Arabs expect to win? They formed a joint command two days before the war started. They weren't prepared for anything except a verbal war.'

Munif, about to finish his course for a Master's degree at the University of California, was already touched by the radicalism of the 1960s so that the Six Day War accelerated his commitment to leftist causes. To him Israel was bound to

win because it was and is part of the militarily superior
American imperialism, a sinister, exploitative force with
operates under many covers, particularly in the Middle East
and South America. His idol was not Nasser. It was Che
Guevara.

For the third generation of Aburishs in the Arab world the
same of defeat was easier. Nasser had crystallized the sense
of Arab identity, the Arabs had incorporated an acceptance
of their oneness in their psyche and they empathized with
each other. My brother Afif remembers many Kuwaiti friends
kissing him on both cheeks and saying, 'the loss is common to
all of us'. Rabah says other Arabs instinctively referred to
him as 'brother' – the new idea of Arab solidarity born in 1948
came of age with the defeat of 1967. The Six Day War was an
Arab war and an Arab defeat, much larger than the 1948
defeat, which could be described as Palestinian, and unlike
the Suez War with no France or Britain on which to lay the
blame. If the men had expected the Arabs to do better, then
the older women were confused; far more than the men,
they had accepted Arab promises at face value.

In Bethany and Amman, Amneh, Fatmeh, Salha Ibrahim
and Mirriam Mahmoud, aghast at the enormity of the defeat,
implored their husbands to explain things to them: some did,
while others didn't know what to say. Aunt Amneh remembers her husband saying: 'The Arabs make me sick. They
stink.' Still, much of the women's concern remained familial,
worry about going back to Bethany, about their husbands'
jobs, and also about Mousa.

Amazingly, the two eldest women of the family, grandmother Rashedah and my own mother, appear to have
reached their own highly individualistic conclusions. Upon
hearing of Mousa's injury and the ensuing problems – he was
the third casualty after Ali and Hassan – my grandmother,
according to Mahmoud, closed her eyes and said: 'Why don't
they stop it? That's enough.' My mother, her horizons
broadened by Beirut's cosmopolitan atmosphere, doesn't
mince her words: 'Why did he – Nasser – start a war he
couldn't win, why didn't he just shut up.' When I told her

Nasser didn't start the war she insistently proclaimed that: 'He played into their hands – he made the war possible.'

But the younger generation of women demonstrated totally new attitudes which reflected their changed positions. My sisters Mona and Alia were in Beirut at the ages of nineteen and sixteen; they went to work collecting donations for people displaced by the fighting: Mona started her campaign by giving the only valuable ring she had, an emerald. The daughters of Mahmoud, Ibrahim, Amneh and Fatmeh went to work in emergency relief centres for refugees; they did everything from cooking to digging ditches.

A month after the Six Day War ended my father came to New York to attend a conference and to rest. We managed to avoid any mention of the war for a few days, but when the subject inevitably came up he produced the right assessment: 'It's all yours from now on. We failed. Your generation must decide what to do. Our time is over – we failed.'

11
The coca cola culture: a people dispersed

Armenian: Take it easy, my friend. Things can't be that bad, what seems to be the problem?
Palestinian: I have lost my country.
Armenian: What else?
Palestinian: My family is scattered all over the world.
Armenian: What else?
Palestinian: Nobody wants me. I have no place to go.
Armenian: What else?
Palestinian: The future looks as bleak as the past.
Armenian: Don't cry my friend, you'll get used to it.

My friend Ibrahim Nazzal is fond of telling this sad story about a kindly old Armenian gentleman who meets a disconsolate Palestinian crouched against a wall and weeping. Certainly, by the 1970s we had grown accustomed to our new lives as unwanted, roaming refugees. Some, like my father, had left as a consequence of the 1948 war, for while he didn't then lose his home, he did lose his business; others left in the 1950s and early 1960s because there were no employment opportunities on the West Bank, and a third group left after the Israeli occupation of Bethany and the West Bank in 1967, in this case because of lack of jobs and because they did not want to live under Israeli occupation, taking jobs that would associate them with the state of Israel.

In the 1970s our combined exposure to the world had given us a broad outlook on life peculiar to all those who do not possess the precious sense of belonging; an outlook which was being transmitted to the very young who grew up thinking of global work opportunities. Only the ones openly committed to Palestinian causes, the ones who channelled their energies into continuing to fight full time for Palestine, escaped the feeling of not belonging to a particular place, of rootlessness.

Many Aburishs who studied engineering took up careers in

the oil-rich countries, the United States and South America, but even non-specialists could not cope with the conflicting atmosphere of Israeli occupation and the equally unbearable burden of Jordanian prejudice, the two countries which were the natural outlets for their talents. We had no attachments to keep us in one place, for even Bethany exercised little pull and ceased to be our anchor. True, we could still live there but it was no longer 'ours'; instead it felt like an occupied town, and those who lived there suffered the unhappiness which goes with being a conquered people. Israel's actions after the Six Day War were explicit manifestations of the attitude of an occupying, stronger power – for example, the Israeli government was quick in imposing rigid control of the school syllabus – though Jordan's rule had differed only in name for they too viewed us as undesirables, unwelcome in our own land – Palestinians were denied jobs in government departments even when their qualifications were clearly superior.

So we went to other countries in search of money and comfort, to live well and without being hounded: that meant personal links had to be sacrificed. While the absence of a sense of belonging in the United States, United Kingdom, South America and other places hampered any quest for a primary position, it was distinctly preferable to being a second class citizen in Bethany. For me remaining in the United States solved many problems: not only did I not relish Israeli or Jordanian attitudes, I refused to accept Lebanon or other Arab countries as an alternative because I thought the prospect of having to plead for a work permit and being denied equal opportunity was emotionally destructive. Better to do this among real alien Britons, Americans or Swiss, than among fellow Arabs who, until they had to demonstrate it, considered themselves your brothers.

Cousin Naim Hamad found working in London less demanding than doing the same in Amman or Damascus, while Hilmi Ibrahim wouldn't have had much of a chance resurrecting his travel business in Kuwait or Saudi Arabia, but managed to do so in Washington DC. Still our ability to mitigate the pain of our plight through financial success did little to eliminate the feeling of not being wanted.

*   *   *   *

During the 1970s Mahmoud's role as mayor was subject to continuous Israeli interference. An Arabic-speaking Israeli army major was appointed by his government to oversee Bethany's affairs and attempted to reduce Mahmoud to an unquestioning instrument of Israeli rule. While Mahmoud had stopped acting as spokesman for Bethanites in dealing with the central government some time back, he was now being asked to transmit the wishes of an alien power, a merciless occupier hated by his villagers. Nobody among the official Israelis paid attention to the wishes or feelings of Mahmoud or his followers, but unlike us they had no place to go.

Mahmoud's humiliation did not stop there; the Israelis reduced him further by expropriating twelve acres of land which belonged to the Aburish family, the same land which Khalil Aburish had refused to sell to the Jewish Agency. The Israeli Government did offer a token payment in return, a sum of money less in real terms than their predecessors had offered in 1928. When Mahmoud refused to sell, the land was seized in accordance with the laws legalizing such seizures. Now it is part of the Israeli settlement of Maale Edumin which strategically straddles the Jerusalem–Jericho road in full view of Mahmoud's house.

My father, who had already overcome all obstacles to his curious position, was celebrated in articles and books which accorded him accolades ranging from 'the doyen of Beirut journalists' to 'the most knowledgeable newspaper man in the Middle East'. In spite of that, perhaps because of it, he too was damaged by his Palestinian identity. He was accused of being a 'PLO plant', of reporting the news with partiality, and other sins.

Ibrahim's problems in continuing to manage the UN refugee camp were similar to Mahmoud's but worse, as the

Israelis didn't trust his refugees at all, and constantly tried to turn him into an informer, to tell them who was opposed to their rule. The previous freedom he had enjoyed in making UN policies acceptable to the refugees was taken away from him because his every move was watched, and the motives behind the smallest act misinterpreted. According to his wife, he shied from uttering simple statements such as 'things will get better' because the Israelis would demand to know what was behind the promise. The result was that his conduct of his job during the 1970s betrayed a lack of imagination which surprised all of those who knew him. Yet the pressure on him was massive for his position as leader of 40,000 Palestinians – the camp's population increased by twenty-five per cent in twelve years – meant that he was courted by all those interested in a solution to the Palestinian refugee problem. Ibrahim was considered capable of steering his wards into accepting or rejecting anything affecting their fate.

Mousa and Daoud, who had returned to Bethany in 1969, weren't subject to direct pressure because they were not important people. Their lives under Israeli occupation were cheerless and they were preoccupied with making ends meet and staying out of harm's way by avoiding contact with the Israeli occupation. Still the 1970s found them, as well as Amneh and Fatmeh, focusing on their children's education and attainments, trying to catch up with their elders through their off-spring. The direction of the children was determined by the atmosphere in which they lived: their parent's constant prodding, the inhospitality of Israel and the relative lack of welcome in the Arab countries meant they had to follow in the footsteps of those who succeeded in far-way lands.

Compared with problems facing the older generation in the Middle East, the ones facing us overseas had an unfamiliar ring to them, they weren't exclusively political in nature, but incorporated peculiarities in our circumstances as outsiders in our adopted countries. My pride in my achievement in the advertising business evaporated when the president of the agency for which I worked told me in a kind, fatherly way: 'What am I going to do with you? You are a senior vice president at thirty-five but there's no way someone with the name of Said Aburish could make it all the way to the top.' Cousin Ahmad Hassan faced a similar problem and gives a good summary of our position within the western body corporate: 'People think of refugees as displaced persons running grocery stores, bowling alleys or restaurants. Nobody is willing to accept them as heroes within a corporate stucture.'

This alien position was a two-edged sword, both limiting and reinforcing the commitment to success. We did resent the people who denied us the right to be 'heroes', whether corporately or in Bethany, Amman, Cairo and Damascus, and particularly resented this denial when it took place in Arab countries which needed our talents and professed brotherly feelings towards us – two elements which heightened our expectations and which were eventually shattered when we discovered that neither need nor verbal commitments to brotherhood guaranteed us equal opportunities.

In the west extra talent and hard work had to compensate for our foreignness, had to make up for a pronounced accent, a lapse in the style of dress, or residual oddities in behaviour. While these characteristics did not matter in Arab countries, there were other requirements to be met, other objections to be overcome, all of which emanated from our Palestinian identity. Fellow Arabs accused us of smugness because we dared claim better knowledge of such things as how the British behaved overseas. We were considered unappreciative of Saudi hospitality because it is against our nature to be subservient, while others complained about our preoccupation with politics, refusing to take into consideration our natural craving to know what the world was planning for us next.

These pressures made us workaholics, and also allowed us to see opportunities not readily visible to our hosts, the people who were comfortable as what they were, where they were. My brother Wagih's explanation of how he talked a Scandinavian bank into investing $100 million in a property development scheme was simple: 'I had the nerve to ask for it ... others were shy.' Hilmi Ibrahim borrowed $2 million without any collateral. 'I had nothing to lose by asking', he says.

During the 1970s all of us found ourselves doing battle against a hostile world; the Aburishs in Bethany had to cope with the harsh Israeli occupation, those in Arab countries fell victim to other Arabs' resentment of their achievements, however modest, and immigrants to western countries stopped being poor refugees deserving of pity. Now we were feared as trouble-makers, as willing or unwilling representatives of the PLO, the group which instilled indiscriminate fear in the hearts of Israelis, Arabs and foreigners alike and reminded them that the Palestinian problem would not go away. Although the label didn't fit most of us, our tormentors didn't care: we were the PLO and that was bad.

Naturally prejudiced western people used our new predicament to justify rejecting us; fellow Arabs feared for the stability of their governments; Israelis excused their harsh measures. Our surroundings became more inhospitable than ever, the problem grew larger, more immediate and more menacing. Every PLO act led to a trial by proxy.

Alone in New York, I learned to deflect rather than argue over explicit or implied accusations. When the head of a major American corporation eyed me funnily and enquired about my origins, I answered: 'I am a Palestinian, sir – but I am not armed.' He didn't laugh.

Most of us have learned to live with our new label, others bear psychological scars; and a third group, unable to face the ugly reality, escaped to other places or other careers. In London cousin Naim Hamad pretended not to hear when both colleagues and patients used the pejorative 'wog' to describe him, though he later decided against ever working in the UK again. Khalil Mahmoud tried for several jobs in Washington DC, but could never answer a question about his 'origins' without becoming upset. He finally gave up and returned to Bethany in disgust.

There was no conspiracy against the descendants of Khalil Aburish, but the problems we experienced were not of our making: on the contrary they were ones with which the world saddled us and in the process confirmed to us that our 'Palestinianism' was inescapable. This, in turn, created reverse prejudices, an instinctive kinship similar to that practised by Armenians, Jews and other victims of homelessness.

Today, most of Hilmi Ibrahim's Washington employees are Palestinian, as he feels an obligation towards them, and my brother Afif's friends at Kuwait Airways were Palestinians who 'shared the same problems'. My sister Mona responded to my description of one of her girl friends as being very nice by saying: 'She is. She's Palestinian.' A PLO cousin took trips to Australia and South America to raise money from the Arab communities there. To him, 'they were all very nice to me but the Palestinians were different. I talked to them as if I had known them all my life.'

But there was more to the 1970s than our ability to realize monetary dreams in the west, adapt and make the best of Israeli rule and overcome the brotherly prejudices of fellow Arabs. There was one unattainable element in all our lives: a sense of dignity.

Our emotional hunger for dignity, and through it for identity is suffocatingly real, although we manifest it and pursue it differently. We emphasize the level of our education in the presence of fellow Arabs to show them that we are more advanced than they are and we take special pride in not being as subservient to authority as the Egyptians and Syrians. We try to pre-empt the tradition of Arab hospitality by being over generous and openly admit that: 'We made the Arab countries through opening their eyes and providing them with doctors, teachers and engineers.' We claim superiority over our fellow Arabs and threaten that: 'We are going to blast this globe to bits.' We are angry and arrogant, and give every sign of being emotionally scarred because we want to belong. This desire to belong has been the one constant in our lives, the one thing which stayed with us in spite of massive changes in lifestyle and attitude.

* * * *

Marriage has been one of the strongest influences for change that has taken place in my generation, for it was the third Aburish generation which was to join the twentieth century, to subscribe totally to marriage by choice and adhere to practices recognized by everyone as modern and fair to all concerned.

When my parents emigrated to Beirut as a result of the 1948–9 war, I was one of thirty-six grandchildren of Khalil Aburish. 'Modern' marriage was even then invading Bethany as girls and boys exchanged letters, even though the girls risked punishment by their parents. Many an engagement was broken off when the intended bridegroom discovered his bride-to-be 'had eyes' for someone else. Cousins still had priority but this custom was being eroded, with girls beginning to say no and boys dismissing the pull of blood ties. In addition to a girl's looks and family background, boys were also interested in her ability to cook, sew, wear modern dress and even speak a second language.

Changes in marriage customs also brought changes in attitudes to divorce, which was previously unknown. Pride in producing children had always been an extremely important stabilizing factor in marriages and barrenness was in fact the only accepted reason for divorce. Now, in the 1970s, there were seven divorces within five years, the direct result of marriage by choice rather than marriage by arrangement. Under the old-fashioned way a women could not divorce even if she wanted to, and her role was limited to bearing children, cooking, keeping house and, lastly, pleasing her man. He provided for her, maintained a friendly relationship with her family and shared with her the responsibility of bringing up the children. Beyond that he was free to misbehave, sneak off to brothels in Jerusalem or have an illicit affair with a foreigner or the odd, willing city Arab.

By the 1970s arranged marriages had slipped into history, in this case unlamented, and wives threw away their implicit vows of silence and became vocal about everything, to the joy of some husbands and the annoyance of others. The distance between the Aburishs and old Bethany ways grew greater; we related more and more to immediate surroundings and less and less to the ways we were brought up.

New horizons were opening up as modern transportation shrank distances and Bethany stopped being a village and became a suburb of Jerusalem. Girls were going to school, and tourists and more aggressive Christian missionary schools had introduced new ideas about the role of women. People's travel to far-away places in Europe and the USA to study and to work broadened horizons which naturally extended to the male–female relationship and consequently to marriage.

My own attitude was moulded by the American school I attended in Beirut after my parents moved there. Cousin Khalil Ibrahim attending Frères College in Jerusalem was three years younger and his situation, the influence of his school superseding that of his parents, was closer to mine. On the other hand, my brother Afif, five years young than I am, absorbed Beirut more readily; he was too young when he left Bethany and its ways left only a superficial impression on him.

The change taking place within us was not isolated, though the degrees of change varied according to where we were. But without exception, our parents were accepting the differences in us because they too were changing in terms of their appreciation of the outside world whose mores they were incorporating into their Bethany background. The new attitudes came too late to affect their lives in their own personal relationships but soon enough to ensure a remarkable tolerance of the young. No one ever suggested I marry a cousin – or anyone else; in fact, a form of disapproval was creeping in on marriage among cousins and the unhealthiness of marrying a close relative was beginning to be mentioned openly.

I met my first wife, Prudence Anne Cooper when we were both at graduate school in America. We met at a student function and danced until the small hours of the morning, which exhausting exercise earned me a peck on the cheek at 3.00 a.m. She came from an old conservative Nebraska family who owned feed mills throughout the Middle West. She was studying for a Ph.D. in sociology, taking part in the prevailing liberal political attitude at the University of Chicago while remaining remote and forbidding in her personal behaviour. Pru Cooper at twenty-three – I was twenty-one – was a virgin, and I loved that, for the importance of virginity was part of my cultural subconscious. An American woman, blonde, pretty, intelligent and highly educated, none the less she appealed to something embedded in the recesses of my mind, and so accidentally she paid tribute to one of the important require-ments of Araby's attitude towards marriage. Because of what she was and because of this specific attitude I loved her and asked her to marry me: she accepted.

Our knowledge of each other's background and family were second-hand and appeared unimportant – we were totally committed to each other and believed that our love for each other would overcome all obstacles, cultural or otherwise. I was enchanted by her intelligence and good looks and she admired my ability to adapt and my worldliness, which included viewing things differently from the usual 'joe college' she had so far encountered. However, her parents' permission had to be obtained; instead of a delegation com-posed of members of my family, I myself had to ask for her hand in marriage from her father, and we selected the 1956 Thanksgiving school holiday to do so.

Pru telephoned her mother to tell her she was bringing me home for Thanksgiving; we saved enough money and squeezed ourselves into a pay 'phone to make a call which proved more amusing than expected:

'Hello, Mom. I will be coming home next Tuesday. I'm bringing Said Aburish with me for Thanksgiving.'

'You're bringing what?'

'Said Aburish, my boyfriend.'

'Is he a Chinaman by chance?'

'No, he's an Arab.'

'A-rab. What is he doing in this country?'

'He's with me at school – getting his M.B.A.'

'Well, bring him along if you want. How does he dress?'

'Like the rest of us. he's a very modern man.'

'Well, I don't care. I hope your father likes him, he's jealous of your boyfriends.'

Humboldt, Nebraska, the home of the Coopers is practically the same size as Bethany, and its people have the same attributes of being part of a community where there are no strangers and no secrets, so my presence caused a stir and a lot of whispering. I am told that people sat at the porch of the Park Hotel, an eight-room building which was also the town's only restaurant and bar, to catch sight of me. They'd never seen an Arab before.

The Coopers were like the Aburishs, local notables, though their money and influence were greater and came from more recognizable sources. They employed most of the local people in their flour and feedmill, owned most of the surrounding farmland and ran a turkey farm which sold close on one million birds every Thanksgiving.

My confrontation with Guy Cooper, a 5 foot 6 inch man with a red moustache, a paunch, a head full of hair swept back 1920s style and a slow non-committal way of speaking, was quite easy.

'I understand you want to marry my daughter?'

'Yes, sir.'

'How are you going to live?'

'We are about to finish school and get jobs.'

'Why do you want to marry her? Is it because she is blonde?'

'No, sir. There are a lot of blonde girls around. I love her.'

'Where will you live?'

'In this country.'

'Do you want to work for our company? My son isn't interested. We'd like to keep the company in the family.'

'I am terribly complimented, sir, but we want to live in New York or Chicago.'

'Oh . . . well get yourself a job. Pru is the apple of my eye. I think you'll be a good provider. She tells me you work part time to supplement what your family sends you. That's good

– it's a good sign. Get yourself a job and make your own arrangements. Naturally, tell me what type of wedding you want.'

Evelyn, his wife, did not take part in any of the discussions, and reminded me of what I had been told about my grandmother at my parent's wedding negotiations. When she was told of my conversation with her husband she gulped a huge portion of sour mash bourbon and announced to Pru that the whole thing was a good idea.

The Thanksgiving dinner ceremony was an all-American affair, where everyone talked about the turkey and the stuffing. Wine was served, an unusual intruder on the American dining table in Bible belt states, and the atmosphere was happy and rather giggly, full of amusing questions about me from Aunt Emma Cooper who, at eighty-two, insisted, without cause, that I was a descendent of the prophet Mohammad and therefore a holy man.

Pru got herself a job teaching at a school in Park Forest, Illinois, a few miles outside Chicago, and I went looking for one. The wedding was to be as soon as possible and we opted, with the agreement of the Coopers, to have it in Park Forest near our friends, with a reception later at the Cooper's home.

My parents didn't attend the wedding: Beirut was too far away. My father was happy but made a point of mentioning that 'the girl is older than you are'. My mother asked for the wedding pictures and sent Pru one of her gold bracelets as a wedding present. According to both my parents, my mother's enquiry about whether she was converting to Islam produced one of their rare quarrels in twenty-four years. Father is reputed to have stared at her and quietly said: 'Soraya, why don't you shut up? There is after all nothing in the Koran against marrying a Christian.'

Pru and I spent two weeks on our honeymoon in Minnesota and while we were there I told her about weddings in Bethany. Being a sociologist she was interested and amazingly agreed that there was much to arranged marriages in a structured society where women and men accepted their roles unquestioningly. She claimed that much argument and conflict was avoided that way.

After the honeymoon we went to Humboldt for the reception. The presents were things rather than money, but except for the absence of an announcer they were no different from the *nkout* in Bethany, as each present had a card with the name of the donor in front of it, and amongst Pru's family, much as in Bethany, there was competition as to who gave the more expensive present. Uncle John Cooper, Humboldt's counterpart of Uncle Ibrahim, got drunk and kept slapping me on the back with: 'Where are the goddamned sheep's eyes ... I want to try some sheep's eyes.'

The difference between my father's wedding and mine was clear and considerable: I chose my own bride and she chose me. She was more knowledgeable in the ways of the world than my mother, expected to participate equally in all decisions and, very importantly, she didn't want children for a while. Otherwise, asking her father for her hand was not too different from Bethany, and given half a chance my friends from school would have sung and danced and drunk for a few days, too, though tribal bragging would not have been part of their carousing. The present-giving differed in form rather than substance. The more fundamental difference came later when her career objectives clashed with mine.

Marrying a foreigner, a liberated American with a Ph.D., was all new to the Aburish clan, but there were others in the family who had one foot in a fast-changing Bethany and the other in a newer and more intriguing world. My cousin Khalil Ibrahim, who lived in Bethany, took a fancy to my sister Mona, so after finishing his university education in the United States and returning home he travelled from Bethany to Beirut to ask for her hand. My father, aware of Mona's inherent stubborness and commitment to Beirut ways, proclaimed he had no say in the affair; Mona turned Khalil down and to his shock a thousand years of tradition embodying cousins' rights gave way without resistance. She didn't have much of a reason beyond not liking him for a husband, and he himself wisely refused to cause problems by attempting to invoke a cousin's privilege. Time eliminated that and both his parents and mine accepted the fact there were no hard feelings; I am pleased to report both Mona and Khalil are happily married to outsiders and are good friends.

Mona later married a man of her choice, Mazen Makki, a classmate of hers at the American University of Beirut where a subdued form of courting, akin to what happens in western schools, existed. He visited my parents to be introduced but never went through the agony of asking for Mona's hand. My father readily approved because that was what Mona wanted, while mother approved reluctantly, not out of pique over loss of influence but because she never liked Mazen.

Mona's wedding took place in Beirut, with an all-male Bethany delegation headed by Mahmoud arriving to attend the festivities. The three stages of a Muslim ceremony were observed, though Mazen and Mona were free to see each other, and much of their time was spent at the Cave du Roi, Beirut's leading discotheque, or at St Michel Beach where bikinis were de rigueur. How far Mazen and Mona's relationship was developed before the wedding is a matter of unimportant speculation: the more important factor is that the immediate families didn't care. Not only were they determined to go their own way, the elders, my parents and Mazen's, people who had never been left alone until the day of their wedding, seemed to accept what was happening.

The wedding itself was an afternoon reception held at the then posh St George's Hotel, with champagne the most popular drink. All Lebanese and Syrian society was there – Mazen came from an old Syrian family – with St Laurent, Carven, Christian Dior and Pucci dresses much in evidence. A confident Mona wandered around greeting everyone with all the usual hugging and kissing we associate with such occasions. The Bethany contingent whispered disapproval when Mona was seen kissing strangers, but as far as she was concerned, they were not entitled to object. When Mahmoud got back to Bethany he didn't mentioned this part to the Aburish women in case they were shocked.

Every guest left with a small box of *mlabas*, almonds

encrusted with sugar, with a blue ribbon tied around it, and much like my parents' wedding and mine, the presents were on view and people vied as to who gave most: it was all silver, except the presents from the bride's and bridegroom's parents, who chose to give Persian rugs.

Other Aburish weddings followed, too numerous to deal with individually. Some involved the people who remained in Bethany, many of whom were still bound by some of its slowly evolving traditions, others connected members of the Aburish family with non-Bethany, non-Palestine Arabs, and these weddings incorporated the attitude of both the bride's and bridegroom's side, while a third variety was marriage to foreigners. In all, sixty-six of Khalil Aburish's grandchildren went to school overseas and eight married foreign girls, Irish, English, Belgian, Romanian, Cuban and three American.

Khalil Ibrahim, Mona's one-time suitor, married a Bethany girl in a two-day ceremony which included all the songs and dances of his parents' wedding but was marked by greater intermingling of the sexes and the consumption of alcohol, champagne included. She is a distant relation but that had nothing to do with it; a person of rare good looks and charm who looks equally attractive in traditional Bethany dress and western clothes. She has an equal voice in everything and is the mother of three lovely children, and like her husband is totally at ease in Bethany, London or Washington DC, where her husband now teaches at university level.

The changes in marriage customs are many and worth summarizing: the first bastion to fall was the parents' right to select a partner for a son or a daughter – even for those who remained in Bethany, though some parents lapse into agreeing to and announcing a girl's impending wedding only to be embarrassed by having to cancel the engagement because she or her intended bridegroom refuse their choice. The days of children being taken totally for granted are gone and so too are cousins' rights. Marriages to cousins continue to take place but less because their parents wish it and more because the couple have grown up with and like each other. This is becoming rare, though with Bethany society still restricted in the possible contacts between girls and boys, a cousin is occasionally attractively familiar, and religiously there are no obstacles.

The *nkout*, giving of money presents, continues but has changed, with most people giving the utilitarian objects normally needed by newly-weds, and closer relations, as in the west, giving money to help the couple along.

For people marrying Middle Eastern girls the dowry and *muta'kher* are still there, as they are part of religion. However, the malady of divorce for reasons other than barrenness, even on vague grounds of incompatibility, has appeared, and more emphasis is placed on the *muta'kher* than on the dowry. There is greater concern with the future, yet the 'name' of whom you marry is still vital.

There is no set pattern to the relationship between the sexes prior to marriage. My sisters married Arabs and western type courtships took place, while some Bethany girl cousins did and do have contact with husbands-to-be well before marrying, though their freedom is limited and 'being left alone' or 'staying up late' is not accepted. One of Fatmeh's daughters married a distant relation of her choice and, as far as anyone knows, the young man arranged the situation well and there was no need for intermediaries or instructors.

Nowadays the Bethany wedding ceremony itself is a smaller affair. People come only by formal invitation and resentment doesn't result from being excluded; there is only one or perhaps two days of celebrations and a Jerusalem hotel is used. Brides dance at their weddings, alone and with their betrothed and very often the whole affair is video-taped for posterity; a dance band is often present, and people sit on high chairs around tables and move around freely greeting members of both sexes. Greater attention is given to the newly-weds having the right start than to giving a legendary shindig which will be the talk of the town for years. Having children, particularly sons to perpetuate a name, remains important, but the wife is no longer viewed as a breeding machine and people worry about the health of mother and children, and afford them a good life including schooling.

Birth control is practised without shame: my brother Afif has three lovely children and when I asked him if more were planned he gazed fixedly at me and said: 'Only a nut would do that. Who could afford to send four kids to college?'

Marriage to a foreigner involves love, something not subject to reason but to trial and error. My brother Wagih (Bill) married an Irish girl. He is an extremely hard-working man who takes an occasional glass of wine; Wagih and Eileen decided against having children from the beginning of their marriage. They treat each other with instinctive deference and open love which transcends their cultural differences; they have lived in a state of bliss for twenty years.

Cousin Taleb married an American girl and proceeded to treat her like a Middle Eastern wife, leaving her behind and going out with the boys every night. She suffered him for three years, bore him two children and then sued for divorce. She gets most of his salary.

Now it is the turn of the new generation, our children. Among the people of marrying age is my daughter Charla Josephine, aged twenty-five, a trilingual college graduate who lives alone in New York and makes a living managing an art gallery on 57th Street. Boyfriends come and go: she gets bored and fires them – occasionally they fire her. Charla and I are very close and visit regularly, but to me her life is her own: I would rather not know.

*   *   *   *

The energetic older generation was still around watching our attempts to extend their leaps forward with combinations of pride, fear and dismay. Mahmoud put our commitment to materialism alongside government interference in his affairs and both became his pet hates: he views the pursuit of money as corrupting, particularly in its destructive effects on family ties. Naturally he champions the old system while knowing that it can no longer apply: he preaches the old virtues to everyone, hoping some of them will take hold.

My father's preoccupations differed from Mahmoud's. He

developed a taste, almost a weakness for power and for what he considered elegance, a natural consequence of the closeness to the powerful and wealthy brought about by his work. Even though he had moved away from the old ways, that did not stop him from lamenting their passing and he retains an endearing reverence for his elder brother Mahmoud in spite of the stronger appeal of new attachments. He takes singular pride in Wagih's financial success, in Munif's rise in the revolutionary ranks and in my work as adviser to two Middle East governments. To him power comes ahead of money; having both is an enviable achievement.

Ibrahim died in 1978 from cirrhosis of the liver, a proud man who could never come to terms with the blow to his reputation resulting from the Hassan disaster. An estimated 7,000 people, including fellow Holy Strugglers, walked in his funeral, a procession, according to Fatmeh, 'fit for a king'. This made doubly sad his belief in money as the only worthwhile thing in life. He lived long enough to see his children successfully follow his creed in making considerable amounts of money. By the end of his life neither old nor new ways interested Ibrahim, only money as a crude instrument of power.

Mousa's uneventful life turned tragic after the 1967 war. He, too, directed his children towards making money, and his sons, who came of age in the late 1970s show every sign of fulfilling their father's dreams.

Daoud was always the quiet member of the family, concerned only with his own life and his environment. Daoud's children became engineers in the 1970s, and like their father their ambitions are modest, but they are happy people with an infectious commitment to the simple, uncomplicated life. The attitude of Daoud's family is evolutionary; they represent slow change which allows them to relate to old and new ways.

To Amneh and Fatmeh, their brothers were to be emulated more than their husbands, so their children grew up idolizing their elder brothers whose achievements the girls admired. The boys are ambitious, relentless in their pursuit of success, and while this is what their mothers wanted, there are signs of unease about what goes with it; the mothers are beginning to preach caution. Amneh expresses her growing misgivings as follows: 'If one isn't considerate of people then the whole thing is worthless. I don't think success should make people hard.'

* * * *

The massive sociological changes and generation gaps and resultant attitudes tell a great deal about us and the older generation. Unhappily, the one trait common to most of us is cynicism, the reflection of lack of belief, perhaps too much exposure to war and politics, the remembrance of unfulfilled promises, the absence of an ability to dream. All of us believe Arab leadership is defective, so political Arabism is highly suspect but not Arabism as a mode of life. Most of us believe in the notion of outside forces controlling our destiny without attention to our hopes; hence the four uninvited occupiers. If, according to our Armenian friends, we have become accustomed to being outsiders then our main preoccupation is in the one area where we might excel, making money.

However, the end of the 1970s showed signs of the re-emergence of a broader vision of life than the strict pursuit of money. Having established that making money is possible, that a comfortable livelihood is within the reach of all of us, we relaxed and began to revert to more human values, however simple and ordinary.

My brother Rabah cannot live without a rose garden towards which he directs time and energy previously used to make money. Cousin Ghaleb Ibrahim freely applies the Jewish joke to various family situations to deflect their inherent morbidity. Khalil Ibrahim's commitment to education proved infectious; others have followed in his footsteps. I put my life on the line and wrote a book about corruption in the Arab world because I believed it had gone too far, and someone had to speak out against abuse. Regardless of merit or moral judgement, those of us who followed the PLO did so at considerable financial cost and risk to their lives.

Though it lingers, the state of mental siege which led to a focus on money as the road to salvation began to show signs of lifting in the late 1970s. This dehumanizing phase, the natural result of being an uprooted people lacking all hope, is being assailed by such down-to-earth values as those which sustained Khalil Aburish. Perhaps the future isn't as bleak as the past.

12
Despair and hope

The Arabs go to war every day, verbally. When Sadat said he was suing for peace, I thought he was being an Arab, saying something while doing nothing. I was wrong – even in this he wasn't Arab.

Soraya Shahine Aburish

There is no way to separate the word Palestinian from the two images which accompany it, though people very seldom merge these two images into a coherent picture which might shed light on a most complex problem. To most of the world the word terror has become part of the Palestinian identity; fewer people see the Palestinians of the refugee camps and the West Bank as the victims of an endless war aimed at denying them their rights and dignity.

The Palestinian attitude towards the use of violence to achieve political ends has undoubtedly governed their relationship with fellow Arabs, Israel and the rest of the world. If the Aburish's acceptance of their Palestinianism is instinctive, spontaneous and totally voluntary, then their attitude towards wars and other acts of violence should tell a great deal about these often misreported happenings.

To my father the armed conflict part of the Arab–Israeli problem falls into two periods – because: 'Before 1967 there was still a chance of a sensible solution but after 1967 all the Israelis want is to dictate to us.' My brother Munif takes the action a step further: 'All wars and acts of terror since the 1967 war took Israeli military superiority for granted. This is accepted by both sides and it is the background to everything which has happened since, including the October 1973 war.'

While my father and Munif tend to be more eloquent and precise then most members of the family, this time division is accepted by all of us. The Aburishs outside Bethany incessantly scold a negligent world, which has shown little understanding of Palestinian claims and less inclination to do anything about them, and retreat into the despair of helplessness against Israel military might. The Bethany Aburishs' problem is infinitely more immediate because Israel governs the West Bank and Bethany and Israeli military power is a harsh reality which has reduced them to a state of subservience near to slavery.

The absence of military parity with Israel has not eliminated the overwhelming desire to do battle. To Munif doing battle is an intellectual stance, keeping Israel off balance, serving notice that the Palestinians 'have not given up their claim – will not give up anything'. This determination to unbalance Israel and be a thorn in the side of the world can be reduced to the ends-justifying-the-means-posture which lies behind the attitude towards the PLO and other organizations.

I can think of no better way to demonstrate the different attitudes towards violence held by the Aburishs outside Bethany than to recall a meeting I had with my brother Munif on 6 September 1972, the day of the Munich Olympic massacre when armed Palestinian gunmen killed eleven Israeli athletes in an act that reverberated to the most remote corners of the world.

Munif was at the Sorbonne writing a Ph.D. thesis after having been deported from the United States by the FBI for 'radical pro-Palestinian activities'. I had moved to London to manage an international business consulting firm specializing in the Middle East, and when in Paris on a business trip I arranged to meet Munif in a bar.

With the ghastly developments in Munich as background it became impossible to have a brotherly meeting full of family news and innocent chatter. Munich created a sinister atmosphere, a heavy feeling that we were being noticed, watched, perhaps judged by other people in the bar. Even our handshakes after a separation of three years were sub-

dued, and we spoke to each other in hushed tones and chose
to sit in a secluded corner in an unconscious attempt to hide
our identity.

There was no way to delay the talk about Munich and the
massacre though we tried our best and avoided it for about
five minutes, after which we succumbed to the inevitable.

'Munif, is this your group, is this the PFLP [Popular Front
for the Liberation of Palestine]?'

'I don't know if it is us, there are so many new groups – it
could be one of them.'

'But why – for God's sake why? Olympic athletes! After this
there won't be a single pro-Palestinian person in the whole
wide world. Why?'

'What difference does the opinion of the world make? We
are already bad guys; they treat us like bad guys. This way we
remind them we haven't gone away, we haven't died.'

'You haven't gone away – this is murder. Nothing can justify this, nothing. Listen to me, someone has to tell your people or whoever did it, that this is murder pure and simple. The
world will not accept this – you will pay for it, do you understand that?'

'I understand that the only thing the world understands is
violence. It's the only thing that changes boundaries and wins
independence. Israel was created by violent means; even
America came into being violently. If they fear us they will listen to us; they will take us into consideration – otherwise they
forget us.'

'Why the hell don't you go to the Israeli border and attack
them – not a bunch of innocent athletes.'

'We can't even reach the border. The countries around
Israel, Egypt, Jordan and Syria won't let us near for fear of
reprisal. We can't do anything except hit them when we can,
however unfortunate!'

'Tell me, do you really condone this? Tell me, I need to
know.'

'Not necessarily but I understand it. If it leads ten more
people to wonder who did it and why, and through that
understand our problem then it's a success.'

'I don't see it – I don't want to see it. I hope the sons of bitches who did it get strung up in the square; they are not my people.'

'Said, don't get all worked up. Just remember you live in a fancy apartment in Knightsbridge and you drive a Mercedes sports car. The people who did this probably come from refugee camps. They can't afford to behave like gentlemen; they don't preach the cause of Palestine at cocktail parties. Israeli planes probably attack their camp almost every day and it's natural that they express themselves through the barrel of a gun.'

I wanted to speak to Munif about our moral position, how it is eroded by the hate which leads to the Munichs in our lives, and how no glib intellectualism can change that, but I decided against lecturing him about morality and thought more and more about his despair. Later, walking down the street after dinner at a late night bistro and an invitation to Munif to visit me in London, I regretted not telling him my inner painful feelings. He had been profoundly hurt, my little brother; so deeply hurt, hampered and humiliated by his Palestinian identity, he had decided to reclaim his lost dignity at my cost. He was my flesh and blood, always so quiet, polite and self effacing and that night so very, very lost. I prayed silently to myself that he wasn't involved in acts of violence against civilians and lamented my inability to transmit my thoughts to him, my utter helplessness. I fought back an urge to telephone him to tell him that I loved him but could not approve or even accept.

Every Aburish felt Munich deeply; even members of the fourth generation like my daughter Charla spoke of her 'shame' and cousin Daoud Ahmad in Haiti found that 'nobody wanted to talk to me about anything else'. Some members of the family took Munif's line openly while others shared their morbid glee only with fellow Arabs whom they could trust. The Bethany Aburishs reacted to these questions in quite a different way.

The mere mention of the Munich massacre, or any PLO act of violence against Israel and its citizens produces instant, silent fear in a Bethany Aburish. Mahmoud breathed deeply, lit a cigarette and asked whether it was necessary to talk about it; Daoud clasped his hands together, shook his head and looked at the floor; Aunt Amneh looked around to see whether anyone else was listening and Aunt Fatmeh said she had nothing to say. Eventually I drew them and other members of the Bethany clan into open conversation which, to protect them, must remain unattributable: 'Every time the PLO does something outside we suffer; Israeli anger is directed at us. Israeli soldiers picked up cousin – because they thought he was a PLO sympathizer and tortured him for three days and it took him two weeks to be able to walk again. Cousin – was picked up by an Israeli patrol after – and they kept him in jail for two days without food and water. We don't have any place to hide; we can't even protect ourselves; we are helpless.'

*   *   *   *

If Munich underscored the divisions in the Aburish family, and dramatized the plight of those living under Israeli rule, then the October 1973 war reinvigorated our sense of oneness in that we all celebrated it as a justified war aimed at restoring Arab rights. Uncle Mahmoud was delighted that 'for the first time ever, they [the Arabs] did something without alerting the enemy'. Hilmi Ibrahim describes it 'like getting a new lease of life – it was overdue and suddenly I was proud to be an Aburish'. A PLO cousin who lives on the West Bank goes further: 'We wanted to rise against Israel; we looked to Jordan for help but that son of a whore [King] Hussein didn't move.'

Hilmi's statement about a new lease of life is the closest thing to the truth; we were reborn. Hilmi himself got so carried away he ordered the oriental orchestra in his Washington restaurant to play nothing but nationalistic songs. When an unsuspecting customer wouldn't stand up to cheer the song 'Palestine' a furious Hilmi threw him out of his restaurant screaming: 'This is a Palestinian restaurant and if you don't like it go somewhere else to eat.' Even my more experienced father told a colleague: 'This is a good one – too bad I am old, I'd like to have another go, it's probably my last chance to fight.' My mother, inimitable as ever, listened to the radio all the time and improvised her own response to Israeli Chief of Staff David Elazar's order of the day promising to 'break their bones' by defiantly asking: 'Where is this Alazar – I'll show him how people break bones.' Later when Munif in full battledress came home to say goodbye before going to southern Lebanon she bade him goodbye with: 'Do us proud ... do us proud.'

Upon hearing the news of the October 1973 war I was incredulous and full of fear that it might turn out to be a short disastrous affair. Every passing day lifted my spirits, broke down the distance which had rendered me remote and sceptical. Eventually I succumbed and could do nothing except listen to news bulletins. On the fourth day of the war, tired and tense, I went to a Chinese restaurant in Soho. I realized the waiter was Egyptian and we smiled at each other, opened our arms and embraced, repeating 'my brother, my brother'.

The eighteen days of the war was a period of hope which all of us wished to extend into eternity. They lifted the despair which had enveloped our lives, for even those who had condoned terrorism had to admit that there was more honour in the open battlefield. This was the longest Arab–Israeli war since 1948 and surely the one that proved that the Arabs are capable of organizing, of mastering the art of surprise, of fielding tanks and jet 'planes in co-ordination and, perhaps more tellingly, of reporting the truth about their battle successes and reverses. We were so touched and elated by it, the thought of the unknown Egyptian waiter in Soho still brings tears to my eyes to this day.

The final battlefield results of the October War did not detract from its overall impact on our lives for it resulted in the oil embargo which served clear notice that the Arabs had had enough, that something must be done to find a solution to the Palestinian problem. Here again our views of what should follow differed dramatically.

My brother Munif, cousin Said Hamad and two other cousins wanted the war to continue, 'to wear down the Israelis until they cry for peace'. Fathi Ibrahim, my brother Wagih and I believed the superpowers would, in Wagih's words, 'never allow another October War. Now, they have to solve the problem.' Reviewing my interviews with most members of my family there is a clear division between the group that saw the October War as a prelude to peace and another group which saw it as a first step towards defeating Israel; but both sides were agreed that a return to the no war, no peace state was unthinkable.

Sadly the unthinkable happened, leading only to greater desperation on both sides – highly reported PLO suicide missions and until 1987 almost totally unreported repression on the West Bank. To Mahmoud: 'The years after the October War, the mid-1970s were pure hell. The Israelis had misjudged our previous attitude as resignation so when our young people began showing signs that they were not afraid, the Israelis threw caution to the winds and began torturing them. At least six of your cousins suffered serious torture.'

The agony of the West Bank Aburishs was coupled with the rise of the full-time activists like Munif and cousins Said and Naim. It is true that terror hadn't moved the Israelis to concede anything but neither has a full-fledged war and the activists argued that the Israelis had no intention of returning a 'square inch of Arab land'.

The rest of us returned to our routine lives and scolded ourselves for 'exposing ourselves', for allowing our true feelings to surface in an open, hopeful way and, in the end for being wrong. We found it easier to pursue the creation of new identities than to continue to hope; we were tired of exaggerating Arab capabilities and through that our hopes.

But you cannot defeat hope; it is very much like a germ that remains dormant in the souls of men, the type that can be contained but never killed. This time the act of resurrection came in November 1974 in the form of an invitiation to Yasser Arafat, the PLO chairman, to speak at the United Nations, shortly after the Arab states recognized the PLO as the sole representative of the Palestinian people.

It is very difficult to explain to a non-Palestinian what this invitation meant to us. An American banker friend, a happy upper middle class person who can make superficial conversation about international affairs was the victim of my unusually potent support for Arafat: 'For over twenty-five years we begged and pleaded and no one listened; they didn't even accept our participation in a debate concerning our own fate; we were sub-human. Now they will listen to our case first hand. Arafat may be the biggest whore in Palestine but he's *my* whore.'

Cousin Said Hamad, a full-time member of the PLO, felt compelled to make the point that: 'Arafat got to the UN because he used the gun; the UN didn't invite a member of the Palestinian intellectual bourgeoisie who are always writing articles pleading for understanding, they invited the head of the Palestinian armed resistance.' The Bethany Aburishs gathered in Mahmoud's house to watch Arafat's UN speech on television and, according to Zakkaria Mahmoud: 'There wasn't a dry eye in the house. He spoke for all of us. I am sure that every person on the West Bank was at home watching him speak.'

The PLO has always captured the imagination of young Palestinians; the more revealing aspect of Arafat's success is what it did to the older generation, the sceptical ones who had experienced all the happenings since 1948 first hand. Mahmoud, who had been dismissive of the PLO until Arafat's UN trip, recognized them as the wave of the future and began to build bridges with their Bethany representatives. Aunt Amneh saw Arafat as 'one of us, not Syrian or Egyptian'. Uncle Daoud admitted that 'you can't deny his achievement; the whole world accepts him'. My father remembers sending Arafat a message stating: 'If you need a public relations man then I am ready to quit *Time Magazine* anytime. Our hearts, thoughts and prayers are with you.' The Aburish identification with the PLO was complete; we accepted it as our representative.

According to Munif: 'Our government in exile [the PLO]

has no form but that doesn't prevent love.' On the other hand one cousin paid the PLO lip service until they asked him for a donation when he took refuge in criticizing their spendthrift ways and some of their activities. Most of us viewed it as necessary; it gave us the identity we craved and we found ourselves preaching its gospel even when we disagreed, because that's all we had.

Munif is right; we were in love with the PLO and as often happens the object of our affection wasn't perfect; but who would ever allow reason to decide that? We exaggerated every diplomatic and military success of the PLO to show that it was worthy of our love, but even if there had been no successes we would have felt the same.

Suddenly, while PLO activity 'promised' the eventual convening of an international conference to settle the Arab–Israeli problem, the old curse of disunity came back to haunt the Arabs. President Sadat of Egypt announced his willingness to go to Jerusalem and while the whole world gasped with shocked surprise he journeyed there to tell the Israelis 'in all sincerity you are welcome among us'.

To us 20 November 1977 is a day of infamy; we were stabbed in the back. Uncle Mahmoud remembers it well: 'He [Sadat] was composed; he spoke well but I really wanted to kill him. He didn't come to Jerusalem, he crawled to Jerusalem. The beggar, the harlot.' My mother told a Beirut neighbour: 'Why doesn't he visit a refugee camp first, then he will get an idea of what the problem is all about. I am an old lady and I am ready to go, can't someone get me to Cairo with a gun – I'd take him with me.' My father remembers my brother Munif being almost suicidal: 'He couldn't shave or do anything; he just chain-smoked and shook his head. Eventually he burst out and wept, but he never said anything – he just shook his head.'

Aware that reporting an event long after its occurrence often leads to distortion and afraid that the eventual failure of Sadat's peace initiative might have influenced people's recollection of it, I tried to find out why all Aburishs appeared to be against it. Most, but not all of us, were against direct negotiations with Israel because we feared the awesome Israeli propaganda machine would turn such an initiative to their advantage regardless of the result. Beyond that, every single one of us objected to the way Sadat did it. My moderate, normally peace-loving uncle Daoud gives a good summary:

> The way he [Sadat] behaved was utterly shameful. He didn't agree to negotiate; he went to Jerusalem to welcome Israel. He wasn't putting forward an Arab point of view; he broke with all the Arabs. Then the way he greeted Israeli leaders – what lack of dignity, what lack of grace. The only thing left for him to do was to hug and kiss them.

That members of the Aburish family, like all Palestinians, manifest an overwhelming preoccupation with their identity and all the hurt which goes with it has been made clear. The degree to which this influences our lives, our ability to go forward as normal human beings, is best told by our foreign wives, the ones who cope with our psychological wounds.

Ahmad Hassan's wife makes a very firm, clear statement when she says: 'My husband feels like an incomplete man. His Palestinianism is a constant quest.' My brother Rabah's Egyptian wife suffered Palestinian anger at its worst during Sadat's peace initiative. Rabah unfairly screamed at her: 'Neither your idiot [Sadat] or anyone else is entitled to give away our rights. We will be a thorn in the side of humanity till they treat us right – with respect.' Cousin Said Hamad's wife reflects his single-mindedness: 'The Israelis are not very clever. Nothing, but nothing will defeat the Palestinians – they should know that by now.'

My brother Munif's words reflect our true state of mind, an attitude of defiance laced with rhetoric: 'We are incomplete – in search of our other self, our self respect. We will not accept everyone else deputizing for us. Our spirits are unbroken, we are ready to continue to fight and adversity has toughened us. We will not go away.'

13
Wanderers with no roots

I preferred the old times when we were one family. We don't know each other any more.

Amneh Aburish

When I asked aunt Amneh the question I had put to all members of her generation – whether she liked life as it is today or life when she was young – she thought carefully before giving me her considered answer. To her the past had meant kinship and personal relationships.

The Aburish family as it exists today is made up of several different geographical and cultural groups, each with its own attitude, and its relationship to Bethany. There are Aburishs who have never left Bethany and who continue to view it as the centre of their lives. Many others work away from Bethany but view the village as their anchor, the place to which they belong culturally and emotionally, while the third group is made up of people who live away from Bethany, physically, culturally and spiritually, and who have made a commitment to what they are and where they are at the expense of their Bethany roots.

It would be wrong to suppose that the uniformity in way of life and attitude in existence at the time of Khalil Aburish is remotely true of any of today's groups. The oneness in social structure that existed at that time is no longer possible even within the Bethany-bound group for even there the multiplicity of vocational choice, advances in communication and emergence of a strong pervasive alien central government and their consequent influence on life-style is far greater than anything conceived of during Khalil Aburish's lifetime.

Bethany is no longer an isolated place where people live off tilling the soil, herding, or even promoting visits to the tombs of Lazarus and Simon the Leper. It is a suburb of Jerusalem with all that that implies – financial benefits to its inhabitants accompanied by damage to their social cohesion, the destruction of their individual community. The number of people who depend on the land as a sole source of income is very few indeed and fewer, if any, herd sheep; most people work in Jerusalem proper in government, trade, professional or service jobs, and go there by car, bus, motorcycle or bicycle. Unlike sixty years ago, the only barrier to the journey they experience is created by people – that unattractive manifestation of civilization, the traffic jam.

My uncle Mahmoud is still in Bethany and so, exceptionally, are almost all his children and grandchildren. Mousa, Amneh, Fatmeh and Daoud are in Bethany and so are Hamdah's children and grandchildren, thirty-five grandchildren and nine great grandchildren of Khalil Aburish. Only nine of the descendants of Mahmoud, Hamdah, Mousa, Amneh, Fatmeh and Daoud are away from Bethany and its atmosphere. The continued presence of the rest means a continued identification of the place with the family name.

Mahmoud's eldest son Khalil, his fourth child, works for the National Tobacco Company and is in charge of production – his father helped him gain employment with this company but his advancement to his present position at the age of thirty-two is due to his talent and hard work. His younger brother Zakkaria is personnel director with the same company, an alert, aggressive young man who, it is generally agreed, will have a successful professional life. Mahmoud's youngest son Rishou is at university studying management. Of Mahmoud's six daughters one is married to the headmaster of the local school, another's husband manages a small hotel in nearby Jerusalem, the third son-in-law is an airline pilot, the fourth runs a tourist office, the fifth is a pharmacist and the sixth works for the United Nations. One of the daughters is a schoolteacher while the rest are housewives. With the possible exceptions of the proprietor of the tourist office and the hotel manager not a single son or son-in-law is engaged in an activity which existed during the lifetime of Khalil Aburish. This is also true in different ways of the daughters – to be a schoolteacher is new for a woman, and although women have always done housework its nature has changed in the last few decades.

Mahmoud's grandchildren appear to be following their happy or unhappy ways and include everything from an electronic engineer to a hoodlum. Their choice of careers is due to their inclinations, what they learn at school and what is possible; they get little direction from their parents, most of whom cannot keep up with the ever increasing options available to their offspring.

Mousa's children are not very different from Mahmoud's children and grandchildren in their professional pursuits and achievements, while Daoud's children, like him, tend to be quiet, and are all mechanical engineers. Amneh's children have a distinct political inclination: one is at large with the very radical Front for the Liberation of Palestine, and another boy is with the PLO Office in Washington. Two of Fatmeh's sons are bankers and the other two are in hotel management. Mousa's, Daoud's, Amneh's and Fatmeh's daughters married well locally: the husbands could be described as 'good providers', the best Bethany can offer.

Mahmoud, Mousa, Daoud, Amneh, Fatmeh and their Bethany-bound descendents along with Hamdah's children and grandchildren are the present-day Aburishs of Bethany. Through the simple act of having remained there, they are the more natural, direct heirs to Khalil Aburish's legacy. The changes which have affected and govern their lives are those which transformed the place and made it what it is today. The most immediate question about how they live concerns their attitudes as citizens of Bethany, for Mahmoud continues to hold the position of mayor and leading citizen, however precariously. Do his children, or indeed any of his nephews, think in terms of perpetuating this hold on the village, or extending

what Khalil Aburish started at the turn of the century? Do
they think the positions 'belong' to them?

The answer is not an easy one. Mahmoud's oldest boy
Khalil would like to be mayor after his father; he is however
fully aware that in pursuing the office he possesses both
advantages and disadvantages. The Aburish name is in one
way an advantage, as there are still people who view
Mahmoud's and Khalil Aburish's long years as Bethany's
unquestioned representatives with gratitude and affection.
However there is no unbreakable bond between them and the
Aburish family or name, nor can they be manipulated. The
drawback lies in the simple fact that the name represents the
old system and there are disadvantages in identifying with
the past. Bethanites no longer want people to deputize for
them, but rather to reflect their point of view; continuing with
the Aburish name is tantamount to perpetuating the old
system.

Khalil Mahmoud can no longer be the power-broker
manipulator his grandfather and father were but he can be
the 'representative' of the people. In order to succeed he will
have to compete with others over what he could do for
Bethany and its people, and that will include the need to provide better schools and a more efficient service in the fields of
electricity, water, road maintenance and refuse collection. He
will also have to discard his father's and grandfather's
arrogant ways; their belief in a simple, local administration.
He openly claims an advantage over potential challengers: 'I
know more about all of these things by osmosis . . . I have
heard my father discuss them all my life.' When I tried to
push him towards an appreciation of Bethany as part of a
larger entity, to determine whether he saw it as part of a country or state, he admitted:

> I know what goes on out there but can't say the roads will be done
> this or that way, because one is a socialist. My attitude is totally
> local – though I must admit others, including relatives, are
> introducing larger national interests and ideology to the com-
> munity – the socialists are always claiming they do more for the

people than others. Many others put the country before local interests. Who knows?

I used my conversation with his son to provoke Mahmoud into a discussion of his present position compared to the past. He is completely and unhappily aware of the erosion of his powers, both as head of the family and as mayor and head of the village.

Within the family he is mostly treated with respect, but he is not obeyed; even his youngest son, Rishou, gets edgy when Mahmoud offers advice about his schooling or career. Rishou is outspoken about his father: 'His views of education are antiquated. Most of the disciplines existing now did not exist in his day and to him anything that doesn't feed directly into a well-paying job is a waste of time – the whole thing is utilitarian.' Mahmoud treats Rishou's study of management with a grunt of derision: 'You are either born to manage men or you aren't – and he was. Why doesn't he learn something useful, be a doctor or engineer?'

Mahmoud's second son, Zakkaria, married a girl disapproved of by his parents. He is very blunt about his decision: 'I loved her and we wanted to marry. I told my parents about it out of politeness and they made unhappy noises. Thank God they didn't object outright because I would have gone ahead with my decision anyway. They have no right to choose a wife for me – that's all gone.'

The eldest son, Khalil, has three children, the eldest, who is ten years old, is named after his grandfather and is the apple of his eye. Mahmoud the elder takes pride in his grandson and would like to see him often and have him keep him company the way my uncles used to enjoy my presence, but his father is totally opposed to this: 'He is a boy who should play with boys and girls of his age . . . football, hide-and-seek and whatever. Spending too much of his time in the company of his grandfather isn't helpful – though he means well.'

Khalil, Zakkaria, young Rishou and two of the six girls smoke: they do it in the presence of their father, and those who drink alcohol do it openly as well. They tease their father about his use of Grecian 2000 to dye his hair, complain when he is late for a meal and poke constant fun about his stories of the good old days. The girls, all in western clothes, notice his stares of disapproval at low-cut dresses and treat them dismissively, and pay even less attention to his undoubted disapproval of the use of contraceptive devices. His own wife, the very attractive mother of ten, is adoring and shows clear signs of acquired independence although she was totally subservient when she married him. When he recently complained about breakfast being late she invited him to 'go to the local hotel if you don't like the service'.

All of these manifestations of change and promises of more to come do not compare with the more explicit diminution of his powers in the traditional areas of reverence and respect. Fatmeh's son Fathi, Mahmoud's nephew and my first cousin, was summoned by Mahmoud to be lectured about his behaviour in settling a dispute regarding his father's inheritance. He listened politely and then announced he would continue employing the same methods, and when Mahmoud objected, invoking his powers as head of family, Fathi impatiently told him to mind his own business and stingingly reminded him: 'The days of being a sheikh are over.'

Mahmoud's sadness at his loss of stature within the family is bitterly explicit:

> They can't wait for me to go. There is no respect any more. I never smoked in my father's presence nor did I dare be familiar with him. As a matter of fact, I almost set myself on fire once. He approached me while I was smoking and I hid the cigarette in my pocket. When I finally depart they will treat each other like strangers; they are already doing so.

The attitude of members of the Bethany family is a microcosm of the attitude of the people of the village. Change has eliminated some of Mahmoud's traditional function, such as settling land and property disputes, and reduced honour problems to occasional oddities. Fear of the state limits the consequences of both, making the traditional containment policy all but obsolete: civil law is supreme. Not only that but the general atmosphere created by the Israeli state is not conducive to perpetuating traditional Arab values. To Israelis Arabs ways are antiquated and not worth preserving and their harsh rule reflects this unfortunate attitude. Even problems which continue to fall within Mahmoud's sphere of influence do not contribute to his position as chief but are part of his 'duties'.

The importance of people's problems used to be judged by whether he chose to address himself to them or not; now people demand that right. A special committee oversees municipal expenditure to protect against kickbacks, and uncle Mousa was forced into resigning his position as assistant to the mayor because it was considered to be nepotism. When Mahmoud recently tried to receive a cut of the settlement payment for a feud, one of the contestants told him his salary was enough. Water distribution is subject to strict scrutiny – he pays his own water rates and can no longer consider using water to coerce reluctant constituents the way his father did with the wells. He is still addressed by the respectful Abu Khalil, but he travels to see and to please people more often than they seek him; his progress towards being a figurehead chief is accelerated by the overwhelming change enveloping his domain: the emergence of a 'state' committed to egalitarianism.

*   *   *   *

The number of Aburishs living away from Bethany while considering it 'home' is greater than the number of those who inhabit it full time. The children of Ibrahim, Ahmed and Hassan belong, for the most part, to this group, as do some of Hamdah's grandchildren and of Mousa's, Fatmeh's and Amneh's children. They live in Saudi Arabia, Jordan, Egypt, Haiti, the United Kingdom, the United States, Canada, Spain and Chile, and range from nineteen to forty-five years of age.

Most of them are self-employed and many of them are millionaires, like cousin Hilmi Ibrahim who owns Washington DC's largest travel agency, and with his brothers a huge limousine service with 170 cars, four petrol stations and three restaurants, all in Washington. Cousin Ishaq Mahmoud, Mahmoud's third son, owns a small chain of grocery stores in Chicago, while Khalil Ahmad is the propietor of four art galleries and three general stores in Haiti. One of Fatmeh's sons owns a jewellery shop in Saudi Arabi. They all do exceptionally well.

Among the Bethany 'connected' as opposed to Bethany-bound, who are not self-employed, there is a predominance of bankers and others working for sheikhs and princes and mon-eyed people from other Arab countries reaping the benefits of oil wealth – they too do well. This group's most noticeable characteristic is the distinction between where they live and work and the place they consider home. Washington DC, Chicago, and even Doha, Qatar, and Jeddah, Saudi Arabia, are places to make money but cannot be home because the inner make-up controlling the lifestyle of the Aburishs, rather than their everyday business conduct, belongs to Bethany. They are seen as outsiders and feel that way: they stay 'out-siders' all day long, but conduct Bethany lives within their homes – many of them have a picture of Bethany as the centre-piece in their living room and they cook Palestinian food.

Almost everyone belonging to this group is married to a Bethany girl or one from a neighbouring village or from Jerusalem; they may leave Bethany unmarried but they return to marry. The explanation of this phenomenon was summed up by cousin Samih Ibrahim who declared: 'It's all right to go to bed with a foreigner but they are not very obedient and they question everything. They make bad wives.' Even girls from other Arab countries don't appear to satisfy Bethany requirements, which include the all impor-tant spiritual relationship with the land.

There is an amusing aspect to this commitment to marry a 'home girl' – because a man living in Chicago or Haiti very seldom spends enough time in Bethany to make his own choice of bride, while marriage for love among Bethany residents has established a solid foothold through cousin Zakkaria and others. It appears that a compromise between an arranged and a chosen marriage has been established for the Bethany-connected group – the intending groom informs Bethany-based relatives of his desire to marry and they in turn prepare a list of eligible girls with full resumés of their family background, education, whether there is barrennesss in the family and the way the girl walks, talks and cooks. The final choice is then left to the suitor.

Cousin Salah Ibrahim described his wife as, 'coming from a good family which is free from disease. She is presentable and finished two years of the university and is a good cook. She respects my mother and gets along with my sisters. She is a Bethany girl through and through.'

Besides continuing the Bethany connection through marriage most members of this group reinforce their links through a surrogate physical presence, the building of a house in the village. Because of their absence this is rented out most of the time but it serves as an important symbol of how well they have done overseas – one cousin got so carried away that he built a huge house which no resident or potential resident of Bethany could afford to rent; he is not at all embarrassed by his impractical ways and views the house with pride. Conversely another cousin told me that he refrained from building a Bethany house because he couldn't build a big one and feared a small one would earn him ridicule.

It is obvious that this large group is preoccupied with financial achievement, 'heroic' capitalism: most of the time they do not have the intellectual make-up to be interested in where they are. They work extremely hard, play very little and when back home regale Bethany folk with tales about how people in their host countries behave; stories as exaggerated as the ones they tell their hosts about Bethany. The real issues for this group are the relationship to the family and village, marriages and the need to identify with the plot of land made famous by Lazarus and Khalil Aburish.

Closer examination of their lives suggest that the Bethany connection continues as much out of their rejection of where they are as it does out of love for Bethany and its ways, since their host countries see them as foreign hustlers who do not integrate. Salah Ibrahim opted for a Bethany girl because his 'instincts' told him that a US girl from 'the right background' was very nearly unattainable, not to speak of his attitude against helping with household chores and wishing to be obeyed. His brother Ghaleb gets satisfaction out of building a big Bethany house which is the talk of the town, something which would scarcely be noticed in a Washington laden with mansions and grand town houses. It is more attractive to be viewed as an achiever in Bethany when others won't have you in their clubs or even inside their houses, and frown at your over-tipping and your gaudy diamond ring. Against this background, the true reason for the affinity to Bethany, the Aburish name and family tradition makes unhappy reading.

The primary force in the lives of the Aburishs who consider Bethany a home base and live as expatriates elsewhere is money, the traditional yardstick of achievement of all displaced people. Their connection with Bethany is mostly forced because their relationship to where they are is superficial; they do no belong to either place and even Bethany is not completely tolerant of their hunger for money. As aunt Fatmeh says: 'Everytime I ask your cousin about his life in Washington he tells me how much money he is making. It's a shame he can't talk about other things.'

Mahmoud, the head of the family and guardian of its traditions and those of the whole village, is not respected by them for what he is and was; his 'old-fashioned' ways are ridiculed by them, all the way from his joy in presiding over a family feast to when he dons Arab robes to go to the mosque. By their own criterion of success he is a failure, because he has no money, having tried to maintain a local grand style of living off capital for a good twenty years or so. He is no longer their head because they have little need for his presence, to protect them against others within Bethany, other villages and even the state. Whereas their fathers saw fit to kiss his hand in a demonstration of respect, even after an absence of only two or three days, the younger expatriates often visit and leave Bethany without as much as a telephone call to say hello to him. Mahmoud's mere existence is a reproach to them and their ways; only in not respecting him can they feel that their achievements are superior to his.

Neither Arab nor westerner, regardless of what they do for a living – they are mercenaries without even knowing it. One of them said, without appreciating the emptiness of his source of pride: 'I can live anywhere and make a good living though working hard. I don't need anything or anyone beyond that.' All of the things which Bethany held together for 2000 years are beyond his comprehension, as are the finer things available where he is, like going to the theatre, enjoying a jazz evening or revelling in a revolutionary piece of architecture – not to speak of the simple act of reading a book. As always with rootless people, what began as an admirable means to gain respect and independence became the end itself; accumulating money for its own sake became a disease which eroded other values.

* * * *

The third group of Aburishs are those who view Bethany in the strict, distant sense of an ancestral home and whose lives now belong totally to the places where they live and work. To be a part of this group can be the result of a conscious and deliberate effort, reflecting a genuine preference for a new culture and its ways, or can result from a natural decay of the link to Bethany through long absences and other circumstances.

My immediate family is the leading example of this group of Aburish descendants, but we are not alone, for there are also Daoud Ahmad, Ahmad Hassan and Mazen Mousa, two of Hamdah's grandchildren and other members of the younger generation. The sample is not a large one but we do represent a group distinct from the other two.

Self-identification is no easy matter, and when I asked my wife Kate what distinguished us from other Aburishs she claimed that we were eighty per cent western and only twenty per cent Bethany Arabs, whereas the others were twenty per cent western and eighty per cent Bethany Arabs. She didn't attach much importance to a physical Bethany connection like owning land or a house there: 'You could own a second house in Bethany and it would mean nothing, you'd use it as a summer place or the like. It's the reason for owning it which matters. You don't need it – the house; your connection with Bethany is intellectual. Both groups are cultural schizoids with different tilts.'

Those of us who chose to adopt western ways did so because our circumstances forced us to make a difficult decision; my brothers, sisters and I were educated in western schools and were boarding students, and beyond that we lived in Beirut, the half-way house between east and west.

Some of us discarded Bethany at a later stage, others forsook their inheritance piece by piece, particularly those with greater initial exposure to Bethany. Ahmad Hassan claims that he never could answer the question of whether he thought in English until it finally happened – after years of absence from Bethany; until then he had no idea what was meant by thinking in English. He and Daoud Ahmad ascribe importance to using English words which have no equivalents in Arabic, and insist that 'okay' is now the most universally used expression denoting acceptance and approval. Both describe their growing acceptance of women as equals – Ahmad's mother looks askance when he stands up for women his age. They treat waiters with enough deference to earn a reprimand from Mahmoud and they speak of buying their first buttoned-down shirts and of eventually finding greater ease in the company of their neighbours and local friends than with Bethany relatives.

Yet even the most westernized of Khalil Aburish's grandchildren appreciate what he and his successor Mahmoud represented and celebrate it for all the wisdom it embodied, particularly the total commitment to human values. Their

ways were patently superior to all the varieties of bureau-
cratic totalitarianism which have followed. My ancestors'
relationship to their children is superior to anything conceiv-
able in western society – love formalized by tradition
embodying enough respect to enhance rather than diminish
the instinctive emotion.

Still there are also those within the group committed to
western ways who are nothing but a reflection of a history of
Arab subservience and misunderstanding to the west. To
them Arabs and things Arab are bad and the west and its
ways are better. This is supposed to justify imitative
behaviour, so to them the west is Gucci shoes, flashy cars, a
comfortable house and other material comforts. They speak
the language of their adopted countries badly, and Arabic
equally atrociously: their most telling trade-mark is an
inability to distinguish between good and bad manners in
either culture – to them chewing gum, wearing crocodile
shoes and speaking of their sexual conquests are acceptable
practices. Their wives and girlfriends are from many countries, are ignorant and undemanding, and concerned with
enjoying the benefits of their spouses' single-mindedness in
the pursuit of money. They lack the grace of a Rashedah and
the good manners of a well-brought-up western girl.

To this group Bethany and what it stands for is unacceptable because it embarrasses them, but their rejection of its
values is a reflection of an overall lack of understanding – just
like western middle class people who equate everything from
the third world with backwardness. They identify with new
places because they have nothing to cling to, in terms of their
natural heritage, and because they attach importance to the
most shallow western traits.

My branch of the family more than any other represents
the group which views Bethany as an ancestral home but has
settled permanently in other places. A dissection of our
attitude is likely to offend but is necessary: Munif, Wagih and
I view Bethany as a way of life which contained many
worthwhile features, a way of life totally capable of justifying
itself, and which contained elements deserving preservation.

We are by nature studious, believers in the work ethic and largely capable of understanding our surroundings and coming to terms with them; money is an important part of life but we do work to live rather than the other way round.

In Wagih's words: 'We may be exiles, but we are not aliens where we are – we understand our surroundings.'

Afif and Rabah can cope with the most superficial aspects of western life: they have no inclination to probe beyond what Wagih called 'waist high culture'. They are 'western' in a barren way within it and, because they totally reject Bethany, they are estranged from its attractive values as well. Their opinion of Bethany is no different from that of a lower middle-class tourist; they think it is backward and has nothing to offer. They totally ignore the fact that they are treated like second-class citizens where they are. Their non-acceptance does not bother them; perhaps they do not even notice it.

My sisters Mona and Alia view Bethany in a kind but distant way. Because they are women who value their total freedom in accordance with western ideas, they confine their negative attitude to the male–female relationship and the relegation of women to a subservient position. According to Mona: 'It is a lovely place and they are closer to each other than we are, but I will be damned if I am going to wait hand and foot on anyone. The wives are still beasts of burden.' Both have a natural attachment to the elegant, and could easily pass for upper middle-class wives in any western capital.

Except for Afif's and Rabah's ill-founded reservations, we like Mahmoud for what he is and respect him for what he represents. Our geographic remoteness helps us to maintain this attitude, for we do not have to contend with his position as head of the family or village, and there are no incidents of direct involvement. He is likeable because he is good company and laughter is never far away when he is around; he is repsected because the system he represents did more good than harm, and he fills our lives with endearing tales of a yesterday which is close in years and far, far away in time. Whatever separates us is overcome by that unmistakeable aura of gentility and liveliness of mind which he possesses.

The relationship of the three divisions of the family to each other is not a close one and is tinged with jealousy and lack of understanding. The Bethany-bound group continues to take pride in its position as leaders of the community, however diminished that position, and its members look down upon the Bethany-connected ones and their ways. Zakkaria Mahmoud is outspoken in his assessment of this group: 'They work like dogs without an identity for eleven months of the year and spend the other month here to feel like human beings. I don't need to do that – it is a happier life being an Aburish here.'

Mahmoud, my father, Mousa, Amneh, Fatmeh and Daoud, the living children of Khalil Aburish have witnessed the changes in the family and resultant attitudes; because they were in the middle of this change it is sometimes difficult for them to take an overall view, and some are very reluctant to do so except after considerable prodding. For obvious reasons Mahmoud's are the more pertinent reflections.

> The people in Bethany changed a great deal . . . education, radio, TV, outsiders, influence of the external economy and oil. Change came fast and became more attractive for its own sake; and there is no one to guard against its harmful aspects like lack of respect for the elders, closeness to relatives and attachment to the soil. Most of the old values are gone. Each is preoccupied with his or her problems – there is no sense of family any more. My brother Ibrahim bowed and kissed my hand in respect – his sons avoid me.

My father reiterates Mahmoud's refrain in a more worldly way:

> People were genuine when they belonged to the land. Now wage labour is the source of income. External forces eliminated the Bethany of old, the young lost their direction and there is nothing to hold on to. We, Mahmoud and my generation, are safe because while in some ways we belong to two worlds, we are more a part of

the old than the new – there was no loss of identity. You are international nomads; you belong to where the grass is greener regardless of family and roots. Soon the only thing you will have in
common is your name.

Amneh's comment about not knowing each other any more
is true and touching, and Fatmeh confirms this very clearly:
'The family is not the centre of life any more. There is no
courtesy any more. Members of the family don't deal with
Mahmoud; they can't. They deal with someone they don't
even know in the government – an unknown person. They
can't be better than before.'

Recently Mahmoud undertook a big trip to visit various
members of the Aburish family in Britain, the United States
and South America, and without exception everyone was
pleased to see him; but they all expressed a singular concern
that he might not understand their need to attend to their
work, and the inevitable limit of how much time they could
spend with him. He tried to be understanding but was
occasionally hurt when small business commitments were
placed ahead of his company – to him this was a corruption of
values and it hurt when he was left on his own in a
strange city.

His arrivals, departures and eventual return to Bethany
were not marked by either familial or communal acts of
loyalty or celebration, and he travelled 18,000 miles to be
met by subdued politeness wherever he went. The people
outside Bethany wanted to hear amusing stories and to learn
of the place's progress in terms of the new local bar and the
jacuzzi built by cousin Jamil: he was reduced to the role of a
storyteller, for whatever news he relayed contained com-
parisons with what used to be.

When he returned to Bethany, after a two and a half month
absence, two of his sons met him while the third took two
days to make an appearance, and no one from the village felt
obliged to pay him homage, for being away is a matter of
everyday life now and besides he wasn't a chief but an elected
official, in all likelihood serving his last term in office. Instead

of receiving the shows of respect which had accompanied his father's return from a hundred miles away, he worked hard to catch up with village and family problems which, as usual now, contained some he had never experienced before. Moreover, he was concerned that some of his constituency complained about his prolonged absence.

If Bethany and the Aburish name no longer afford us identity then what does? Are we still Palestinians – as opposed to holders of sixteen nationalities? The answer is a qualified yes: we are Palestinians.

However well-meaning the British colonial attitude, it was one of master and slave that was followed by the oppression by Jordan when it ruled us, rejection by other Arabs, and the Israeli insistence that we do not exist: it is these elements which have created the Palestinian identity. My nephew Ziad Munif is a tri-lingual six-year old who one day asked his father what a Palestinian is, and when Munif explained that it was an Arab who came from Palestine Ziad persisted with: 'Why do we want to be Palestinians?' Munif's sad answer tells the story: 'It's not a matter of choice. When everyone thinks you are something then you are that thing.' This is true of all of us – even the ones to whom Bethany is nothing but a distant memory.

Some of us pay this identity-label lip service without ever doing anything to help the Palestinians realize their vague aspirations – to them their Palestinianism is fashionable. Others object to being relegated to nonentities and describe their misery in the vague context of human rights. Thus Wagih's description of the Arab–Israeli conflict is bitter: 'The victim is being asked to apologise.' Yet others have gone further and adopted Palestine as their only identity. 'It is *the idea* of Palestine that we love' cousin Said Hamad once said. In all cases this real, superficial and hypothetical attachment to Palestine replaces Bethany, the Aburish name and all the things they stood for.

*　*　*　*

In 1979, Rashedah Aburish died at the age of ninety-two and people from near and far marched in her funeral procession and paid their respects, most of them old people who remembered Khalil Aburish and revered his memory and his sons and what they represented. She was an illiterate woman full of love and respect for her husband, a good mother and grandmother, a woman endowed with natural grace and common sense which transcended the complex forces of economic change and social revolution.

Two days after Rashedah's death my daughter Charla Josephine telephoned me from New York with good news. Having written a sparkling paper on the influence of the Tunisian sun on the painting of Paul Klee, she had won a competition to work as an assistant to the curator at the White House. Charla is the great-grand daughter of Rashedah and Khalil Aburish.